Off Script Therapy

*When You Are Off Script And I Am Off Script,
We Are Alive To Each Other*

By Luc Watelet

~ ~ ~

Joyous Yogi, New York

Published, in the United States, by Joyous Yogi
www.innerwearth.com

Joyous Yogi is Luc Watelet's publishing company.

eBook ISBN 978-0-9977741-0-8
Paperback ISBN 978-0-9977741-1-5

Book design and photographs by Luc Watelet.
Front cover photograph taken on 8/15/2012 at dusk by a Lumix Simple Viewer digital camera.
Author photograph is a self-portrait (selfie) taken on 11/05/2015 with a Samsung Galaxy S4.

The poem "I Am Me" by Virginia Satir reproduced in Chapter 3, Love, is used with permission of the Virginia Satir Global Network www.satirglobal.org. All rights reserved.

The poem "Autobiography in Five Short Chapters" by Portia Nelson, reproduced in Chapter 7, Understanding Mental Illness, is reprinted with the permission of Beyond Words/Atria, a division of Simon & Schuster, Inc., from THERE'S A HOLE IN MY SIDEWALK: THE ROMANCE OF SELF-DISCOVERY by Portia Nelson. Copyright © 1993 by Portia Nelson. All rights reserved.

First Paperback Edition

INSIDE EACH OF US

Inside each of us
Shines a light

It needs us to notice it
Until then we feel in the dark
in a script we think is our own
disconnected
lonely
abandoned
disrespected
and empty
deeply – seemingly forever – empty

That light does not know Illnesses
It does not know Disorder
It only knows Love
and Joy and Peace

We think we are this script
But it holds us in darkness
We are everything but
So we need to dare to get out of it
To be able to see
Who we really are

That light lets us see
the treasure chest
of our most cherished dreams

And when we connect with it
We start Healing

Then we can see depression
and anxiety and emptiness
and all darkness
as the result of
not noticing
our very own precious light

The Dark moves us
to search the Light

Until we find it
Searching for our light
is our most important life purpose

With Determination
Courage and Infinite Faith
We remember small fragments of
forgotten self
that light up some of the way forward

And, as we remember our light,
it starts shining like a lighthouse
for people around us
to dare take a peak
outside of their script

~   ~   ~

To those who seek lasting healing
To the future of psychotherapy
To all of our relationships

CONTENTS

ACKNOWLEDGMENTS

I knew I would write books "someday," and had made some attempts that did not come to fruition. The original idea that led to this book was to write a paper about my psychotherapeutic orientation. It came from Dr. Robyn Trippany, one of my teachers and mentors toward the end of my master's degree in mental health counseling at Walden University. I had no idea that Robyn's idea would send me on a very personal journey of self-discovery and self-belief. The obstacles were many and in surmounting them I grew as a human being and as a therapist. One of the difficulties for me was to find the right voice and the right purpose for writing the book, because I soon found out that much of what I wanted to write had already been published by Ron Kurtz founder of the Hakomi Method.

I thank Walden University for giving me a training that helped me see the difference between mainstream approaches to therapy and how I saw my work as a psychotherapist. This contrast helped me clarify what I wanted to contribute to the field of psychotherapy.

I am grateful to the agency that offered me an internship. The director gave me a chance of a lifetime to be myself including encouraging me to bring yoga to our staff and clients. I enjoyed working with my supervisor who also encouraged me to be myself and taught me to recognize steps in the evolution of recovery from addictions and mental health challenges. I am also grateful to the rest of the staff for welcoming me on board, for sharing their experiences with me, and for sharing their clients with me. I keep all the names to myself to protect the privacy of our clients.

I thank all my students and clients who put their trust in me. Our work together convinced me that my therapeutic instincts work. Thanks for your questions and the experiences that helped me sharpen my clarity as a teacher, and my craft as a healer.

I thank all the people with whom I engaged in conversations, not only about psychotherapy, as they often helped me clarify my thoughts in ways that influenced the writing of this book.

Luc Watelet

My friend and colleague Andrea Niedererr has been encouraging me since the beginning. She is currently president of the Respective Solutions Group and read my first drafts. Her love and support were invaluable in finding my voice. As my book is getting ready for publication she has invited me to give a presentation to her group about trauma and self-care. Giving presentations feeds the book and the book feeds my presentations. It is wonderful synergy. Thank you Andrea!

With time, other people joined my encouraging team.

Lisa Giudici, from Blossom Therapeutics Family Massage & Wellness, and I had many discussions about Mind-Body Medicine that were an early inspiration in putting my thoughts together as I was finding my voice to write this book. Lisa made me aware of author Lissa Rankin's work and, in particular, her important message from the Q'eros (see Chapter 10).

Jennifer Sutton, president of What If Wellness, edited, with love and in true service to my voice, this entire version of the book, and prompted too many rewrites to count. After all these rewrites she proofread, yet again, the second half of the book. She also made me aware of the article by Deborah Becker (see Chapter 8) about meditation in the treatment of people in addiction recovery. I wish for every potential author to receive the support of someone like Jennifer who thoroughly believed in the importance of my work.

I want to thank friends who are local therapists: Tonya Girard and Tom Porpiglia for their stories of clients I have included here, and Dale Goldstein who put me in touch with several of his clients. I selected two of their stories for this book. They have not been published elsewhere.

Thanks Tom also for proofreading the final version of the first half of this book.

My working title for this book was *Psychotherapy and Healing: Aligning Mind, Body, and Soul with Self-Love, Mindfulness, and Mindlessness*. It was a good title for an academic audience. But I wanted this book to reach everyone and started looking for a more approachable title. I brainstormed ideas with my friend and colleague Nicole Waldschmidt. She was very encouraging and a wonderful listener. I thank you Nicole in helping me make my final decision.

Kathy Weber, a friend I met on Facebook, was my first supporter in wanting to purchase this book and asked me many times: "Are you there yet?" Others followed. Jessica Fischer and I chatted at a time when I was wondering how to promote my work and, thanks to her encouragements, I created a Facebook page to start sharing ideas from this book. I thank Kim Conrad, friend and author of *Vice Versa Verse: Inspiring Twists on How to View Your Life and Fill Your Soul*, for her encouragements as she suggested someone who could help me navigate the road to self-publication at a time when I was strongly resisting the idea!

Friend and author Cindy Schuerr read my book from the perspective of a potential reader. She encouraged me by letting me know my book was readable (not just by psychotherapists!) and would help many people heal.

Writing a book is only part of the journey. After writing comes publishing. Regularly, friends suggested that I self-publish. I had a strong resistance to self-publishing because my first inquiries into receiving permission for my quotes met with some obstacles. I wanted to quote some authors and needed permission as in two cases the length of my quotes went beyond fair use. Author Stephanie Marohn gave me permission to quote the entire story of Alex (see Chapter 10). But I also needed permission from her publishing company which I did not receive in time. I decided to paraphrase the story. I tried looking for a publishing company to save me some work, but that did not come as I was hoping for. Finding an agent I did not have to pay up front did not come either. Andy Grant, author of several books and in particular of *Intro to eBook Publishing for the Heart Centered Entrepreneur*, encouraged me to start with an eBook and his words were convincing at the time I received them.

Thanks to my sister in law, Marie-Noëlle Massé, graphic designer, who helped me shift up the cover photograph of this first paperback edition so the sail boat is a little higher than I had it

I thank all therapists, whether I mentioned them in this book or not, whose works have contributed to my thoughts about therapy – some because I celebrated their ideas and some because they helped me see who I did not want to be. Both are important in our human exploration of who we are and how to improve our relationships with each other.

I thank my teachers and spiritual teachers, whether they taught me in person or by way of their work.

Thanks to Life for guiding me toward joy and love.

I thank my parents, brothers and sisters for being a continual source of love to me. My father modelled being a truth seeker and my mother modelled faithfulness to family and especially the value of beauty of a finished work. I had not fully appreciated beauty because I did not know it opened the heart.

I thank the women who joined me for some of my life for the many beautiful moments we shared and the lessons you taught me, in particular the balance and dance of holding one's space with love in relationships.

I thank my son, Evan, for teaching me from an early age what it means to celebrate oneself. I love him for being who he is: passionate about music, loving toward all, and a wonderful person to share ideas with!

Finally, I forgive myself for all the mistakes and lack of clarity I have left scattered here and there in this book. With each reading, I find more ways to improve the grammar or the clarity and elegance of speech! My friend Sue McGorray said to me, "Yes, hurry up - get it out there, mistakes and all. It will never be perfect. I am looking forward to it." She said she knows many people who suffer, "We need new ideas." Thanks Sue for allowing me to give up perfection for being of service! That made it a simpler choice!

PROLOGUE

The Anti-Self Help Book

I present this book as a self help book. But it isn't. Your genuine self is pure and whole already. It does not need any help. What we need is a book that shows us how to let go of what isn't who we are, but that we have come to identify with and robs us from our self, our anti-self. This is an anti-self help book.

Real Therapy

In my introduction as an intern in a substance abuse treatment facility, I was asked to lead a men's group. The director of the center sat in and watched me lead the group. At the end, his private comment to me came as a surprise, "You do real therapy!" I did not quite understand the full meaning of his statement until later. What where others doing if what I was doing needed the name real therapy?

The next hint about the current practice of psychotherapy came from a long time counselor at that center when he told me, "Our clients would not make any progress here if it wasn't for going to Alcoholics Anonymous." Attending Alcoholics Anonymous (AA) or Narcotics Anonymous (NA) meetings was strongly recommended. I wondered what the point was to being a psychotherapist if one did not feel that one's practice made a difference.

After a few weeks, I understood that counselors in a substance abuse treatment center have a heavy case load of 35 to 40 clients and can only spend 1/2 hour per week and sometimes every two weeks in individual meetings. They ask questions requested by a third party payer (insurance) such as: "Did you relapse since our last meeting?" or "What do you do to avoid relapse?" or "Do you practice staying away from people, places and things that trigger relapse?"

I was learning about the current practice of most substance abuse treatment centers in the USA.

I saw immediately that I cared about what was genuine about people, not their poor behavior. I started to ask my clients about what they loved, if they remembered having fun as children. I discovered that what I was doing was *self-discovery* work with them. Those who worked with me at the center stopped using drugs or alcohol within two weeks of working with me (i.e., no relapse). They were tested. They all graduated. Some of them refused to go to AA or NA meetings during the period of their treatment.

There was another counselor who believed in *self-discovery* as the proper way to help our clients as well. Our backgrounds were opposite in many ways and gave value to the practice of *self-discovery*. He had learned about life from the streets' culture, and I learned by wanting to heal from old haunting wounds (See Chapter 2, Life Lessons). So I was not the only one interested in *real therapy*.

I discovered that only addressing the disease or the misbehavior with clients is not talking about who they really are and so, at a subtle level, they don't feel heard and eventually they rebel or relapse.

More recently, I talked with a retired psychiatric nurse who understood exactly the kind of therapy I was doing. She said that they used to do *real therapy* prior to the 1980s, and then everything shifted with health insurance companies dictating the pace of therapy and, at the same time, came a push for psychotropic medication. They could not do *real therapy* after that and it was difficult to practice as one wanted.

The Script

I have come to believe that the problems we face in life come, for the most part, from interpreting life through a filter of beliefs, a worldview, instead of experiencing life as it is. Albert Ellis (1913-2007) expressed a similar idea. These beliefs come from the meaning we gave past experiences, or from family, teachers, and society. We work very hard at creating a more or less coherent story from these beliefs, and it becomes the script of our life. That script may be very different from our soul's needs. Our life script rules how we think and what we do consciously and unconsciously. It expresses itself in our body and our external life, and it is usually in conflict, at least in part, with our soul which holds our dreams and life purpose. This conflict can explain most cases of mental health challenges, depression, anxiety, post-traumatic stress disorder (PTSD), delusion, etc., or physical diseases, cancer, any chronic diseases, etc. That is what is meant by problems being psychosomatic. Lifestyle and nutrition habits are also important, but if the script we operate from does not change, it will still express itself in our life. While we are seeing things from inside this script, we can only see its internal logic which is very compelling, and it keeps us trapped within its painfully limiting view of life. But there is hope because solutions become possible when we look at life from outside of this script.

A famous example that may shed a little light on my claim is the story of Tom Shadyak who made several successful movies with Jim Carey. He was living the life of the rich and famous until he had a bicycle accident that led him to the hospital with a post-concussion syndrome that included terrible headaches and depression. Tom was contemplating suicide. Before ending his life he had a thought: "What would I want to do before I die?" And it occurred to him he wanted to answer two questions: "What's wrong with the world? What can we do about it?" After he became clear of what he wanted to do, he started healing. Then he made a documentary film called *I Am* attempting to answer his questions. While making his documentary film he had a profound transformation that led him to want to live simply and he sold his expensive mansion.

Being willing to die shows how much he believed his life script was all there was about him. But it also showed he was willing to let go of it and allowed him to start looking at life from outside that script. Then, everything changed. He healed physically but also spiritually. It goes together.

We may choose to fight the illness, mental or physical, that we face, but what we are fighting are the symptoms that arise as expressions of the script we have identified with. It is like fighting against a shadow, not realizing that the shadow only exists because something is blocking the light. Illnesses are only shadows which exist because something is blocking the light. From within the script, there is absolutely no way out. As long as we identify with it, we don't realize there is any other part to us. As soon as we are able to look at the content of the script from an outside perspective, we can start seeing the collapse of its internal logic. The practice of looking at one's script from the outside is mindfulness, and when the internal logic of that part of the script collapses, that part of the script disintegrates, and the light gets in which brings freedom from suffering and, ultimately, enlightenment.

This is a book about how to get outside of a script we have internalized which drives our thoughts and actions, and can make life seem as if it is predetermined. It is a book about how psychotherapy can bring healing. The means toward healing come from becoming aware that we have very different parts to us which can pull us apart if we don't become aware of what is taking place. We need to align our mind, body, and soul, otherwise we are filled with internal conflicts that lead to stress. Stress weakens our immune system which makes us prone to illnesses. At a deeper level, stress becomes so intense that it may lead to a variety of mental health challenges. The way to align our mind, body, and soul is to practice self-love, mindfulness and/or mindlessness.

The idea is simple, the practice not always. And it leads to healing and personal/spiritual growth. We do not have to keep believing that we have no power and that the only solution is through psychotropic drugs.

Note: I prefer the term mental health challenge to mental illness. In this book, I use the term "mental illness" when I am referring to the way our culture calls it and use "mental health challenge" when I refer to the condition.

The way this book is organized is as follows. I start with an introduction for those who have some knowledge of psychology and want to know where the ideas expressed here fit in the general field of psychotherapy. I then tell my story in order to explain how I came to understand how to heal. I continue by exploring various themes I find important such as Love, Nature, and Human Nature so as to lay out a foundation from which to understand notions of psychotherapy, mental illness, and mindfulness. I describe methods of healing in psychotherapy which are embraced by the Western world and approaches of healing from the non-Western worlds. I propose a unifying model for all of psychotherapy, which was believed to not be possible a few years ago as I was getting my master's in mental health counseling. I conclude with ideas for a new curriculum for the teaching of psychotherapy.

Currently, the field of Western psychotherapy is fragmented into schools and models, and different associations. As therapists, we have little communication across schools and associations. To put it plainly, the family of psychotherapists has not yet found inner harmony. How can psychotherapy offer harmony to people if it has not done the work for itself? Therefore, this unifying model of psychotherapy is the foundation for harmony among the fields of psychotherapy which can then be in a better position to offer healing to people who seek help.

Why Write this Book?

I was first asked to write an article about my therapeutic orientation by my teacher and mentor Robyn Trippany toward the end of my program at Walden University. Although what I wanted to say was new to the mainstream schools of psychotherapy, as I did some research to place my work in context, I found out it was not new to body-oriented psychotherapist Ron Kurtz. It took me a while to figure out what I could add to what he and others had already published. One of the key factors in my decision to write this book was my experience that I could help clients beyond what their former therapists were able to do with them. And the decisive factor came when Robin Williams committed suicide and, as a result, how people talked about depression on the radio.

I am a Kundalini yoga teacher and I have a master's degree in mental health counseling. I started teaching Kundalini yoga in 1995. I received my master's degree in mental health counseling in 2010.

Luc Watelet

From the practice of Kundalini yoga I started to experience a relationship between my mind, my body and my soul. As a result, I started feeling more joy and I was able to connect more deeply with my intuitive side. I also learned how to tune in to my students' energy so I could help them pay attention to what needed attention within them. This practice led me to discover how I wanted to practice psychotherapy. I was able to help people who sought my help. In particular, I witnessed how I was able to help someone who had suffered from depression for more than 30 years. After we started working together, despite years of therapy, she was able to reduce her need for anti-depression medications and started saying she was happy, both, for the first time in her adult life.

When Robin Williams' suicide became public and radio shows covered it, I heard on the radio someone repeat, as truth, a common belief that is rarely challenged in the media: "Depression is caused by a chemical imbalance." I thought it was time to put my thoughts together. I posted the following paragraph on my Facebook page and it created a stir of responses:

> Lots of talk about depression after Robin Williams' passing. Still hearing the same message that depression is caused by a chemical imbalance in the brain. Need to challenge this. Depression as all "mental illnesses" are a disconnection from our soul and from nature. Chemical imbalances are caused by this disconnect. We can heal by listening to our soul's needs.

Although most people who responded to my post agreed with it, including some counselors, some people responded with concerns and one with disbelief that I should be so ignorant.

I have grown used to people healing from physical conditions as well as mental health challenges such as depression, anxiety, addictions, and even schizophrenia. My mother healed herself from a hyperthyroid condition that doctors wanted to take care of with surgery followed by supplements. I write from experience, not from theoretical knowledge. And I also seek what science has to offer that sheds light on what I know from experience.

I have learned two things from this Facebook experience. One, if I voice my conclusions without explaining how I got there, I am likely to meet with resistance. And two, in order to write how I got to my conclusions, Facebook was not the right forum – I needed to write a book.

The two main concerns from people who commented on my post were: 1) In some people's experiences, depression and other mental health challenges had been so devastating and no solutions were found, so they had come to trust the explanation that those diseases had to be genetic or at least physiological in nature, and 2) some feared I was completely dismissing Western medicine.

So let me address this because I know that a reader with such concerns will not be able to read one more word that appears to go against all logic and/or cultural common sense.

Chemical Imbalances and Genetics

Could mental illnesses be genetic in nature? They seem to run in families don't they?

My first answer is that I have been able to help people reverse their dependence on medication and rely on mindfulness to overcome depression, even for someone who had been suffering from it for over 30 years. Thus, personal experience tells me that chemical imbalances or genetics cannot explain all cases of long term depression.

A Scientific Look at the Chemical Imbalance Argument

I have a Ph.D. in biostatistics. My training tells me that in order to show causality between variables that are correlated, one has to demonstrate that the causal event came before the dependent event and demonstrate a convincing pathway how one event causes the other. There are no studies demonstrating that a chemical imbalance causes depression. There is a study that demonstrates that the two conditions are correlated. In 2006, a study[1] led by Dr. Jeffery Meyer demonstrated

---

[1] Retrieved on October 22, 2014, and still active on July 1, 2016, from http://www.camh.ca/en/hospital/about_camh/newsroom/news_releases_me dia_advisories_and_backgrounders/archives/2006/Pages/new_depression_mo del_nov_2006.aspx.

that an enzyme, Monoamine oxidase A (MAO-A), is, on average, 34% higher for people having a major depression episode. This enzyme breaks down chemicals called neurotransmitters like serotonin, norepinephrine and dopamine. These neurotransmitters are essential for many functions including sexual desire, mood balance, the fight or flight response, and being alert. It is clear that if this enzyme level is too high, the essential neurotransmitters that contribute to our positive outlook and experience of life will be dangerously decreased.

The correlation between the chemical imbalance and depression was demonstrated for the subjects in that study. But this correlation does not tell what came first, the chemical imbalance or the depression. That the chemical imbalance came first is merely an assumption. Depression and the need for antidepressants can be reversed in the people I work with, as well as in people participating in other mindfulness programs. If the need for anti-depressants is reversed with mindfulness, the chemical imbalance is reversed with mindfulness.

In my clients, I have found that there is trauma at the source of the depression. As the trauma is released so is the depression and the chemical imbalance. Thus, my best hypothesis at this point is that the original trauma at the source of the depression and our response to it are together somehow responsible for the brain's chemical imbalance.

The Genetic Argument

The argument that something runs in families and therefore must be genetic is not convincing. Obesity, for instance, runs in families where people learn to live in the same nutrition environment and share the same nutrition worldview. That experience already starts in the womb. A similar argument that mental health challenges may be the result of a family environment can be made.

Scientists have been very creative in trying to discern the difference between the genetic and the environmental (nature vs. nurture) influences. They thought of studies on twins separated at birth. But,

Note: Remember that any link provided in this book may no longer be active when you try to open it. If it isn't, please search for the quote you are interested in online to find the new site it may be on!

unfortunately they were not entirely valid because the twins had shared the same environment in the womb prior to being born. A more careful approach was devised called the classical twin study which compares true twins with fraternal twins to control for the womb time and environment.

Looking for classical twin studies that show a genetic influence on mental health challenges, I found that autism may be explained genetically. And genetic markers have been found that are associated with several mental health challenges.

> Genetic maps have been used successfully to find the single gene responsible for relatively rare inherited disorders, like cystic fibrosis and muscular dystrophy. Maps have also become useful in guiding scientists to the many genes that are believed to interact to bring about more common disorders, such as asthma, heart disease, diabetes, cancer and psychiatric conditions.[2]

But even the classical twin study may not detect true genetic differences between genetic twins and fraternal twins because the family and social environment in which genetic twins live may reinforce twins similarities whereas fraternal twins may live in an environment that reinforces their differences. In other words, the environment of true twins may still be somewhat different from that of fraternal twins in ways that cannot easily be differentiated, measured, and controlled for. Therefore we still need to be careful in interpreting classical twin studies.

The other side of the genetic argument is that there is scientific evidence (Bruce Lipton, *The Biology of Belief*) that we control the activation of genes with our emotions. Positive emotions activate beneficial genes and negative emotions activate genes that can hurt us. So we have to be careful when we say that a problem is caused by genes.

> *"Medicine does miracles," [Lipton] said, "but it's limited to trauma. The AMA protocol is to regard our physical body like a machine, in*

---

[2] Retrieved on September 21, 2014, and still active July 1, 2016, from http://www.genome.gov/10000715.

the same way that an auto mechanic regards a car. When the parts break, you replace them — a transplant, synthetic joints, and so on — and those are medical miracles.

"The problem is that while they have an understanding that the mechanism isn't working, they're blaming the vehicle for what went wrong. They believe that the vehicle, in this case our bodies, is controlled by genes. "But guess what? They don't take into consideration that there's actually a driver in that car. The new science, epigenetics, reveals that the vehicles — or the genes — aren't responsible for the breakdown. It's the driver."

~ William James interview of Bruce Lipton.[3]

In one of my mental health counseling courses, we used a manual called *Psychology: A Topical Approach to Life Span Development*. In it, there is a section acknowledging the epigenetics view describing the current understanding that our relationship to our genetic material is a two-way relationship.[4] This scientific field establishes that we are not necessarily controlled by our genes. We have to understand that the messages we hear in the media, even sometimes from experts, may not be complete. We have to use critical thinking.

In some cases, like Down syndrome, it seems accurate to say that the condition is determined by the genes because of the extra chromosome in the genetic make-up that is responsible for the condition. Even in this case, we have healing options. I know of no cases of reversal of Down syndrome. The Bruno Gröning Circle of Friends is an organization that teaches healing on the spiritual path for free around the world according to the teachings of Bruno Gröning. Its medical scientific group keeps records of healings verified by medical doctors that were experienced by people using these teachings. The organization is currently active in about 140 countries. There are no accounts from that organization, to my knowledge at this point, of healings from Down syndrome. On the other hand, I have heard accounts of families who feel blessed by their children with Down syndrome and would never wish them to be different even if a cure were available. Loving their

---

[3] Retrieved September 21, 2014, and still active July 1, 2016, from https://www.brucelipton.com/resource/article/epigenetics.
[4] *Psychology: A Topical Approach to Life Span Development*. Third edition published by McGraw-Hill, 2008, p. 81.

children, as they are, transformed the family's understanding of what it means to love and the meaning of a fulfilling life.

Some families who have children with autism have also discovered that love is transformative and they would not wish for their children to be different.

Depression is different. It drags people down and can affect people close to them. So if there is a chance to understand how to reverse it, I wanted to find it. And I found that mindfulness is a way that can lead to healing from depression. I also found out that depression is not the only mental health challenge people can heal from using a mindfulness approach. I have personally helped or spoken with people diagnosed with addictions, anxiety, bi-polar, post-traumatic stress disorder (PTSD), and delusional and paranoid schizophrenia for whom mindfulness was very successful in the identification 1) that at some unconscious level the person chose the illness, and, hence, 2) that the person could also choose to be healthy.

Reframing the Genetic and Chemical Imbalance Concern: We Are More than Our Genes!

Whether a human condition is due to a chemical imbalance or a genetic influence, the key question to me is: Is the person affected by the condition living a fulfilling and happy life? If the person is, then why seek to change that person? If the person is not, and really wants a happy, fulfilling life, that person usually feels powerless to change the experience, but why assume that the person really is powerless?

In my life, whenever I felt down, anxious, apathetic, or depressed, my underlying realization was that I was disconnected from myself and from life. The question has always been to find out how to reconnect. The solution has always been: self-love, meditation, going for a walk in nature, or being of service to others. Wouldn't this be true for others as well?

There are cases that challenge my claim. The case of dementia for instance which includes Alzheimer's and Lewy body diseases. I have been close to and cared for people with such diagnoses. As the disease progresses, it becomes increasingly hard to establish and experience a heart to heart connection with them. It is hard to imagine people with such diagnoses to be experiencing a happy fulfilling life.

From my experiences with healing, my basic question has two sides. The first side asks: "What leads someone to need the experience of a particular struggle for his/her spiritual growth?" or, when a condition becomes an epidemic, "What does our society have to learn from people with such experiences?" These questions relate to looking for the metaphor in our lives that the disease represents. More on this topic in Chapter 8, Mindfulness Psychotherapy. The second side asks: "Given what a person's situation is, how can one help him/her find satisfaction and even happiness in life?"

Caregivers of people with dementia have asked themselves this last question. It is very possible that the lessons are more for the caregivers than they are for the patients. Caregivers must enter the worlds of their patients and learn to love them where they are and as they are. The patients appear to behave more and more like children. At the same time we need to remember that they have lived rich lives. They still have a spirit within them. They may, at times, have flashes of memories come back to them and may even sometimes show signs of being present. Caregivers must never give up on the possibility of having a fulfilling experience with a person affected by dementia.

I visited a few times and cared for a person with an Alzheimer diagnosis. She had not had a clear and present connection with her daughter, with whom she lived, for at least a year. One day, I was giving her a routine sponge bath. She was on her commode. I was preparing her for bed when I heard her hum a tune faintly. So I asked her, "Do you like singing?" And she said, "Do Si Do!" So I said, "Oh! You like dancing!" And a most beautiful smile lit up her face. So I said, "Well then, I'll dance you to your bed when we are done!" Her daughter witnessed the whole exchange and was baffled. That had not happened in over a year. She then confirmed that her mother loved to dance. These are moments when I know the real person is "still in there" and I just happened to notice an opening with my client that evening so I could experience a connection with her. An Alzheimer's or Lewy body diagnosis does not mean the person is losing his memory or spirit, he is simply losing the brain's ability to connect with them.

After that experience, I heard on the radio the interview of a doctor who shared a similar experience with a patient with an Alzheimer diagnosis.

Moments like these show me that we are more than our genes; there is a spirit lurking in each of us, needing to be acknowledged. Like the woman who had a diagnosis of Alzheimer's, as soon as I told her, "Oh! You like dancing?" her face lit up with a smile we had not seen in a year. She was acknowledged. The spirit of people with dementia may not have received the attention it needed prior to the development of dementia. Now it is up to us to see if we can create that connection. Time will tell if dementia can be reversed if we focused on connecting rather than treating. But, even if we can't reverse dementia, by looking to acknowledge our patients and clients' spirit, we develop our connection to, and become aware of, our own in the process.

People with dementia give us that opportunity and if we take it we receive a gift. Dementia and mental health challenges may be symptoms of a culture that has forgotten the importance of the inner-self, the importance of consciousness, the importance of the soul.

Looking for a genetic or medical solution to dementia and mental health challenges has the potential for incredible advances in our scientific understanding of the human physiology. But by addressing the symptoms only, we run the risk of ignoring the inner self who craves to be acknowledged, that faint voice of our own spirit and that of our clients asking softly: *"What about me?"*

We need to change our illness driven focus and learn to be soul driven, infinite possibilities driven, miracle driven. Anything else is limiting to our clients/patients and to ourselves.

Western Medicine

It is not my place to judge Western or Allopathic Medicine. I can only tell what happens when symptoms are taken care of by Allopathic Medicine.

I mentioned that my mother healed herself from a hyperthyroid condition. She decided to address the stress in her life in two ways:

emotionally and physically. She figured, if she relieved her body from as much stress as she could, her immune system would take care of the rest. She dealt with the emotional stress coming from her daily interactions with people and dealt with the physical stress by eliminating foods from her diet that she was found allergic to with a blood-based allergy test. In the process, she learned how to deal with stresses in her life. She grew spiritually. It took two years for her thyroid tests to be back to normal. Had she taken the surgery route recommended by doctors, she would not have understood so quickly how stress was affecting her body and would not have experienced her own power to let her body heal. And she would be taking supplements for the rest of her life believing that her body was aging and that she had no power against that process.

I had a hernia condition that I tried to heal with mindfulness. The tear in my abdominal muscle wall was increasing dangerously and surgery was necessary and successfully done. Hernia repair is a successful medical procedure today. Yet I have met older men who had undergone surgery due to a hernia years earlier and felt pain again in that area of their body when I met them. Thus, I was also very aware that there was a source of stress that led to the hernia condition that neither they nor I had fully addressed. I could still feel internal pressures in that part of my body. With experience, I know more clearly what triggers the internal stress and I can address it better. Western medicine did not heal me. It took care of the major symptom which needed to be addressed to avoid deeper immediate damage. It is still important to address the source of stress to avoid what could lead to a relapse of the hernia condition.

I never discourage my clients from taking psychotropic medications because they help us have coherent conversations. But in time, my clients themselves feel when their need for medication decreases. Dr. Brian Weiss, psychiatrist and past life therapist, has a similar experience as he mentions in his workshops how past life therapy has been successful in making his patients less dependent on medication. Dr. Breggin, psychiatrist, is also a proponent of reducing the need for medication in his patients.

Western medicine is wonderful for emergencies and addressing immediate dangerous symptoms. However, it is important to know that it does not address the real cause(s) of the problem. We need to recognize that Western medicine is a symptom-based modality, it is not a healing modality.

This Book

My Facebook post is an elevator speech of a key message of this book.

> *Lots of talk about depression after Robin Williams' passing. Still hearing the same message that depression is caused by a chemical imbalance in the brain. Need to challenge this. Depression as all "mental illnesses" are a disconnection from our soul and from nature. Chemical imbalances are caused by this disconnect. We can heal by listening to our soul's needs.*

It is one message that I feel needs attention today because the current message having people believe that mental illness is the result of a chemical imbalance or due to genetics is misleading and disempowering when it is generalized to all cases.

It is not a new message as the following comment about Jung recognizes:

> *With the hegemony of the biochemical approach to so-called mental disorders and the rise of an endless succession of "wonder" drugs such as Prozac, Jung's insistence on the psychogenic and symbolic significance of such states is even more timely now than then. As R. D. Laing stated in this regard: "It was Jung who broke the ground here, but few have followed him."*[5]

I want to remind the reader how one can reestablish the inner connection needed to achieve healing. I framed it within the context of psychotherapy because I want to help us reclaim the field of psychotherapy as a healing discipline. Reclaim it from the limitations of medicine and sometimes science, and from the controls of health insurances and the pharmaceutical industry. If you talk to therapists who were active before the 1980s, you may have a very different idea

---

[5] S. Shamdasani. From the introduction of C. G. Jung, *The Psychology of Kundalini Yoga.* Princeton University Press. Edited by Sonu Shamdasani, 1996, pp. xxvi, xxvii.

of the practice of psychotherapy from the way it is today. We need to do better and we can.

When we understand that illnesses are an expression of one's life script, we see that we have to extract our identity from this script. In order to do so, we need the tools of meditation. This leads to a mindfulness approach to psychotherapy. The basic principle is to learn to reconnect with oneself. This approach to therapy can be used in all aspects of psychotherapy from addiction recovery to mental health challenges recovery, from family therapy to vocational therapy, in mediation in the corporate world to facilitate better relationships between co-workers or between management and the people they manage. This approach transcends illnesses because it is not dependent on illness. Instead it is focused on wellness. The work toward deeper wellness leads to personal growth and enlightenment: Know who you are and let go of the rest. You are not your problems, so let them go, and connect with those parts of you that are infinite and eternal. That's who you are.

The role of the psychotherapist becomes that of a midwife of the inner world, helping to give birth to the healthy you that is ready to be born. It is not about changing you. It is not about fixing you. It is about helping you reconnect with the healthy you that is already there so the illness can leave and the circumstances can heal.

This book at its core goes beyond therapy to the very basic ways in which we relate with our self, with each other, and with the world at large. If we can learn to be more present to our self and to each other by adopting a caring/loving attitude and by developing an ability to truly hear each other, we may create a culture in which mental health challenges and addictions no longer exist, and therefore lead the way toward a culture in which psychotherapy may not be as needed as it is today. If you have any doubts, a glimpse into Chapter 10 indicates that there are cultures, for example the Q'eros, where mental health challenges do not exist. They are not genetically protected from them as individual members of their community can still get mentally ill when they move out from their original community.

~ ~ ~

To people seeking help and healing: Help and healing are available if you look in the right places. This book can help you find the understanding and inspiration you need to find what you seek.

To the future of psychotherapy: We are at a fork on the road. One path leads to prescribing medication to people for the rest of their lives and the giving up of our inner powers. The other path leads to empowering people to know they can heal and the end of unnecessary suffering. Which path will we take?

To all of our relationships: Mental health challenges, physical diseases and our circumstances all point to what we need to do in order to heal. They are all blessings in disguise if we only pay attention to their blessings. As a culture we have forgotten to love ourselves, and each other, and to love all of life, and the sky, the air, the mountains, the waters, and the grounds. We have a chance to remember to dare to love.

1 INTRODUCTION

This chapter places my work in the context of psychotherapy today and, in doing so, points to the internal fragmentation of the field of psychotherapy and the need for an integration within the field. I discuss the importance of working with the mind, the body, and the soul. I question the notion of an abnormal psychology. I discuss the position of the therapist who is traditionally supposed to be objective and yet needs to explore the subjective world of a client and the implications this has on therapy. And finally, I discuss therapy from the perspective of a healing paradigm.

This introduction is for the reader who already has some notions of the history of psychotherapy and wants to understand where this book fits in that history. The person who seeks how to heal from illness may skip to the disclaimer at the end of this chapter and start reading the next chapters immediately and may come back to this chapter later.

A Parable on the Origin of Psychotherapy

I imagine the three medical doctors, Freud (1856-1939), Adler (1870-1937) and Jung (1875-1961), having a beer in Vienna. Freud brings up the case of a man on the edge of suicide after a year of marriage with a woman diagnosed with hysteria.

Adler chimes in: "The man is obviously discouraged; he is ready to give up. He lacks a supportive and encouraging environment!"

"That's too simplistic my friend," says Freud, "This man had a death wish long before his wife developed hysteria; he is now using his wife's desperate situation to justify his death wish!"

After a moment of silence, Jung says, "You may both be right; all I know for sure is that neither one has established a healthy relationship with the unconscious. The woman's relationship with her animus is hanging by a thread as is represented by her suicidal husband, and the man's anima is getting crazy because he is not interested in her, as is represented by his wife's hysteria."

I see them shaking their heads baffled by the differences between each one's perspective, and holding on to their own position. In real life, they parted ways to create different schools of psychotherapy. These schools are still separate today.

Freud went on to be the father of a psychotherapy based on the medical and scientific paradigms. Adler created a school of understanding the individual in her social context, inspired feminist therapy, for instance, and became the father of brief psychotherapies. Jung became interested in people's relationships with their soul and became the father of spiritually-oriented psychotherapies. If I can be forgiven for overly simplifying, they represent the archetypal trinity of the origin of psychotherapy: Freud, focusing primarily on the mind/personality and its *drives*, Adler on the body with the experience of the human being in his environment, and Jung on the soul, and, therefore, the human being's relationship with what is bigger than himself.

Jung explained the difference between their approaches to therapy by his personality types. That means that their approaches are not interchangeable, they are complementary, as each one contributed to a different aspect of human nature and is worth paying attention to.

Many psychotherapists have since elaborated on the efforts and work of these three men and their schools. Many ways have been described to apprehend the mind, the body, and the soul, but we need to address all three together. Currently, in the USA, there are many psychotherapy related professional associations: the American Psychological Association (APA), the National Association of Social Workers (NASW), the American Counseling Association (ACA), the American Mental Health Counselors Association (AMHCA), the American Association of Marriage and Family Therapy (AAMFT), and the American Psychiatric Association (also with acronym APA). There is an association to advance somatic psychology called the United States Association for Body Psychotherapy (USABP). And there is a separate association for a spiritual approach to therapy called the Association for Transpersonal Psychology (ATP). There is also a Society for the Psychology of Religion and Spirituality which is a branch of the American Psychological Association. To me, to group together religion and spirituality shows a misunderstanding of spirituality because a spiritual life is simply the outcome of engaging consciously with life, therefore it cannot be escaped, but religion is a specific philosophical approach to living.

Why do we have so many associations related to psychotherapy? It seems to indicate that psychotherapy is a fragmented profession that has not yet learned to integrate its internal disagreements and differences. How then could we expect such a profession to be able to help clients and patients resolve their internal conflicts?

During my master's level coursework in mental health counseling, the notion of religion and spirituality in psychology were not fully addressed, neither were the body-oriented approaches to therapy. As a whole the field of psychotherapy shows a separation between cognitive behavioral, somatic, and spiritual approaches to therapy. Behavior therapy is typically addressed through the mind not the body. In its education system and by the number of its associations, the field of psychotherapy acknowledges implicitly a fragmentation in the way it thinks of the human being. At the same time, more therapists seek a holistic approach to psychotherapy. This trend will open new doors.

The Notion of Spirituality and the Notion of the Soul

Before I say more about the importance of the mind, the body, and the soul, I want to address the notion of spirituality. Jung stressed its importance throughout his writings, but for the most part psychotherapy evolved more toward a mind-oriented discipline.

The notion of spirituality made a resurgence with pastoral counselors such as Clinebell. Many after him discussed the importance to address spirituality in counseling. But the definition of spirituality remains vague perhaps because the experience of spirituality is very personal. Paul Ceasar and Judith Miranti[6] (school textbook) describe various definitions of spirituality all dependent on something that we experience such as "highest level of development line" or "attitude of openness or love" or "peak experience."

To me spirituality comes from living consciously. In that sense, spiritual growth is the same as personal growth. The only difference is that it acknowledges that an unforeseen dimension of life results by engaging with life. And because engaging with life is the very substance of therapy, there should be no separate field of spiritual psychotherapy. Religion may be one way a person chooses to engage with life, but, in and of itself, spirituality is not dependent on any belief. Instead it simply comes from experience. This definition of spirituality paves the way for a unifying model of psychotherapy.

Some may want to argue that we do not have a soul. It is relatively easy to believe in the importance of working with both the body and the mind as there are more and more accounts indicating that it is not enough to work with the mind only and one needs to pay attention to the body. But where in my mind or my body do I find my dreams and my purpose? In order to access these, I have to do some "soul searching" that goes beyond just thinking, and beyond the memories in my body. I have to access my heart which opens me to something beyond my mind and my body. As a result I enter the realm of my passion and my spirit, something that is more purely me than anything else. That's what I mean by the soul. Not including the soul in therapy would be avoiding an essential part of me. In this sense, the idea of a soul does not need to be attached to the belief in the existence or not of a deity.

The Integration of Mind, Body, and Soul

I envision a holistic form of psychotherapy that brings harmony between the three different aspects of the trinity of human nature: the mind, the body and the soul.

---

[6] P. Ceasar and J. Miranti (2005). *Counseling and Spirituality* in An Introduction to the Counseling Profession, 4th ed., edited by David Capuzzi and Douglas Gross, Pearson Education, Inc.

How many of us treat our body's symptoms as though they are unrelated with the problems we face in life? We treat headaches with an aspirin, migraines with more powerful medicine, knee problems don't get addressed very well until we need knee surgery and so on. It is not that we don't have the knowledge. Louise Hay's book, *You Can Heal Your Life* (1984), is more than thirty years old. The idea that the mind and the body are not distinct entities was already argued by Parmenides in the fifth century BC (found from several internet sources). Yet I remember that my father did not believe in a connection between the physical symptoms he experienced and his life's circumstances until my mother healed herself from the hyperthyroid condition I mentioned in the Prologue. My father's way of thinking was representative of the culture in which we live. In our culture, we may address the mind with teachers or psychotherapists, we address the body with sport coaches, medical doctors, chiropractors, or physical therapists, and we address the soul once a week mostly with preachers, ministers, rabbis, imams, and sometimes with a spiritual practice or a spiritual teacher. So in our daily lives we deal separately with our mind, our body and our soul.

There are individual professionals who work holistically with their clients/patients, but, as discussed above, psychotherapy as a field does not yet have an integrative view of the mind, body and soul.

Bringing harmony between groups of people comes by seeing the underlying truths that bring them together and/or push them apart from each other. Similarly, bringing harmony within a person comes from discovering the truths of the relationship between the different parts of a person. Our mind, body and soul have different roles to play. We need to bring them to converse with each other so we can create integrity in our lives. In psychotherapy, we have a unique platform to bring harmony to our relationship with all three parts of our trinity, and with each other. I'd love to see psychotherapists invited at the United Nations' discussions concerned with bringing peace between nations! For a wonderful approach to healing world conflicts check out Worldwork with Arnold and Amy Mindell.[7]

The disconnected view of our mind, body and soul is represented in our culture's accepted beliefs about addiction and mental illness. They are

[7] http://www.aamindell.net.

voiced unchallenged in the media. For instance, "Depression is the result of a chemical imbalance," "Depression is a genetic disease," "In schizophrenia, the disease makes clients not take their medication," or "An addict is always an addict." These are blanket statements that leave little room for hope of a complete healing and have little to do with a holistic view of human nature.

My natural inner thirst for truth led me to check if these statements were true with my clients. I found people could reverse the diagnosis of depression; people could discover that they chose not to take their medication and it wasn't the disease that made the choice for them; and people could heal from alcoholism – that is, after being healed, they could drink a half a glass of wine and not need to drink it all. These cases are counterexamples to and challenge our mainstream cultural beliefs.

Abnormal Psychology

I came to ask myself: What if there is no such thing as abnormal psychology? What if, instead, every behavior one observes in human beings is either 1) an opportunity for compassion or 2) the natural consequence of a worldview?

Let's consider the psychological view of sexual preference. It recently stopped being considered abnormal. We are led to understand sexual preference as a personal, a family, or a societal challenge to compassion or opportunity for compassion. One may also include people born with Down syndrome, autism, or physical disabilities as personal, family or social challenges to our ability to love people just as they present themselves to us. All these experiences fall outside of what we have been considering "normal" as a culture. Yet they are opportunities to open our hearts to a new "normal," a normal based on the naturalness of diversity of being and self-expression.

In the second instance, depression for example, may come to an individual as the natural consequence of ignoring (having forgotten) one's deeply buried inner wants, or one's life purpose, and/or as the natural consequence in a culture that does not value the soul and spirit and their purposes in our lives.

In *The New Peoplemaking,* Virginia Satir expresses the seed of a similar idea as my point #2 above:

> *When I am in any of these troubled atmospheres, my body reacts violently. My stomach feels queasy, my back and shoulders soon ache, as does my head. I used to wonder if the bodies of these family members responded as mine did. Later, when I knew them better and they became free enough to tell me what life was like in their family, I learned that they did indeed have the same sensations. [...] Their bodies were simply responding humanly to a very inhuman atmosphere.*[8]

Other people also challenge the mainstream view on mental illness. Dr. Michael Cornwall gave a talk in 2000. He started: "Hi, I'm Michael Cornwall and I don't believe in mental illness!"[9]

Although my belief is that medication can be helpful and is even necessary to have coherent conversations with some people, it does not mean we have to think of them as ill for life.

In this book, I explore the kind of psychotherapy that derives naturally from the premise that our human symptoms and diseases, physical or mental, are not abnormal and instead are natural consequences from how we see our experiences. This suggests a client-centered approach to therapy.

Subjectivity and Objectivity

Freud was a big proponent of presenting an objective front to his patients. He was known to have his patients lie down on a couch such that they did not see him. This facilitated his work with hypnosis and also prevented patients from seeing, and be affected by, his body language. The therapist was supposed to remain an objective presence. Reflecting in his memoirs, Jung questioned the notion of objectivity, describing Freud as being emotionally involved in his sexual theory.[10]

---

[8] V. Satir (1988).*The New Peoplemaking*, Science and Behavior Books, p. 10.
[9] Retrieved on Sept 28, 2014, and still active July 1, 2016, from
 http://www.madinamerica.com/2012/03/i-dont-believe-in-mental-illness-do-you/.
[10] C.G., Jung (1965). *Memories, Dreams and Reflections*, Vintage Books edition,

When I was a child, I remember feeling hurt by objectivity. I wanted my subjectivity to be acknowledged. My father was a historian who worked diligently to deal with historical research in a scientific manner. Many historians used the filter of some –isms (socialism, Marxism, liberalism, capitalism, etc.) to understand and reflect on history. Historians can use history to promote their views and not simply be of service to the truth. My father reacted to this and instead wanted to let the facts speak for themselves. He searched all the records he could find to paint the clearest picture he could to understand the questions he was studying. He would use records in geology, social circumstances, economics, and politics in his detective work. As a result, objectivity became his guiding light. In contrast to this, I discovered that my subjectivity mattered deeply to me. There is a place for both.

Later, when I studied statistics, I started to understand the need to find general trends and therefore the importance of eliminating individual differences unless they pointed to a problem with the hypotheses being tested. Statistics and science were methods to establish underlying truths shared by systems, communities, and large groups of people. However, in my therapeutic work, I wanted to hear the very subjectivity of my clients. Science could inform therapy, but subjectivity needed a prominent place. Therapy became a dance between the subjective and the objective. I had to have an objective view that cares for a healthy ideal for my clients and I needed to understand my clients' subjectivity that prevents them from being able to live their ideal.

More recently, when I discussed my thoughts on subjectivity and objectivity with my father, he agreed with me. He had done a similar journey from developing an objective scientific way to research history to becoming fascinated with social history and the experience of individual workers who worked in a mine he had studied.

The involvement of Arnold Mindell[11] with Worldwork, either with small groups or large ones[12] or with Deep Democracy, all points to the importance of the subjective, the importance of the shyest voice which,

---

pp. 150, 158.
[11] http://www.aamindell.net.
[12] A. Mindell (1995). *Sitting in the Fire: Large Group Transformation Through Diversity And Conflict.* Lao Tse Press.

when spoken and heard, can change an entire group's dynamic.

We live in a smart culture that knows how to be practical and logical. Why say that chemical imbalances cause depression when there are no studies demonstrating this causality? The discussion of the dance between the subjective and the objective is, therefore, crucial. Using science, or a position of authority, to make claims on mental health issues that sound objective is abuse of power and disempowering.

When thinking of the paradigm to frame psychotherapy in a context that can be communicated and taught, remember that human nature is not ruled by statistics, science and medicine, it is ruled by universal laws. Healing happens best when we work with life, i.e., with universal laws.

I went to see a client-centered therapist with the question of how I could make a living with my therapeutic knowledge. At the time, I felt frustrated with my inability to create a successful business. Client-centered therapists are supposed to believe more than any other therapists that clients have their solutions within themselves. I went for a few sessions during which I told her my story and she took copious notes. Meanwhile, I received notice from my bank that my house was being foreclosed and I shared this information with her. She told me we had to stop doing therapy, that I needed to use my money for my son, and I needed to go back into statistics. I will tell more in my Life Lessons' chapter about that difficult part of my life. I had left statistics knowing that I had to dive into the future of my life. After a while, my income did not support me. I tried to get back into statistics without success. That's why I sought the help of a therapist so I could gain clarity about myself. Not only was she trained to help me find my own answers and was not supposed to tell me what to do, she did not help me gain clarity about myself. And to add to the problem, I saw her at a health fair a week later and she asked me if I had started to search for work in statistics. I felt very vulnerable. I had no answers and I did not know how to sound assertive and convincing to her or how to tell her she was misreading me. This experience made me even more aware of the importance as a psychotherapist to work with the subjective of the client and not judge that experience from an apparent objective worldview.

Eight years later I know why Life happened the way that it did for me and that the therapist was wrong – the solution was not a return to statistics. But the experience was instructive in that it taught me that I had the answers within and did not need to rely on outside help to know what to do. Life was unbeknownst to me supporting me on my quest.

Around that same time, a yoga teacher had also urged me to go back into statistics even if I had to live thousands of miles away from my son. And a friend accused me of being a leach to society because I had accrued credit card debts and then applied for bankruptcy. I did not use bankruptcy to get out of my own debt, but because of a credit card fine print, I had been made responsible for someone else's $10,000 debt.

Because I received no help from those I thought could be helpful, I had to find the strength within myself to pull myself up by the bootstraps. I don't blame anyone who did not support me or who gave me the wrong advice. In the end, the lack of help from the outside pushed me to find it inside. This experience informed me at a deep level of the importance of the subjective as I found the answers I needed within me. In the process, I found friends who did not judge me and listened with their heart, or offered either some care giving job or a roof over my head. I was not alone. I was only alone in trying to put order in my financial life. This brought me on quest to find meaning from struggles in my life which led me to work with life instead of trying to control life.

That a client-centered therapist would go out of her way to give me advice that was wrong in the end shows a deep mistrust in our culture in the individual's inner-self. This is why I spend so much time in this introduction setting up the need to care for the subjective, the need to listen to individual circumstances and to withhold judgment. This is why this book is centered on stories, my own and those of several clients. I trust these stories lay out a solid foundation for understanding the benefits of trusting in everyone's inner knowing and that the best approach to this inner knowing, short of having access to a spiritual master who can see directly into someone's soul, is to embrace self-love, mindfulness, and mindlessness (see Chapter 8).

One more aspect of the subjective versus the objective concerns the use of theory in counseling. When I was a master's student studying mental health counseling, I was struck by the emphasis some of my teachers placed on the need for theory, in particular that we cannot do therapy without a well-established theory. I felt an inner rebellion inside. I feared I would only be allowed to be a smart robot whose only job was to master listening skills and to choose the right theory, at the right time, for the right client. Their argument was that the role of theory is to lay out a system of therapy that can be communicated to other therapists in a way that others can implement it and that scientific research can be done to evaluate its effectiveness. The idea is that ethically we want to help and do no harm, and therefore it is essential to provide services that are already known to be effective. We were told that we needed to find our own voice as a therapist, but that we also needed to use evidence-based theory. It sounded very convincing and coming from a client wellbeing point of view.

My problem was with the use of *theory*. Theory is a construct that is neither true nor false; it needs to be tested. What if I know of a therapeutic orientation that is based on truths rather than on hypotheses? Any psychotherapeutic theory, by definition is bound to limit our human understanding of experience. My goal, if I have any with my clients, is to help them find freedom, not be bound by any theoretical filter of their experience. My clients may have goals; in my experience, such goals are ways to get moving, to have a motivation and a life canvas from which to grow. Therefore, my goals for my clients are as unlimited as I can make them to be: freedom (from suffering and to create), passion, peace, unconditional love, bliss, harmony... and I support my clients as they work toward their personal goals as a path of least resistance toward these loftier goals.

M. Scott Peck explains very succinctly why theory is not the best approach to therapy and why the subjective is so important:

> *Each one of us must make his own path through life. There are no self-help manuals, no formulas, no easy answers. The right road for one is the wrong road for another. [...] The journey of life is not paved in blacktop; it is not brightly lit, and it has no road signs. It is a rocky path through the wilderness.*[13]

---

[13] M. Scott Peck (1993). *Further Along the Road Less Traveled: The Unending Journey Toward Spiritual Growth*. Touchstone, p. 13.

A Paradigm of Healing

People I meet are often surprised by my claim that they can heal. They say: "No, my problem is just this…." It is partly that we are so used to our own life that we don't question our experience unless it is unusual to us. I was so used to worrying that I believed I was happy enough when I was not. But life has a way to remind us. In my case, it did not flow as smoothly as I expected. When I found ways to notice I was worrying and release the worry, life started to flow better. The lack of flow was what drew my attention because I could not tell I was worrying. That is why it is so important to not dismiss our triggers and see them instead as signs that we have something to learn. Our emotions can point to where we could heal.

When I was seven or so and I thought about Jesus being able to heal people, I thought that if he could do that anyone could learn to do it too. It felt a bit sacrilegious to think that way and I did not say it out loud. But as a result, I don't believe I have to live with problems, such as poor teeth, limited eyesight, the flu, etc. If I haven't healed yet, it is because the healing process is not complete, or there is something I have yet to learn. If I have not changed my worldview after the problem came up, the problem is likely to stay or be recurrent. I use no excuses for myself. I come from a place where I believe that anything can be healed and that I am the only one limiting my experience. I have to be humble though and accept that timing is important with the universe, otherwise I would easily become a tyrant commanding the universe for everything I want.

The experiential mindfulness approach to therapy is based on the integration of one's life experiences and is an attempt to move us beyond theories into the sacred space of healing where freedom comes by letting go of what we think we know as therapists and by entering innocently into the sacred unknown with our clients. This is where we connect intuitively with each other. I know many therapists have actually experienced this.

We need to acknowledge this in the open so we stop giving our students the impression that therapy is just an application of the right theories. Theories, but also a more complete understanding of life and human nature, personal experiences and experiences with clients, and intuition, can be used as spring boards into a space that transcends theories... the sacred space of healing where we really connect with our self and our clients. This is where we all heal.

This freeing experience in therapy may not be easy to tap into for a beginning therapist, but it can be aspired to. One does not learn to be a tennis professional without studying what has been achieved by the best.

What I know from direct experience is that healing from mental health challenges is possible. It depends on the willingness to heal by the person affected. It also depends on the limitations and openness of the therapist. Healing is deeply linked to personal and spiritual growth as it is linked to remembering who we are. And remembering who we are is a doorway into our relationships with each other, with nature and with the universe. This is a huge paradigm shift from using therapy to treat illness and help people be functional in their cultural environment.

The healing paradigm works like this:
1.   Do I want to heal?
If I want to heal, then
2.   Am I willing to receive healing?

If a person does not receive instant healing, then there are three worlds that can be explored: self-love, self-knowledge, and selfless service to others.

Do I Want to Heal?

This addresses the conscious will to heal. Some people don't want to heal because they benefit in some way from the problem they face and don't want to imagine a life without these benefits; it might take away the attention they get from family, friends, or the health care system, and/or the financial benefits they may be receiving.

Carolyn Myss's book *Why People Don't Heal and How They Can* is a wonderful exploration into the mysteries of healing and resistance to healing.

Am I Willing to Receive Healing?

This addresses the unconscious will to heal. A person might say they really want to heal, but they don't realize that they are really attached to being angry toward a person or a system, or toward God. The need to remain angry prevents the healing from taking place. Sometimes the benefits for remaining ill or having a disability are unconscious and are not easy to see and therefore to let go.

This question really asks: Am I willing to accept the consequences of being healed?

Self-Love

Self-love is not a switch that propels us instantly into the space of 100% self-love. Each time we face a challenge we have an opportunity to access more self-love than we knew was necessary prior to the challenge. I think self-love, and compassion, is ultimately what we are in this life to learn. When we are fully loving and compassionate, we have grown to the next level of personal and spiritual growth beyond what life on earth has to offer.

Self-love includes an exploration of self-acceptance, self-worth (self-esteem), forgiveness, letting go, not taking things personally, and extracting our self out of negative perceptions and stories we tell our self to explain our experience. It is an exploration of peace, joy, celebration, inner harmony, and being loved and loveable.

Self-Knowledge

Socrates reminded us to *know thyself*. He was right. It is often easier to love one-self when we understand why we acted a certain way, or to forgive others if we understand why they acted a certain way. If you are driving and someone cuts you off, you may be angry with the other driver. But if you learn that that person's spouse was just hurt badly and sent to the hospital you might be more open to forgiving him. Understanding helps, but what really heals is to learn to love without the need to understand, to learn to love unconditionally.

On the other hand, an active pursuit of self-knowledge is an aspect of self-love. Self-knowledge can be explored through formal meditation: mindful or mindless. It can also be explored through creative disciplines: journaling, writing fiction, practicing any of the arts, and activities that require finding solutions, because when we pay attention intensely to something other than our self, we allow new solutions to come in if we are open to healing.

Selfless Service to Others

None of the activities we engage in should be used to avoid our core issues. Some psychologists become psychologists to help heal others from the very trauma they themselves suffer from without having healed their own trauma. Some caregivers experience burnout because they forget themselves. Burnout is a sure sign that we forgot to pay attention to our self.

We cannot be of service and be helpful to others if our purpose is self-serving. Avoiding our issues is self-serving.

But if we are selfless and recognize our own issues being triggered during our service to others, our service becomes a meditation, it becomes healing to our self, and thereby healing to those we serve. For instance, Patch Adams, MD, talks about his discovery that the depression that haunted him no longer had a hold over him when he started paying attention to others.

My Purpose in Writing this Book

In writing this book, I wanted to give a central place to the inner world of human beings. I wrote this book not for the purpose of developing new theories, but from the purpose of honoring the human spirit. I used my stories of healing as my truest source of knowledge. It is always possible to distort the meaning of experiences and that is where our unhealthy scripts come from. Truth comes from healing experiences. They showed me a picture of human nature that I would not know of otherwise. As a result, I honor other people's experiences because they lead to their gold. As they share their experiences with me, some of them become gold to me. In honor of our inner worlds, I lay out a foundation that shifts from the medical and scientific paradigms to a healing paradigm, a paradigm that has been long known by spiritual masters and traditional healers.

We can heal from addiction and mental health challenges. These stumbling blocks in life are actually pointing to what needs or seeks healing in us. In the process, we grow personally and spiritually. The foundation of the work to heal from addictions and/or mental health challenges is the same as that of growing more and more toward peace, joy, love, and ultimately enlightenment. Thus, this book lays out a foundation of the work toward enlightenment.

Seen in this context, it is time to change our traditional perspective of mental illness presented in the *Diagnostic and Statistical Manual of Mental Disorders*, which is now in its 5th Edition (DSM-5). This manual is the gold standard for psychiatrist and trained psychologists to give a mental disorder diagnostic to their patients and clients. I submit and hope to convince the reader that mental illness is not a personality disorder and instead is a symptom of a disconnection between the mind, body and soul in an individual and depends on the culture. I wish for the next edition of the DSM to take this into account and no longer talk about illnesses but instead talk about symptoms, and substitute the phrase *mental illness* with *mental health challenge*.

As you read this book, know that I did my best not to lay claims without justifications. I was honest with my assumptions when I made them. In the end, I am not asking that you believe anything I say, but please hold your criticisms until after you have made an honest attempt at experiencing your inner world and that of others. This is the difference between a book about theories and a book about experiences. Anyone can argue about theories, but not about experiences.

I am writing this book because this information has been put aside and needs to be reintroduced into the mainstream of our culture – which in my view is where the core healing of a culture occurs – and because I feel joy at the thought that *our culture can grasp this better today than ever before and can heal*!

Disclaimer

This book is not meant to cover all aspects of healing in psychotherapy. It is meant to introduce the topic from my perspective in a way that is accessible by anyone interested in his/her own healing. My goal is to foster curiosity and discussion. I encourage readers to write their own thoughts on the subject and if someone's publication reaches more people than mine, so much the better for humanity; I will have accomplished my goal in writing this!

Note: For the reader interested in the context of some of the quotes I provided here from the internet, it can be that the link I provided no longer works by the time you are interested in it. Then search online for the quote I mention in this book and see if you can find another site that gives you the context you are looking for.

2 LIFE LESSONS

The most important knowledge may not be in books but in experiencing consciously. Since this book seeks to honor the subjective as part of the journey to personal growth, I am starting with key experiences life gifted me with on my journey.

Becoming Aware of My Body

More Than a Car Accident

It was July 1984. I was 24. It was a month before leaving my parents' home for graduate school. I was carefree, driving to join friends to do some sailboarding at the beach. Instead, I had a car accident that would become a crucial piece in my understanding of human nature.

I was driving and the traffic light at a major intersection ahead was green for me. Then my memory stops for a while. When I slowly became aware again, my eyes were closed. I remembered I had been driving so I knew I had had an accident. I opened my eyes and had the thought that my windshield was gone. I extended my right arm to check it out and heard a man's voice on my left telling me not to move – I knew he was a medic. I became aware that my driver seat door was open. I did not turn my head to look at him. Everything happened quickly. He asked me to stay awake and, in order to help me, he asked from which lane I had been coming. My car was facing the direction from which I had been driving. I recognized that and I saw many lanes in front of me and thought I could deduce which one I had been on before the accident, but the whole thing was too much effort to consider and I thought I'd much rather sleep. The intersection looked like a spaghetti junction but I was very familiar with it and, driving on it later, I knew without effort which lane I was using the day of the accident.

I tried to remain awake, but I was unsuccessful. I woke up in the hospital on a stretcher by a reception area. I saw a phone and asked to call my parents. The receptionist must have dialed the number for me given that I could not reach the dial. She handed me the phone receiver. I told my parents what had happened, in which hospital I was, and that the medical professionals were going to check on my vital signs.

My parents told me they'd come to the hospital right away. As I was handing the receiver back, I noticed blood where it touched my left ear and told the receptionist. I touched my ear; it was still bleeding. I thought the impact of the accident must have sent my head against the left inside frame of the door in my car which was metal and not padded. That must have given me a concussion.

A nurse passed by and I asked him if I could meet the people from the other car. He said he would ask and came back to tell me it was against hospital policy. In retrospect, there was no way for me to know at that time that there were other people involved in the accident and that they were also at the hospital. So what made me ask the question? That question did not occur to me until later.

I was moved to a bed in a room with other patients. My parents arrived shortly after that. I don't remember how long I was there. From memory, it could have been two or three hours. I had a headache. I did not remember how the accident happened. I was told that the memory often comes back after a while. It never did and the headache lasted a week.

My car was totaled. I started driving, again, almost immediately, to not let the fear of driving win. I did not have a fear of driving, but I was very cautious at each intersection. The police report said I was not at fault. I felt good that I remembered correctly that the light was green for me, that I could still trust my memory, even though I did not remember everything.

As I reflected on the accident at the time, I thought that I could have died, that my life was now a gift to me and I was free to live it as I chose to. I saw it as a gift as I was starting my own journey away from my family. I did not particularly like biostatistics, but that's what I was going to study for my Ph.D. I liked psychotherapy, but the couple of psychology courses I took and aced as electives (Introduction to Psychology and Child Development) bored me to tears. I could not have said why at the time. I loved Jung and felt I could argue with Freud. It took me 15 years or so to understand that it was not psychology I did not like, it was the way it was presented – all theories and nothing about human nature. I felt no connection with what was taught to us. I did not pursue the academic study of psychology. I had excelled as an undergraduate and master's level math student and received scholarships to study biostatistics. I could have chosen to stop all that right then, aware that I was in charge of my life, but did not know what else to do. I was looking forward to leaving home and traveling.

Who Am I?

I moved 3,000 miles away from my parents' home. For the first time, I had to figure out how to navigate my life. I had no clue what I was doing in biostatistics. All I knew was I was good at it and I had received a scholarship for several years to study it at a graduate level. It gave me an opportunity to explore the world.

After a couple of years into the program, I had passed all my exams and was working on my dissertation research. Recurring symptoms made me see a doctor who was wise enough to tell me it was due to stress. I went to the university psychiatrist. He could only see me for three sessions at the end of which he gave me a diagnosis that I was not assertive enough. I could then see a social worker who could see me for up to 15 sessions. I did not understand what being assertive would look like differently from what I was doing. It did not seem to hit the mark. The social worker was nice, but I was not noticing any progress.

Then, I had a dream in which I was going to my social worker for therapy, and I took the elevator to the second floor where her office was in reality, but the elevator went to the fifth floor which did not exist in reality. The elevator doors opened a little shy of the fifth floor. The space was empty from the second to the fifth floor. I climbed out of the elevator somehow easily enough to reach the floor. There, I noticed, among others, a graduate student standing with a glass of champagne. In reality, he was ahead of me in the biostatistics program. He was looking at me from a distance and invited me to join in the celebration. I waved at him and, instead of joining them, I turned to my left, climbed a rope ladder up to a half of a floor higher. When I reached the top, I was greeted by people in business suits who had risen up from an oval table as I arrived. The dream ended here.

I deduced it was time to end therapy, finish my Ph.D., and work on something that would lead me to professional success.

I saw my therapist that day and she agreed it was time to end our sessions. The symptoms for which I went to see the doctor in the first place had not subsided. At that time, they occurred daily.

I started to keep a daily journal of the occurrences of symptoms and their intensity and what happened during each day. It took a few weeks to start seeing a pattern that I was ignoring any negative emotions such as fear and anger. I was so good at ignoring them that I did not know I was choosing to ignore them! I practiced being more aware. At first, just noticing anger and fear was enough to prevent symptoms from occurring. In time, I needed to do more than notice. It took four years to completely stop the symptoms. In more than 20 years since then, they have occurred only a handful of times. I healed myself by paying attention to my feelings and by learning to listen to their messages in my life.

There were days during that period when I could not feel anything and I would get angry just to muster some feelings. I also listened to songs that made me cry. It felt as though a part of me was dead, or numb at the least, and I wanted so badly to feel alive. I wasn't living, I was surviving. I did not like it. I was discovering that my body was like a map sharing with me information I needed to pay attention to. Body problems only occurred if I did not pay attention to emotional warnings.

Healing 101: The Feeling of a Sword Through My Heart

One night, around two in the morning, I experienced a pain going through my chest that felt as sharp as a sword. I knew it was not a heart attack because I felt no numbness. I chose not to go to the hospital, but the pain took two hours to subside. So the next time I experienced it, I went to the hospital. It took two hours in the emergency room before I was invited into the doctor's office. The pain had gone and he told me he could not do anything for me. "Come back when it occurs again," was his advice. I thought to myself, "Not a chance!" Who else can make you wait two hours and charge for a co-pay without offering any services?

The pain occurred a third time. I was home. I was determined to figure it out. I did not have a plan. I simply rested comfortably on my couch and felt everything about the pain with total curiosity, no judgments and complete patience. The pain went away in 20 minutes this time and, as it went away, the memory of an interaction with my Ph.D. advisor came back. It had happened a couple of weeks before. I saw that I had not taken responsibility for what I was struggling with in my research and waited for my advisor to rescue me. That had caused a subtle tension between us. I saw that I had to take responsibility for my needs. My relationship with him never got tense after that and the pain never came back.

Is that what the psychiatrist meant by I needed to be more assertive? Perhaps. I would have understood better if he had said that I needed to take responsibility for who I am and what I wanted. Instead, my body told me… but I had to learn its language!

My experiences taught me three things. 1) My body was not against me. All the symptoms to which I had started to pay attention were guiding me to new self-awareness and when I got the message, the problem disappeared. I learned later that this is called healing. 2) The messages were of a personal growth nature. 3) I had discovered an aspect of mindfulness: listening to my body led to healing.

Later I learned that what I had done on my own is used in many healing traditions and in particular is an aspect of the healing tradition practiced in Kundalini yoga called *Sat Nam Rasayan* (Relaxing into the truth), a practice I studied as a Kundalini yoga practitioner.

Empathy

I also learned something else during those years. I was having a discussion with a friend which led to talking about how we felt. She seemed to take a guess about what she was feeling. I told her I was feeling something else coming from her. I felt it in my heart. I shared what I was feeling and she agreed I had perceived it accurately. She knew what she was feeling but could not find the words for it.

I had never heard of people being able to do that before and I had never thought it was unusual either. I thought it was odd that I could feel something about her more accurately than she could. Later, when I studied healing work, it all started to make sense.

This ability showed me that we are not separate from one another. I started to see how children get "difficult" when the adults around them feel tense and most times end up being blamed for their "being difficult." The invisible communication of feelings happens all the time; we simply do not necessarily recognize that it is happening.

I experienced anger one day that I could not figure out how to address, until I asked myself if it was mine. I suddenly realized it was the anger of someone I had just met. As soon as I made that realization I felt free of it.

Helping My Grandmother Back to Reality

My father's mother had received a pig valve transplant whose life expectancy is about 10 years. She had just returned for a replacement valve in 1994 and immediately after surgery went into a coma which lasted a couple of weeks. When she came through, she was not always in touch with reality, sometimes mistaking people's identities. My mother called me to let me know that if I wanted to have a shot at talking with her, perhaps one last time, I should not wait too long. My grandmother lived in Belgium and I was in upstate New York. I could not easily afford to make a trip to Belgium on such short notice, so I called her. She thought I was Bernard, my uncle, her youngest son. I wondered how to get her back to reality. I found myself telling her that her husband, André, who had long passed on, was waiting for her, as if I knew this was true. "You think?" she said, in French. "You know who I am!" I said, recognizing by her tone that she was back. "You are Luc!" she said as if she had never mistaken me for her son. It did not matter what I thought about the afterlife or whether I was right or wrong about her husband waiting for her. Talking about death was what brought her back because something about it had scared her and had sent her into a state of confusion. But we did not need to talk about it. I had entered the world she felt trapped in. That brought her back to reality. Once she saw more clearly, she made the decision it was okay to move on. I actually knew something had shifted for her during our phone call so, right after the phone call, I called her son who was closest to her at the time to let him know I felt she might be close to dying. She passed on a couple of days later.

I had worked with my grandmother in a way described in *Coma* by Arnold Mindell. People in a coma, Mindell hypothesized, are trapped in a world of indecision, not knowing whether to live or to die. He describes in his book ways he communicated with several comatose patients. By asking them questions, they became aware of where they were trapped and were able to make a decision to either come back to life or pass on. I became aware of this book and read it in 1990, a few years before my conversation with my grandmother. I was not thinking about the book at the time of our conversation. I had simply had an intention to bring my grandmother back to reality; the answer came in the words that I expressed as if they had been given to me. Ask Life and answers come. When I am aware of this, I have a sense that I am working with the whole Universe. I am not alone.

Synchronicity

Synchronicity and Psychotherapy

Jung coined the term *synchronicity* as meaningful coincidences. Many times in my life, I became aware that some events were happening beyond my control and they were meaningful to me. At those times, there was nothing I could do to change the course of events. I felt either elated because everything was going my way or I felt as though I was in a train heading for a big wreck, and all I could do was remain alive and alert and watch how life would resolve the whole matter.

How life guided me to discover the kind of psychotherapist I wanted to be is key to the discussion of this book because it helped me see that synchronicity happens all the time. Synchronicity happens both as a result of our conscious questioning and our unconscious quests. We are all "guided" via synchronicity toward our deepest wishes whether conscious or unconscious. I am not saying that this "guidance" is external to us and yet it may feel like it.

If you have heard of the Law of Attraction made famous by Abraham-Hicks, I use the term synchronicity as a similar concept. I prefer using the term synchronicity because it was used first and because it came from within the field of psychotherapy. What Abraham-Hicks popularized was how to engage synchronicity in a direction we want.

Some people I gave talks to asked if I mean to say that I believe in fate. I don't. I don't believe I am separate from Life, so I see everything as part of a dance. I think of it as my soul attracting what it needs to itself by Law of Attraction. This is not talked about because the Law of Attraction is typically used to attract something consciously to oneself via a collaboration of the mind and the heart. But the soul does not have changes of heart like our heart and mind do. The soul has a consistent energy and so it attracts what it needs consistently much better than we can do consciously sometimes because we are not able to remain pure in our intention. We have doubts, we second guess ourselves, etc. I am only using the word guidance because that is how it feels.

As therapists, we can take synchronicity into account as we help our clients through their life challenges. Once we understand this, we learn two things: 1) We see that if we judge events before truly understanding them, we will likely miss the guidance we are receiving and we will likely miss the meaning in the coincidences. So the role of the therapist is less to help clients find solutions and more to help clients raise their awareness about the guidance they are receiving. 2) Trust that as the clients reorganize their self-awareness and self-acceptance, that synchronicity will continue to guide their life accordingly. So there is not always a need to set up therapeutic objectives with the client in order to change their life, unless there is imminent danger, because life will naturally bring the elements needed for the healing via synchronicities. That will be more efficient than whatever the therapist or the client may be able to devise cognitively. 3) Instead of setting up objectives, I prefer to set intentions: Who do I want to be? What would I love my life to be? What would I like to see healed? 4) In some situations, nothing seems to move in a client's life, then it may be time to try something, anything that brings joy, in order to reengage with Life. Life cannot push you in the right direction if you are standing still!

Life Guidance Toward Psychotherapy

At 17, I was a busboy in a classy French restaurant. After lunch, one of the waiters with whom I had become friends asked me what I wanted to do when I grew up. I had not really thought about it but it came out of my mouth as though I had given it a great deal of thought. With total confidence I said, "I want to be a psychotherapist."

I had read some Jung and some Freud and already felt a profound interest in Jung's ideas and formulated my own criticisms of Freud's ideas. For instance, I found Freud too theoretical. I could easily imagine other dream interpretations than his for his patients and could not see why his would be more accurate than mine. I wanted dream interpretation to be patient driven, not one-size-fits-all in the way I perceived in Freud's approach. Jung, from my point of view, was more interested in human nature and built theories empirically. I felt free reading Jung and put aside reading Freud.

I mentioned my realization that I wanted to be a psychotherapist to my father. He had been interested in psychoanalysis and read some accounts from writers who had experienced it. He suggested that I do psychiatry to understand the body as well as the mind. I thought that was a good idea and enrolled in pre-med. After two years of biology during which I learned to be a student, but felt little excitement for biology, I had come to realize I could never be a medical student. Something in me had woken up about what I was willing to do and what I wasn't.

Instead, I renewed my passion for mathematics when I started to answer puzzlers from emeritus mathematics professor Linus. These puzzlers were posted in the science buildings. I answered some of them with success and received prizes from professor Linus. I had no more mathematics background than the usual courses required in science therefore winning these prizes seemed like a door opening up to me. As

Luc Watelet

a result, I decided to transfer to mathematics after my third year in biology.

I excelled as a student in mathematics. I was on the Dean's list, which came as a total surprise because I did not know it existed until then. I was happy. A student I had not met yet passed by a classroom one day where I was doing my homework. He said I looked spiritual to him. He said there was a light about me. I had never heard such language.

I did not go to church. I had lost interest in being preached to. I had been raised in a Catholic family to a pious mother and an academic father who mistrusted the Church and its leaders and who was mainly atheist, but acknowledged that he did not know about God. At the time, I would say to people who asked me if I believed in God, "What does it matter? It won't change how I choose to live my life. I want to help and change the world." I was a humanist. So the notion that I looked spiritual came as a bit of a surprise and made me smile. The student invited me to a religious gathering he attended regularly. I joined him once, but it did not interest me and I did not go back. I understood later that the light he saw about me came from my happiness. Mathematics is a world I belong to and I enjoyed playing in it like a kid in a sand box.

Since I had to take electives, I chose to take them in psychology. I took the Introduction to Psychology and the Childhood Development courses. I could not attend all the classes because of a conflict with some of my math courses, but the teachers accepted my situation as long as I did all the homework and the tests. I got As in both courses but, as I said before, I did not find either one exciting.

In retrospect, it is interesting to me that I gave up so easily on psychology and therefore on the last path to psychotherapy of which I was aware. I did not seek advice from an academic advisor who knew the field and could have opened my eyes to other possibilities. I can only assume that being happy in mathematics distracted me from what I truly loved. I completely let go of the idea of becoming a psychotherapist during the seventeen years that followed. So how did I get back there and discover the kind of psychotherapist I wanted to be? I can only attribute this to a series of synchronistic events that opened my eyes and reminded me of who I am.

1. I experienced confidence and happiness in mathematics. Money came easily in the form of scholarships. I had a wonderful master's degree advisor in probability, Ben B. Winter, who spent hours helping me rewrite my thesis until it was worded with a level of clarity that made it possible to have the rest of the committee read it. It took me a while to see that my lack of attention to detail reflected how poorly I felt about myself. My work was worthy of my advisor's attention and I felt worthy in return.

2. At Ben's suggestion I planned to get a Ph.D. in biostatistics. It was the practical and logical thing to do. It combined my academic backgrounds in mathematics and biology. I was not interested in pursuing the tenure track route in math, and the field of biostatistics was becoming popular and would offer me plenty of work for a lifetime and more.

3. I made the decision do my Ph.D. in Seattle, at the University of Washington. The transition into biostatistics and the move to the US, including having to learn English, was my initiation into adulthood. I had to figure out how to find an apartment. The language shift gave me headaches for about a year. I was learning to take responsibility for myself. I started my first relationship.

4. Abundance and Life's support continued to come easily to me. Financial support went from scholarships to teaching assistantships and fellowships. I also had several publications as a co-author. I already had one from my master's thesis and it continued. All this with very little planning on my part.

5. So on the one hand I was happy enough doing something I liked, felt good at, and was rewarded financially for, on the other hand, I felt confused. I felt I was not the conductor of my own train. I wondered who I was and what I wanted out of life. Why should everything come so easily when the inner joy and innocence I had felt in mathematics were now soiled with uncertainty about what I was doing and where it would lead me?

6. I had the dream I mentioned about going to my therapy appointment, seeing I would complete my Ph.D., and then move on

to something that would require my own efforts. That dream in itself did not hint at psychotherapy in any way as being in my future.

7. I kept wondering where I was going. I had a vision one afternoon while at home sitting at my desk, working on my dissertation. In this vision I was drawn to a cathedral. As I approached the cathedral, I thought the front doors would be locked, but they were not. I entered and it was very bright. Opulent chandeliers made of gold and diamonds hung over the central aisle. The pews were filled with people. I walked down the middle aisle to find a place to sit down. As I got closer and closer to the front, I realized the only possible place left was at the pulpit where I was expected to stand. I walked up to it and faced the crowd. The vision ended there. I would not have known what to say at the time. I did not even think of myself as having a spiritual message to offer. So this vision took me a little by surprise and yet a part of me felt very comfortable with the idea. I knew there was more to me than I had experienced yet. I craved to know more. Again this vision did not hint at psychotherapy but instead to spirituality and opulence.

8. I got married. That gave me access to a green card. My wife was a fellow graduate student and we finished our schooling at about the same time. She was clear that she wanted to continue in biostatistics and I was clear I was not going to continue on that path. We moved where she was offered a position.

9. I decided to be a writer. My writing led me to spiritual experiences I did not expect. I experienced unconditional love on two separate occasions, accessing a beautiful space simply through the process of writing, thereby learning there was more to the world than I knew, and getting two clear pieces of wisdom: "The world does not want to be changed, just loved," and "Disgust is fear of love." I will share those experiences in my chapter about Love.

10. My wife and I grew distant and neither one of us understood why. After two years of crying, including four months of therapy at the end, seeking answers that were not coming, we separated.

11. I asked myself, "Now, where do I go?" I needed to move. The series of events that followed were an amazingly well orchestrated series

of synchronicities. A friend of mine had recently given me a book about Buddhism which included a section on meditation. I was curious about it.

It was around Thanksgiving 1993. I had no plans for Thanksgiving where I was so I asked two friends, one in upstate New York and one in Florida, if either one was available so I could join them for Thanksgiving at the end of November. Both welcomed me, but the upstate New York proposition was a surer bet. Thinking about it, since my parents' anniversary was at the end of November, I could drive a little further north to my childhood home to pay them a visit and celebrate their wedding anniversary with my siblings. When I met my friend she suggested we do Thanksgiving dinner at a local church. That sounded great. It was less work for us and would be community-oriented! We met P. a woman who belonged to a monthly meditation group. They were meeting the next evening. My friend and I attended the gathering. It was a guided meditation followed by a vegetarian potluck dinner.

I drove up north to visit my parents in Canada. I was surprised by a snow storm about 20 miles south of Watertown, New York. I did not slow down enough before moving to the slower lane and my car could not handle the little ridge of snow that had piled up between the lanes. Despite the brand new all season tires, my car spun around on the highway and went into the downhill median where it hit the stump of a tree. A couple of people waved like angels from the side of the highway, asking, "Are you okay?" I yelled back that I was. They told me to come up and wait in their car with them to stay warm. They'd already called the police and an officer was on the way. They probably had a CB radio.. I thanked them. The police arrived.

The policeman took a look at my car from the road and said it was probably totaled. I was hoping not. He had already called the tow truck and we waited in his car. The mechanic confirmed the policeman's guess. So we followed the tow truck with my car to the garage where I signed the title of my car to them. And the policeman drove me to a nearby rental car shop where I rented a car to continue my trip to Canada.

The celebration with my parents and siblings was fun. I had brought percussion instruments and we all jammed together and laughed a lot. I went back to upstate New York. I called my friend from the car rental place, and told her that my car was totaled and that I did not know how I'd get back home. She laughed and told me to call P. I was surprised my friend took it so lightly. I called P. and she told me that she and B., a friend I had met at the meditation group, were going where I lived for a five-day workshop. They asked if they could sleep at my place to save on hotel costs. They were planning to take B.'s car. I explained that I totaled my car and that I would need a ride with them. She thought it would be okay and said to call B. He invited me to check his car and all my percussion instruments and bags fit. They were leaving for their workshop the day I had planned to return home!

The workshop they wanted to attend was about learning to develop one's intuition. It started with a private 45-minute psychic reading. For two weeks prior to the workshop, the participants were supposed to follow a strict diet with no sugar, no caffeine, no red meat, no alcohol, and no medicines or drugs unless pre-approved by the teacher. The teacher's husband was handling all the phone calls, so the first time you met the teacher was the day of your appointment where she immediately scanned your pineal gland to see if you had been disciplined with your diet. If you had not been disciplined, she dismissed you. If you had been, she started her psychic reading and gave you a copy on tape. P. failed the pineal gland test and the teacher was right as P. had taken some meds that were not pre-approved. B. passed it and, when he came back at the end of the day, he had me listen to his psychic reading. I was stunned. I had never heard anything like this. I was totally new to anything "spiritual" and did not have any experience that told me whether to believe in psychics or not. This tape was very impressive… enough that I wanted to take the course at the next opportunity, six months later.

My new friends and the meditation group were already more meaningful experiences to me than I had experienced in the last three years since the end of my Ph.D. I decided to move to upstate NY as soon as I could. The opportunity came on the weekend of the 15th of January 1994.

12. I moved to upstate NY to be close to my new friends. I did not want to do statistical work, so I was looking for any kind of work possible from waiting tables to tutoring and then being a substitute teacher. When I experienced being a substitute teacher several times with teenagers, I had to put a stop to that nonsense. If I was to be a teacher, I had to teach material more advanced than what was taught in high school, otherwise I was bored to tears. At that time, the department of biostatistics was looking for postdoctoral students. I applied and was welcome. Yikes! I could not escape biostatistics. Why? But this gave me a salary I could live on. I had not found a way to go very far with writing fiction. I had written a lot since I finished my Ph.D., but nothing that made a complete story. It had been the beginning of my healing journey, but I did not have enough experience yet. Childhood pains still haunted me.

13. The story of how I took my first series of yoga classes is worth mentioning because yoga became such an important link for me in my conceptualization of psychotherapy. I had made up my mind as a teenager that yoga was not for me, even though I had never tried it. There are things we decide without true knowing. P. had a vertebra that protruded out of her spine. In April 1994, she was drawn to a yoga series for people with back problems and asked me if I would support her and take the series with her. Since I always make myself available to help others when it feels right, I enrolled. There were postures that were easy for people with back problems, but not for me. I completed the series.

14. In May, I was invited by B. to audition to live in a vegetarian and no alcohol community where he lived. The housemates took care of a yoga business. We referred to it as "The Yoga Society." I had been trained in Reiki I and II (a spiritual healing practice), I was taking my first yoga series of classes, and I was about to take the course on getting in touch with and developing my intuition.

I had enough personal experiences to believe I could get answers intuitively. At 15, I wanted to talk about Life and about Love with my classmates. I could not find friends who were interested in talking philosophy with me. I felt lonely. An answer came to me that I would make such friends in my twenties. That answer came true. At 17, I also asked about when love would come into my life. The answer came in the form of a poem which said to not wait for love, to simply give love, then love would come on its own.

I did not know intuition was a field human beings dedicated their time to. I never knew it could be taught. I was discovering a new world.

I said earlier in this book that when I was a child and learned about Jesus, the healer, I thought secretly that if he could do it, I could learn to do it too. So it is not surprising that at the first opportunity I became curious to study healing. But it was interesting that I did not seek it consciously.

Once I moved into The Yoga Society, I had an incentive to try more yoga classes because I did not need to drive to them and they were free for the housemates living there. I learned there were different styles of yoga and experienced several.

15. By the end of 1994, I was dating a woman who became my second wife and the mother of my only child. 1994 was a turning point spiritually in my life.

16. In January 1995, I took my first Kundalini yoga class and there was no turning back. My experience was as though I'd entered graduate school of yoga. And then I started studying Sat Nam Rasayan (see earlier section titled *Healing 101*). It stunned me that it was describing the practice with which I had healed myself back when I experienced the feeling of a sword going through my chest. That experience had come to me without a teacher as if I knew that practice but not remembering where it came from. And now I was told where it came from. Missing pieces of my life puzzle were coming together.

17. In July 1996, I took the training to become a teacher in Kundalini yoga. I would not have done it if a friend had not encouraged me to take the workshop I felt drawn to the most in Española, NM, that summer, where Kundalini yoga is headquartered. I needed that push because I lacked money and would have ignored an unspoken dream. The dream was to meet a spiritual master. My friend advanced the money I needed. During the training, I had a private

meeting with the Master of Kundalini yoga, Yogi Bhajan. There was only one such master on planet earth at any given time in history until Yogi Bhajan. No one replaced him after he passed. He completed another piece of my puzzle by telling me, after asking for my birthdate and looking at my aura, that I was a reincarnated teacher. He did not know about my vision of the cathedral that showed me facing a crowd to talk about spirituality. I wished I could remember more about who I am that Yogi Bhajan could so easily see on our first meeting.

18. I taught weekly classes of Kundalini yoga after that. Toward the end of 1999, I started a series of yoga classes after which I offered an hour of Sat Nam Rasayan healing for free to my students who wanted to stay. They stayed and I could practice healing work on them. I soon noticed that I did not want to do strictly silent healing work, I wanted to talk about the experience. That sharing became the foundation of my counseling approach. I experienced my students' energy in my body, released the tension I felt, which helped them release tension as well, and then shared what I had experienced with them. What I described made them share their own experience of the healing received and the conversation led them to a new place of clarity. After practicing this for a year I felt ready to start offering this service professionally.

19. The crows

Let's backtrack. In July of 1994, I had just started a postdoctoral degree in biostatistics. I was struggling in the fall as I kept falling asleep trying to read statistical literature to do the research I was required to do. Something was blocking me inside. I could do the consulting easily. So I became extremely confused as to what to do. I approached the chair of the department to describe my situation to him and he asked me what I wanted to do. I told him I did not know, but it felt like I should quit. He told me he respected my decision, but that if I did quit it would be very hard to justify giving me another fellowship if I wanted it back. He suggested I give it a month to reflect on it. I was to give him my decision on December 15, 1994. When the time came I had no more clarity than I had a month earlier. I decided to quit.

I was diving into the unknown. I did not know what to do. The day after I quit, I had an appointment with a psychic. Not knowing what to do, I was ready to try something, anything. He did not know about my work in biostatistics. Among many other statements, he said he saw me working in a university environment, like a medical field, by the fall of 1995. I was even more confused.

At the end of February of 1995, I still had not found anything to do. I was walking home on a trail when suddenly hundreds of crows swirled noisily over my head. Needless to say they had my attention – I had never seen so many crows and so close to me, and so loud. I certainly had never heard such a racket. Their noise was going straight to my heart. I leaned against a strong tree and cried. "You gotta be kidding!" I said to the skies. I *knew* I had to ask for my postdoc back. I had to swallow my pride and face the words of the Chairman that it would be next to impossible to get a scholarship after quitting. But I knew that if the Universe wanted me back in biostatistics, there would be a way. I trusted.

The next day, I went to talk to the Chairman and told him I had come to realize I needed to make the effort to go through whatever hurdle I was facing. I have a lot of respect for this man. He was visibly feeling in a bind. I cannot imagine this was easy for him. But he remained thoughtful. He looked for a solution that he could live with. Then he told me that he would like me to write a paper from my Ph.D. dissertation. I told him I would, but that I needed access to a computer. He gave me permission to use the students' computer lab.

I finished my paper by June of 1995 and gave it to the Chairman. He told me he would get back to me.

My paper was difficult to write. It was a theoretical paper that begged for a practical example I could never find. I had generalized a well-known theory in biostatistics. It was clear to see how it was a generalization of this well-known theory. The paper would be difficult to publish without an example.

By the end of August, I had not heard from the Chairman. I went to see him and asked what he thought. He told me he still did not know what to do. I told him I needed to work and I asked to be allowed to teach a course. He referred me to the professor in charge of selecting teachers for the various graduate courses. This professor gave me a course in probability theory to teach. I could not believe my luck. This was my favorite course of all the courses I could have been asked to teach.

I was given an office. I realized that if I was to show I was serious about coming back and overcoming my difficulties, I would need to attend the monthly seminar. I could never follow seminars very well. The research presented was never close to what I was familiar with and, as a result, I did not know what questions to ask. I wondered what I could do.

It turned out that one of the presenters during the fall was a statistician from Quebec I had heard of because I knew his sisters although I had never met him personally. When he came to visit us, I immediately introduced myself in French and told him I knew his sisters. Then we talked about his research. And when I went to his talk I was prepared. I had a question or two. Life was really supporting me.

By Christmas, the Chairman called me into his office and asked me if I wanted to do a postdoc in biostatistics. He told me to think about it. I would have to finish it this time. I told him I wanted it and I would finish it. I thanked him. I knew I would finish it because if I was given a message from the Universe, I knew to follow through. If I have to commit to something, I knew that, if I could find a spiritual reason for it, it would be more effective than any human reason.

Not only did I get to finish my postdoc, I was then hired as an instructor in biostatistics. I kept teaching the course in probability theory every fall and did some consulting. I was also to do some research, but that never went very far.

My officemate with whom I got along very well was hired mid-1999 by a pharmaceutical company and I thought my turn would come. And it did... six months later.

I love this story. It is not directly related to how I became the psychotherapist that I am today, or the spiritual teacher. But it shows how Life worked with me through a series of synchronistic events. It wasn't easy, but, in retrospect, it was fun. I learned from it that for some reason, biostatistics was not an accident in my life. It taught me to trust Life, have patience, and accept it, as it happened, in order to learn from it and receive its support. Because of this, I knew I could help someone looking for his or her life purpose when the time would come.

20. Early 2000, I was hired as a statistician by a pharmaceutical company that made bacterial vaccines. My income doubled. I knew that, at some point, I'd make my transition to teaching yoga and healing full time. I did not want to quit this time. So I was curious how Life would make it happen. My wife and I bought a house. In 2003, the company I worked for announced that our group was going to join the viral vaccine group in New Jersey. I was invited to join. As a family, we decided not to move. I inherited the studio of The Yoga Society for a very low price. The Yoga Society had gone through many changes by then. It was no longer an intentional community and the studio was at a different location from where I had lived. Everything seemed to be going wonderfully well for me... but it did not take long before I noticed I was not able to make a living out of what I loved.

21. What happened then was like a card castle that crumbles. My marriage fell apart. I kept the house but there was a flood in the basement that destroyed all of my mathematics and statistics books and course notes. My house was foreclosed. I filed for bankruptcy and did not know how to make a living. The help and advice I received from my wife, from a yoga teacher, and from a therapist all pointed to my going back into statistics. I had tried and I knew that was no longer for me. If I was not clear yet, losing all my math and stats material in the flood was the nudge forward prompting me to leave everything behind. I did not want to leave upstate New York because of my eight year old son, otherwise I was free. I had to find the strength to trust in myself enough to go against what seemed like the logical path according to all of the people of authority around me who knew me only from the outside and did not try to get me from the inside.

22. A sequence of events led me to consider being a home health aide. Because of the low pay, I took the master's program in mental health counseling online with Walden University in order to build a brighter future. To finish the program, I found an internship at a local addiction recovery center. My intention had been to study family therapy, but that did not open up. I learned instead that I could help people struggling with addiction and mental illness diagnoses. This experience expanded my understanding of who I was as a therapist.

23. After that coursework, Dr. Robyn Trippany, my teacher and mentor from Walden University, told me I should write up my therapeutic approach because it was different from what the school had taught me. After some research, I discovered Ron Kurtz whose ideas were surprisingly similar to mine. Kurtz had received a lifetime achievement award from the US Association of Body Psychotherapy. He was at the end of his life and I was just starting mine. How would I write something about psychotherapy that had already been published by someone who'd received a lifetime achievement award? I felt stuck. I decided to send an e-mail to Ron. He never responded and I found out online that he had passed away within three months of my e-mail to him.

24. After I received my degree as a mental health counselor, I tried over a period of several months to get an interview with agencies, so I could get hired as a mental health counselor. That was the only way in NY State to be supervised and apply for a license as a mental health counselor. But I could not find any agency to give me an interview. I decided to network with all the counselors who would talk with me, but that did not lead to any opportunities. I was disgruntled. I knew I was good at what I was doing. I believed in the ways of the Universe to give us exactly what we need. I was still trying to be "assertive" thinking I was not trying hard enough. But I found myself becoming aggressive instead. I could not make sense of what was happening to me. After a year of trying to make ends meet, I was ready to quit. I did some deep soul searching and felt very strongly my passion for my style of psychotherapy and that I had to make it my life purpose. Otherwise, I was losing my desire to live. Then I realized my approach to psychotherapy was very different from the mainstream's in that I was not diagnosing and

treating diseases. I was using mindfulness and working as a yoga teacher. I decided I did not need a license to do what I was doing. That freed me. I slowly realized that the reason all this was happening was that I had to believe in myself independently of circumstances and to continue despite the odds. With time, having to find a way to make it work with no outside support, my self-confidence built up as I had never imagined possible.

I only mentioned the most important of an intricate set of synchronistic events. Every step I mentioned was essential in awakening me to who I am and/or how I want to practice psychotherapy. It also solidified my relationship with Life, as I would not have known how to move forward without my constant seeking.

In essence, what I had learned from my experiences was that our bodies hold pains that hold us back, our minds hold beliefs that are connected with those memories, and our souls hold our dreams that want to be fulfilled. The trauma, when accessed, can be released and, when it is, a new awareness comes which challenges some of our beliefs, and our life moves on energized by a new freedom. Our true purpose becomes clearer as a result and had to be accessed by releasing the trauma. The trauma is our waking call to remembering who we are.

The order of what needs to be released is already a part of each of us. Our body memories and life experiences catch our attention so we can release trauma and limiting beliefs. Because of this, we do not need to guess the therapy direction. The only guide necessary for the therapy process is who the client wants to be and what dreams matter to him. The only question necessary for the client is: How can I be more myself? The pain/trauma that seeks to be released will show itself. Mindfulness puts us in touch with what needs to be addressed next and love is essential in supporting the changes that need to happen. Our heart needs to be open to what we experience. That is Love, a combination of acceptance with what is, releasing judgment, not taking anything personally, not second-guessing ourselves, patience, reconnecting with our natural joy, and being our best friend/advocate. The therapist is like a midwife in that process.

Wayne Muller explains it this way in his *Legacy of the Heart:*

If we believe that this particular pain is the one that will push the baby out of the womb and into our arms, we somehow try to make a place for that pain in our heart. Pain is still there: excruciating, terrible pain. But at the moment of birth, we rarely feel betrayal or rage; we somehow feel that this is simply pain that has come with life.[14]

The other aspect to this therapeutic approach that became more and more obvious with each new experience was that every mental health challenge, every problem, can be approached the same way because, by accepting our experiences, we reconnect with who we really are. Addictions and mental health challenges are simply symptoms of the specific kind of disconnection from which we suffer.

The following quote is attributed to Virginia Satir by many without a reference (e.g., by AZquotes.com):

The problem is never the problem! It is only a symptom of something much deeper.[15]

And then it occurred to me that *there is no such thing as a personality disorder* because the personality is just fine when the trauma is released.

Intuitively, I had always agreed with Jung in his assessment that spirituality was the cornerstone of psychotherapy via a process he called individuation. From experience, I now knew he was correct.

A Glimpse into Human Nature

A home health aide is a person with specific state-regulated training (in the USA) on how to care for people who cannot completely care for themselves. It involves housecleaning, cooking and personal care. Personal care means cleaning them by giving them a foot bath, sponge

---

[14] W. Muller (1992). *Legacy of the Heart: The Spiritual Advantages of a Painful Childhood.* Fireside, p.2.

[15] I could not find the source of this quote. I love it though. The author deserves a proper reference. If someone knows the origin of this quote please contact me (see copyright page).

bath, a bath or a shower, or just being present during their bathing for security, and changing their absorbing underwear. Aides employed by an agency were not allowed to take care of bleeding wounds... although who would not? A nurse always needed to be called in that case. We also needed to use gloves and clean our hands regularly in order to not pass on germs to other clients or to ourselves.

I had a Ph.D. in biostatistics. I had a mind that could grasp, hold, and solve complicated problems. I felt deep humiliation needing to do home health aide work to make ends meet. What kind of *accident* led me to that position? What a profound mistake in my life! But there was also a very satisfying feeling in being able to pass on some kind of peace and caring to the people to whom I was assigned.

All my life, I had a deep fear of being judged negatively by people. Visiting new people in their homes triggered that fear over and over, and I had to remind myself they would be angrier with me if I did not show up than if I did. After a while, that fear left me. I could even go visit anyone unannounced. Being a home health aide was healing for me.

But that was only one of the benefits. Another was that it expanded my belief about the kind of people I thought I could help. First, I thought I was only to help those who could attend my yoga classes with able bodies and minds. As a home health aide, I was being made aware that I could be helpful to people with physical disabilities and dementia or simply old age. Later, when I was doing my internship at a substance abuse treatment center working with people with addiction including many also diagnosed with a mental illness, I discovered my ability to work with them as well. *I was led to experience the whole gamut of human experiences and how I could be helpful with everyone who truly wanted help.*

Within a couple of weeks of working as a home health aide, the man who had interviewed me and given me my new job, stopped me in the hallway. He said, "Luc, I had a dream last night that the phone was ringing off the hook with clients asking for you. What are you doing?" I answered, "I don't know. I don't know what others aren't doing!" He was promoted shortly after and I never saw him again; I never was able to tell him what it was I was doing. But I needed to ask *myself* that question.

At the time of his dream, clients had not started to ask for me. I was not known yet. During the first six months, I was, for the most part, assigned to the same four men. After that, things started to shift. After six months, I was known as a reliable aide so I was offered to be a "senior aide." The responsibility of a senior aide is to accept assignments wherever they are within the county and during one's work schedule. So a senior aide does not have regular clients, although there are exceptions. I replaced aides who could not make it on time to their clients and I did office work when I had no clients if the office was open. When I started to be sent to different clients every day, some clients started to ask for me even after they were told I was not available for regular care. Some said that if I was not available right then, they would wait; they did not want anyone else. The number of aides always varied but to give an idea, in the agency, at one point, I was one of five male aides out of a 150 aides. I was not the only aide who was liked, but I was doing something many others were not.

When I started asking my clients why they wanted me, instead of other aides, I received many answers, "Oh! Other aides don't do as good a job as you do!" But the answer I think was the most enlightening was, "You give me dignity!" This was also reflected by feedback from family members of my clients.

That answer gave me food for thought. My car accident from 1984 came back to mind. The memory of what happened in the ambulance on the way to the hospital came back as though I had always known what happened, not as if I was remembering it for the first time.

I could see myself on a stretcher from above... my body completely inert, my mind unconscious. I was watching everything from above nestled in the corner of the roof of the ambulance and the separating panel behind the passenger seat. I was a consciousness, an awareness. I saw two women facing each other sitting on benches along the side of the ambulance cabin. They were by the rear door. The woman on my right had a nine or ten-year old boy sitting next to her on her left. But neither woman was engaging with him. He remained quiet the whole trip to the hospital. They talked to each other about the mall and other daily things. They did not talk about the accident and they seemed

59

oblivious to my body or my presence. I remembered that, when I first remembered that story, I could have given many details about their actual conversations and the clothes they were wearing. But now what was most interesting was who I was. What was this thing with which I could see and hear, and was invisible to the human eye and separated from my body and mind? It was not judging or reflecting, it was simply observing. It had not been hurt by the accident. It had no gender, no race, no socioeconomic status, no disability, no sexual orientation, no religion or ethnicity, and no age. It felt more real to me now than my body/mind that lay unconscious. Also, I recognized this consciousness as me the same way I could feel that the consciousness of the child or the women in the ambulance were not me.

The most important part to all this for me was that since I now identified more with my consciousness, my true identity had nothing to do with identities we study in psychology (age, sex, gender, race, etc.) and this consciousness was alert and not affected, like my mind and body were, by the accident.

Remembering that experience told me what I was doing with my clients. I saw them as having a consciousness that was not affected by their age, disability, or illness, and that is what I related to. I talked to anyone as though that consciousness was able to see and understand what I was saying. I only catered to the disease or disability, if the client asked me for help with it. That is why they felt dignity.

I was soon invited to talk for 15-20 minutes about my home health aide experience to aides in training within the agency for which I worked. I shared with them my out-of-body experience and how, what I learned from it, changed how I see others and therefore how I care for them and how they feel cared for.

Reflections

The experience as a home health aide helped me care for people and their spirit. I saw firsthand that diseases and disabilities never define a person. So why should a psychotherapeutic approach put so much importance on diseases and disabilities? Why not care for the person directly instead?

The experience getting a master's degree in mental health counseling helped me understand how mainstream counseling works. It was not so much that what they are teaching is wrong, it is simply that it lacks a true understanding of human nature. It is as though people who acted as therapists in the past found helpful ways to deal with problems and defined theories and practices to approach them. These theories and practices became the foundation for mainstream therapy today and the standard psychotherapy curriculum. It surprised me that the work of my favorite psychotherapists was never mentioned. When my teacher first suggested I publish my therapeutic approach, I slowly discovered that my approach as a therapist was not new, that my teacher had simply not heard of it before, and that I was in a position to create a bridge between the dramatically different worlds of psychotherapeutic approaches.

It was Freud who envisioned psychotherapy within a medical paradigm. And it appears his legacy has left the most impact on the mainstream therapy paradigm today. Jung operated within a healing paradigm and many therapists since such as Virginia Satir, and Carl Whitaker, who each have a prominent place in mainstream schools of psychotherapy, and Ron Kurtz and Arnold Mindell who deserve to be given a prominent place in mainstream schools of psychotherapy. And others I mention in this book such as Richard Schwartz and Wayne Muller.

Mainstream psychotherapy operates from the medical paradigm but also from the scientific paradigm. The coursework I took emphasized the scientific model and the need to diagnose and treat as in the medical paradigm. In contrast to it, my key therapeutic tools were: intuition, synchronicity, and mindfulness. This made me want to envision psychotherapy within a paradigm much closer to the life process than a scientific paradigm built on evidence-based theories. Evidence-based theories sound great in theory but do not address the inner world of the client directly; they can only be a lens through which to view anything. Only the client has access to his or her inner world. So why use a theory when we can have direct access to someone's truth? I am not discounting the scientific mindset needed in one's approach to therapy. But I do not want science to tell me who I am. I am the only one who can really know that. It is not that I think we should eliminate the medical and the scientific paradigms; it is that psychotherapy can do much better within a healing and life process paradigm.

Luc Watelet

There is a similarity between my father's approach to making history research more scientific instead of driven by the need to prove the supremacy of an –ism (Socialism, Marxism, Liberalism, etc.) and my approach to freeing psychotherapy from the medical and scientific paradigms. We are both seekers of truth. We don't want to be limited by or in service of a filter in the study of our subject.

Reflections on Human Nature

I was part of a forum of student counselors around my time of graduation from the mental health counseling program. The discussion pointed to a lack of understanding of human nature in what we were taught.

Memory

One misconception from some of the budding counselors was that all our memories are in our brain. How do I know something is stored or not in my brain? How can I have an experience of what is in my brain other than stimulating different parts of my brain and watching what is triggered into awareness? Without instruments, perhaps I cannot have a direct experience of what is in my brain. But I can pay attention to something in my body other than my brain and remember an experience I was not thinking about before. For instance, if someone is complaining about a difficult emotion, I ask them where they feel that emotion in their bodies. Usually they'll feel it in their chest, their shoulders or even in their belly. I ask them to stay with the sensations and give them all the space in the world without judgment. That usually leads to a memory they did not have in mind prior to the mindful attention to that particular part of their body. That leads me to believe that memories are stored in our bodies. This is an important piece of information that shows that talk therapy is not enough. We also need to access the memories of trauma stuck in our bodies so we can release them. We need to work within a mind-body relationship perspective, not just a cognitive-behavioral perspective, in order to heal.

During a Rosen healing method training, I volunteered for a demonstration by our teacher in front of all the students. I was invited on a massage table. My teacher asked what I wanted work on. I had had cold feet, sometimes icy cold feet, as long as I could remember. I asked that my teacher help me with that. The teacher first put her hands on my feet and asked me if I could feel her hands. I could feel the warmth of her hands but could not let that warm energy into my feet. She also did not feel energy moving in my feet. She moved her hands to my lower back. That was an area from which I could partly let the warmth of her hands in me. It was partly blocked and partly open. She could feel it too. As I let the warmth of her hands inside my lower back, I remembered an infant memory I had not yet remembered.

I only knew from my mother that early on in my childhood, if I was fed and clean, and I still cried, she and my dad would play some classical music really loudly so they did not have to hear me. It was what they had learned they needed to do to teach me independence. They learned that that was not the right approach in time for my siblings. I was aware of all this from talking with my parents, but I had no direct memory that showed me if their response to my crying as an infant had any lasting effect on me as an adult.

During that Rosen healing demonstration, I found myself experiencing that memory from the infant's perspective. I had tears in my eyes. I could hear the music from Beethoven playing and I could feel the incredible need to be physically held and cared for by my mother. The new piece of information was that I could see that I had a choice to let the music give me the soothing I was seeking, because I loved it, or long for what I thought I lacked and feel miserable. The music was my path to a heavenly feeling. But I could not do both at once. As an infant, I kept feeling miserable. As an adult, I now had a choice.

My teacher stopped the healing process and I never had cold feet again.

The memory came back as a result of allowing the energy flow more freely in my lower back. The block of energy in the body seemed to block access to the memory. The different aches and pains in our bodies point to various stuck memories. That is why yoga is healing. It forces us to access where pain has settled and the stored energy gets released, sometimes with emotions, slowly by practicing postures and meditations regularly. Release can happen on the massage table or in the presence of good healers or therapists. These can also be accessed with mindfulness. The deeper trauma is better released in the presence of someone with experience so the experience of release is done in a safe environment.

Out-of-body Experience: How do I Know It Was Real and Not a Dream?

When I shared my out-of-body experience with the students from the forum, some students challenged my experience saying it was a dream. I mention this because I am certain some of the readers may have had the same reaction when I described that experience.

I can say that the experience of a dream gets my emotions involved or my mind active. An out-of-body experience is not like that. In an out-of-body experience, I am not the central figure as I am in any dream I have ever had. My body and mind are not engaged. If functional magnetic resonance imaging was performed at the time of an out-of-body experience, there would be nothing to record because the experience is not happening in the brain. In the out-of-body experience I had, I simply witnessed two women talking with each other. It was like viewing a documentary. I have never had a dream like that before or after. The perspective was simply different. Not only did this feel real, but I did not wake up thinking, "I had the most realistic dream!" as people usually do when they have realistic dreams. Here, I simply acted and lived from the knowledge I received from the experience as we all do when we have just experienced something in real life. Then later, at the hospital, I asked a nurse to see the people from the accident because I had seen them in the ambulance on the way there. Unlike the transition between a dream and reality, there was continuity between my (out-of-body) experience and my (in-body) question to the nurse. The nurse did not tell me there wasn't anybody from the other car at the hospital.

Let's take the opposite take on this. One can assume we only have a body and a mind and there is no such thing as a consciousness that is separate from the body/mind. Without an experience like mine, how would one know for sure? Under such a premise, one would think that what I experienced was a dream. With this assumption, I had a dream that gave me the experience of having a consciousness that is separate from my body/mind and that has no gender, no age, none of the identities that we usually assume we have. So even if it were a dream, it was pointing to something about human nature of which I had never thought or been aware before. It was a shift of paradigm.

At any rate, my experience was what it was and it led me to see that we must all have a consciousness that is disease-free and disability-free, whatever the condition of our body/mind. So there is always a sane part to each of us. That is very different from our mainstream worldview that we have personality disorders and that we are genetically-conditioned.

In therapy, we can use that knowledge to help our clients reconnect with their sane self. Spiritual teachers teach of such a place in us which we can access by being in the present moment, by meditating, and by quieting (not engaging with) the mind.

Summary of Life Lessons

1. I received meaningful dreams and visions shedding some clarity on my life. They pointed to some kind of clarity about my life that was not conscious but became conscious. Life was not simply what I wanted in the moment; there was a higher purpose. I was being "guided" at some level. We usually think of guidance as external to us. I am not assuming that.

2. I could heal myself. There is a connection between my physical being and my life. If I ignore important emotional information, my body hurts, but when I pay attention without judgment and with compassion to my body, I heal. By paying attention to my body's reactions/symptoms, I can become aware of the way my behavior can be hurtful to me, I gain wisdom, meaning I change my script, and my behavior changes in a way that is supportive of who I am.

3. I can feel what other people feel, sometimes with less confusion than them. We are not as separate as we think.

4. My experience with my grandmother told me I could help other people sometimes when they can't help themselves. Human nature is such that we sometimes get lost, disconnected from consciousness, and when something or someone brings our attention back to what matters to us, we regain clarity.

5. The synchronicities I experienced are intricate and when I look back I am amazed at the realization that I did not know how to navigate

my life and yet every step and every decision were in constant contact with Life in a way that shows that there was a meaningful path being presented to me at all times. I was never abandoned, just given opportunities to check out and to learn and to become aware. My free-will was respected always. Synchronicity is not just the experience of a few meaningful coincidences here and there. Synchronicity is constant and continuous. It involves all of humanity and all of nature, the whole universe! Synchronicity is Life itself, there is no separation.

Life is a finely tuned multidimensional representation of who we are. If we learn to participate in its dance and accept where it flows, with a little grace and gratitude, we will get where we want. And this is true even if we rebel each step of the way against it and live without grace and gratitude. But when we learn this dance, we can teach it to others. Psychotherapy can be seen as a stage where people learn to dance with life again; that is, with themselves first and then with others toward the fulfillment of their destiny.

6. I learned a bit of the intricate relationship between my mind, body and soul and the importance of becoming aware of how they relate to each other as that awareness leads to an experience of clarity and freedom. Clarity about who I am. Freedom from confusion and suffering. And as a result being more aligned with a sense of purpose, having something to learn and contribute before I die.

7. I learned that there is no separation between my personal growth and my spiritual growth, and no separation between healing physically, emotionally, mentally, and spiritually.

8. I learned that psychotherapy can be much more than treating an addiction or a mental health challenge as though these experiences were pathological. Instead, I started to see that addictions and mental health challenges are expressions of our mind, body and soul being disconnected from each other. That is, they are symptoms, or warning signs, of a disconnection within the self. Therefore, healing is possible by facilitating an inner reconnection. We can do it alone or with the help of someone who acts as a spiritual midwife, someone who understands the mind, body and soul nature of human beings.

3 LOVE

Love in the therapeutic relationship is almost a taboo topic in psychotherapy. Carl Rogers used a phrase that sounds very technical to refer to love: To see one's client with "unconditional positive regard." His phrase has the benefit of describing an aspect of love precisely, but it is a mental aspect of it, it isn't the total experience of love because it misses the presence of one's heart to another person. It is true that the word love can be used with a multitude of meanings and we need to be very precise as to which meaning we want in a therapeutic relationship. In our culture, the separation between love and sexual feelings is often blurred and the lack of clarity in the therapist can lead to, and has led to, abuse at the expense of the client's sense of self.

I have talked to people who have been asked not to be too close to students in the school environment. Their open caring toward students was frowned upon by the administrations. In one case, when the person withdrew his caring as requested by the administration, a student wrongly accused him of sexual harassment. The withdrawing of affection from the person in authority led to a feeling of abuse in the student. That would have been a great discussion for a round table at the school. Instead, the person in authority felt he had no other choice but to give his resignation. In another case, the person gave her resignation instead of having to withdraw love in her interaction with students.

In the home health aide world, we are instructed during the training not to get too close and not to get attached to our clients. One of the reasons given is that some are likely to die and this instruction is meant to make it easier on the aide as many clients are likely to leave this world over time. But the aides I talked to, who were recognized by clients and the supervising nurses for their wonderful work with their clients, all told me the same thing (I paraphrase): *"You have to care, you have to allow yourself to get close. You know they may die, but how can you not create a human connection? You have to be real!"* And all of them also knew how to let the clients go when it was their time to go. Caring deeply for a client who dies, rarely comes in the way of caring for any of the other clients.

When I give workshops to people in the caring profession, including counselors or social workers, and I touch on the importance of love in the therapeutic relationship, people talk to me privately afterwards about their desire to be loving but their fear of repercussions from authority and from the culture. It begs the question, where does this fear of love come from? Is it simply the confusion between love and sexuality? Or is there a deeper fear? I am reminded of Freud's instruction for a medical distance and objectivity toward patients. It has left a deep legacy in the world of psychotherapy and it is important to question it.

When we have experienced that love heals, and that a loving environment helps support the most difficult of projects, there is no turning back. Love is key to helping clients heal.

Spiritual Experiences of Love

"Jesus Loves You"

The first time I had an experience of pure love was unexpected. I had been annoyed at a common bumper sticker that said, "Jesus loves you!" As a kid, I wanted to be a healer like him. I wanted to be my own version of Jesus. As a teenager, I grew my hair long and other kids teased me by calling me Jesus. I did not mind. But for people to tell me that Jesus loves me resulted in an inner reaction that translated into something like, "How dare they? They know nothing about me!"

One day, I noticed my reaction in a different light and I thought, "What if Jesus loved me?" So I closed my eyes and opened up inside to check if I would feel his love. I immediately felt filled with love. It was like a light that helped me feel loved like I never felt before. I suddenly saw that my parents loved me. As a kid, I did not feel loved, yet what I was experiencing, by allowing Jesus to love me, is that my parents loved me. It was I who did not perceive it as a kid because I was looking for specific signs of love that I was not experiencing. It changed how I saw them and it changed our relationship forever. I was no longer a kid waiting to be loved when I was with them, or pushing them away because I did not get what I wanted from them. They were my parents but also we were equals as human beings, each one looking to fulfill something and each one wishing to support each other.

How Do I Get Back There?

The second time I had an experience of pure love was a couple of years later, in 1992. I had been talking with a friend who told me her parents had loved her unconditionally as a kid. I was not convinced of it due to other stories she had told me about her childhood. I made a decision not to argue this with her as it may have robbed her from her good feeling. Yet, for a whole month, I observed my mind arguing that she did not experience unconditional love from her family. I did not understand; I was not going to argue this with her, so why was this obsessing me so? And I suddenly thought, "If unconditional love exists, I want to experience it!" I was never obsessed with my friend's story again. In fact, she had a great relationship with her parents and seemed to understand love at a deeper level than I did. Perhaps I'd been judging her. In those days, I was writing daily about my childhood in a fictional way to try and find some peace and healing. Two months after my request to experience unconditional love, I found myself writing about an event in my childhood with which I had been grappling several times before without success.

I was six or so and my father picked me up regularly after school. But he picked me up about a half an hour after the last kid was picked up. It was hard, but I did not pay attention to how I felt. One day, the superintendent who waited for me to be picked up expressed out loud a negative comment about my dad and I suddenly realized that I could no longer hide what was happening. My father had been criticized by others and I lost, that day, the last piece I was holding on to: the desire to feel proud of my father. I suddenly felt deeply alone. I was not able to find peace with that. I had tried crying my heart out, I had tried expressing my anger about it, and I had tried making it all better. Nothing worked. But that day I found myself following a different approach. I wrote about the physical walk I could take as an adult to meet the child I was, in the exact spot he was waiting for his dad, on the front steps of the school. I had learned that to be in touch with the childhood wound, I needed to feel everything in my body and let that feeling guide the writing, not let the intellectual memory guide the writing. Twice, I lost the feeling. But I found that I could reconnect with it and start from there to approach the boy I was. At my third attempt, I was able to get close enough to open my arms to him and hold him in a heartfelt embrace.

Instantly, I found myself sobbing, but not out of frustration or pain, my heart had just opened up like it had never opened before to that particular experience, like a dam had been opened. I was crying while feeling a freeing feeling of unconditional love. A sunny meadow scene with the wind blowing over tall green grass and golden wheat showed itself to my mind's eye. Words came to me as though engraved in my mind, *"The world does not want to be changed, just loved."*

This was an answer to my heartfelt wish from my teenage years to contribute to changing the world. It was showing me how. I had just done that exact work with that event in my childhood that had bothered me for so long. This time, I had no longer tried to change it. I had accepted it and loved the child I was, in his pain, as I remembered it. And it gave me an experience of pure love. This happened a couple of years before I started meditation, formal healing training, and yoga. My writing was my meditation, but I did not know it then.

This was a lesson in healing which would be one piece of the foundation of my psychotherapeutic work years later. I had to love my clients until they could love themselves; I had to find a way for them to love themselves, that part in them they could not accept that was hurting and/or haunting them.

I could have enjoyed the experience and left it at that, but when I was back to my former state of being, a half a minute or a minute later, I asked, "How do I get back there?" "Let go of worries!" came the answer. At the time, I did not know how to do that.

Disgust Is Fear of Love

After the breakup of my first marriage, I felt particularly disgusted one afternoon and my writing was getting me in a very dark place. I thought I was doing good work to try and get to the other side. Instead, I was feeling more and more tired. My mind was shutting down. I went to bed and asked just before falling asleep, "What is this disgust about?" I woke up two hours later with words engraved in my mind: *"Disgust is fear of love."* I had never thought I was scared of love and yet this was what was given to me. I immediately went to my desk lighthearted and threw away what I had written. I took a blank piece of paper thinking I would write about love. But nothing came. In such situations my approach was to close my eyes and tap into the feeling I wanted to write about and a story would emerge.

But this time it was different. Instead, I saw a face. But it wasn't as before when I saw characters and a story coming together. This face felt independent of me, and very real. The face was really invisible and I could only be aware of it because its contour was shaped perfectly by a ribbon surrounding it in a spiral with spaces between each spiral. The face came close to mine and our lips touched in a kiss. I immediately felt filled with pure love as though it was breathed into me. I no longer wanted to write about love. I wanted to go out and hug everyone – which I did not do, so I would not be sent to a psych ward. I went out and walked around the block. It was fall and there were beautiful colored leaves on the sidewalk. The sunlight went through between the leaves still held on the trees and sparkling light sprinkled the sidewalk. I was in heaven, beauty all around me and peace in my heart.

The lesson here was that I did not need to go through the darkness to come out of it. I could just change from thinking to tapping into pure love. It was always there and accessible. But at times, I found that to be the most difficult choice to make as though parts of me feared that light and love were simply inaccessible where I was.

Luc Watelet

Human Experiences of Love

Ben B. Winter

I told before the story of my math master's degree advisor, Ben, and how much time he spent helping me rewrite my thesis. I was not aware of this as love at the time. He was extremely patient with me without ever getting irritated at me in my presence. I was amazed at that. Later I recognized that as an act of love. He told me that as much as I had been one of his best students, working with me had been his most difficult experience and he never wanted to have to repeat it again.

Carol Lee Lorenzo

At the end of 1991, I had decided to take a couple of courses in writing. I wanted to take a course about writing fiction for children because I had a sense that, in order to heal, I had to make my stories simple so a child could understand them. The second course was in poetry. For some reason the two courses were scheduled at the same time so I could only take one of the two. Life was forcing me to make a choice. I chose the course in writing fiction for children. The teacher expected us to write two to three pages every week based on some event from childhood and we could write the true event or turn it into fiction. She planned to read some of our work in class to show us examples of what works. Thus, if we did not want our work read to everyone, she asked that we write on the front page of our work that it should not be read in class.

I wrote my first story about how I felt as a young boy experiencing vertigo. My parents, my younger brother and I were walking over a bridge. My brother did not mind being held over the stone wall separating the bridge from the empty space over the river, but I had terrible shivers in my thighs and groin. I was envious of my brother and felt left alone and behind. I was crying as I wrote that story and I could not find a resolution to it. I left the story feeling deeply alone in my vulnerability. I wrote on the front page "Please do not read in class."

The following week when I received my work back, the teacher had written in answer to my request: "It's a good thing you said 'don't read' if you didn't want to hear it cause I would have read it in class." And she continued: "I really appreciate this work – it is very open and special."

And she went on describing how my writing worked with specific details and that I could turn it into a picture book. She wrote a response about three times the length of my story.

That day everything shifted for me. My vulnerability was accepted, my work valued. After that I told the teacher she could always read my stories in class. The class had about 25 students, and the teacher read my stories week after week, except for one I had not completed.

Carol Lee Lorenzo, you gave me what no therapist has ever given me, no matter how kind they were: self-acceptance for one of my deepest wounds. You did not try to fix me. You just accepted me and gave me the kind of feedback about my work I had never received before and that helped me love who I was in the world and what I had to offer. Thank you.

This experience helped me see that it is not necessary to help find answers as a therapist, what matters more is to love the person just as she is.

A Baby's Response to Opening My Heart

A friend trusted me to watch over her infant son one day. While she was gone, I thought of carrying him to my bed to play there. On the way, I got distracted and the baby's head hit the sharp corner of a paper cutter sitting on a piece of furniture just before the entrance to my bedroom. He started to cry and I felt terrible at the thought of telling his mother what had happened. I touched the baby's skull and there was a dent in it which made me feel even worse. Everything happened very quickly, as I was feeling extremely scared and sorry for myself. I realized what I was doing and how that was insane given that the baby got hurt, not me. I laid him on my bed. I stopped worrying about myself and I turned my heart to him and how he was feeling. The infant stopped crying instantly and made playful little baby sounds.

It was an incredible experience for me as I realized that it wasn't the pain of the wound that made him cry so much as my disconnection from him while I had turned inward and worried about myself.

That instant experience of connecting without words left a profound impression on me. So much love is exchanged just by opening one's heart to someone. And it hurts when a heart closes to you.

A Relationship

I was in a relationship. We lived in separate homes and, at times, my companion needed time off, but would not necessarily let me know. So I was left guessing that she needed time to herself. Often, those times would leave me feeling filled with self-doubt. I learned to feel the source of self-doubt. It was a quest for my own truth in the relationship and to be able to not let her time off become a manipulative tool against me. I learned to be at peace with myself. And every time I found my peace, my friend would call back within minutes and asked if she could see me.

I was learning something I call: holding my space. This had started with my first relationship but I was now able to give it a name as I was recognizing it as a key step in having a healthy relationship and in my personal growth. Holding one's space is part of the individuation process where you become aware of yourself as a separate person from your mother first, and also separate from others. But apparently it is not a one-step event, it is a process.

One of the ways I was not holding my space was to believe that I could not be joyful if my significant other was unhappy. My joy had to always come second. The first time I chose to stop doing this was with a girlfriend who I was going to go out dancing with one evening, but just before leaving she started pouting and said she did not want to go anymore. I felt a pull inside, like she wanted me to stay with her but without saying it. In the past I would have asked: "What's wrong?" and let myself be pulled by her state of being. But this time, for some reason unknown to me, I just accepted her at her words, I wished her a good evening and told her I was still going out. I had a great time. That night I had a dream.

A big African American pianist was playing jazz. He was having the time of his life. The tune was not one I recognized and it was beautiful. I noticed the keys of the piano and saw them up close. They were made of pieces of fruit. I woke up still enthralled with the music. I wondered what the fruit were for and the immediate thought was "fruit for the soul." I understood I had fed my soul by taking care of myself and having fun instead of catering to my girlfriend's feelings.

This was an experience of self-love.

Self-Love

What Do You Feel Humanity Is Missing?

In Chapter 2, I mentioned a workshop I took in 1994 to develop my relationship to intuition. In that class, our teacher asked us a question, "What do you feel humanity is missing?" We each had to answer that question for ourselves. People wanted to see more unconditional love, community, connectedness, peace, harmony. Mine was that humanity needed Joy.

Then she told us that what we see missing in humanity is what we need to bring to it. That is part of our purpose. But of course to be able to bring it to humanity we needed first to find it in ourselves.

This was a great gift and, although I did not recognize it right away, it was my answer to letting go of worries.

How Do I Become a Master?

In 1996, when I took the training called *The Master's Touch* to be a Kundalini yoga teacher, we were offered the opportunity to meet with Yogi Bhajan one on one. We could only ask one question. The meetings were very short, up to five minutes. Our group had over 100 students and, even though not all of us had requested a private meeting, the line to see him was long. I did not want to waste my time with a question that would be resolved easily so I asked, "How do I become a Master?" Yogi Bhajan looked at my aura and he gave me a meditation to practice for two and a half hours per day for 1,000 days in a row. The mantra I was to repeat out loud was "Wha Hey Gu Ru." It was to be repeated in a monotone in four separate syllables. The mantra is similar to "Hallelujah!" for Judeo Christians. It is the experience of ecstasy when one leaves darkness and enters a state of grace. Then he was quiet for a moment and I thought I may have time for a second question, but he interrupted me and I realized he'd been exploring my aura. That's when he told me he wanted to give me a spiritual name and asked for my birthdate. He considered it and said, "Awtar Singh." And he added, "You are a reincarnated teacher." Then he dismissed me.

After the teacher training, I started practicing that meditation. But I kept falling asleep within 10 minutes. My mind could not sustain that energy. I could do other meditations and stay awake. But not that one. I stopped for a few months and tried again and this time I could stay awake for a half an hour. For some reason I do not recall, I stopped practicing it for quite some time at that point.

Reflections

I had not recognized right away that, within a period of four years, I had received three answers that were almost identical and from totally independent human sources. First, in 1992 after my unconditional love experience, I was told through inner guidance to let go of worries. Then, in 1994, I was inspired by my teacher to find joy within myself so I could bring it to humanity. Finally, in 1996, I was told to meditate on the ecstasy of letting go of darkness and embracing the light.

There was a deep darkness in my heart I did not acknowledge to anyone, or at least not directly. I tried to acknowledge it through fiction writing. One of the reasons I did not deal with it openly is that I did not have words for it. Now, I can say it was a form of gloom and doom that could be described with fears such as: "I don't matter to the world." "God hates me." "Nobody will want me on their team." It resulted in a fear of not being supported for who I wanted to be, a fear of lack, and, in particular, lack of material support.

I addressed the money issue by opening up to and accepting employment in the pharmaceutical industry as a statistician. And I was well paid for a period of time. But being well paid did not heal anything. The fears remained untouched. The experience of financial ease though remained a gift. I knew I was able to attract it to myself.

When the company branch I was working for was moved to merge with another branch of the company, my wife and I decided we would not move. I had an opportunity to build my own life the way I wanted to.

My company had left me with a six month severance package. I saw it as a gift. I thought I was full of trust. I received another gift: A yoga studio ready to use with pillows and blocks and blankets and mats, and a brand new original painting on the wall, all for $250. I was grateful. But my trust was wounded by fears I was not aware of and I did not know they affected my ability to attract wealth. So even though my students loved my classes, I could not make a living. Slowly, I felt drained and my business went down.

At the time, I did some spiritual inner search and the same answer kept coming: "Your problem is not about money, your problem is love!" I did not understand what that meant. How could opening up to love change my luck with money? I had recently been separated from the mother of my son. And I met a woman who became a lover and everything was wonderful for almost a year. Then she asked me to love her enough to let her go. Then I met another woman who had access to quite a bit of money and we became lovers. That relationship lasted a few years. But it ended, as well. I was given an experience of love and money but somehow it did not translate into my ability to generate a higher income. I was not anti-rich, I was not anti-upper class. At the same time, I was also not attracted by the wealthy lifestyle.

To survive while my yoga business went down, I became a home health aide. That did not pay enough to make a living. I resolved that by becoming a student in mental health counseling with a student loan. But at the end, despite my efforts, I did not get any interviews to work in that field.

The whole experience, as I described it in the previous chapter about my life lessons, led me to find self-belief, and self-confidence. My solution was not to wait for others to believe in me. I had a few friends who kept encouraging me throughout that very difficult and lonely time. I found out that my situation was the perfect setup to learn that I could rely on myself, and that I had the strength to make it. I simply needed to believe in myself, stop trying to find a solution from others, and behave accordingly.

Money came more easily after I started believing in myself, but I was still not generating enough. I had accrued some debts and I felt out of my wits as to what to do next.

In June 2013, I suddenly remembered all three experiences that started 20 years earlier telling me to meditate on joy. I realized that my stumbling block to meditating for two and a half hours a day was that I would not be spending that time toward being practical and creating a career. Since nothing practical worked, I felt I had nothing to lose. I had tried everything I knew. I let go of the fear and started doing the "Wha Hey Gu Ru" meditation one hour every morning and one hour every evening. Within a week, I received $500 cash unexpectedly on a Sunday to help get a new clutch for my car. The failing clutch died two days later.

Also, I had been asking the Universe for help getting clients who would pay me the full price of my sliding scale instead of having clients paying the middle or lower end of the scale. My prayer was not answered in quite the manner I was expecting, but the result was that circumstances shifted so that I started being reimbursed for my work by a third party at a higher rate than the upper end of my scale. And money continued coming month after month after that. I was able to start paying off debts and even started to pay off my student loan.

In the end, the solution to my financial struggles was multifaceted. I had to really believe in myself, I had to start living for joy and not for paying my bills, and I also had to stop being afraid of not being supported for who I am. It was easy to be supported while I was doing what others wanted me to do (my life as a statistician). I had to learn to trust that being me was enough. The third party agency started to require narrative notes of the work I did for my clients. I believed in what I did, but I did not trust that a mainstream agency would accept my work. I had to learn to trust more and more. And Life gave me ample opportunities to learn that lesson.

My financial dark phase was an incredible lesson about self-love. I was stuck with a belief that our culture does not welcome our true nature, but Life led me to trust that it was possible. I just had to trust that who I wanted to be, including the way I wanted to practice psychotherapy, was welcome, not just by my friends and clients, but also by the whole culture.

Love in Psychotherapy

Clifford Whittingham Beers

Love is not often acknowledged in the literature about the psychotherapeutic process but it is important. In *A Mind That Found Itself* (1908), Clifford W. Beers talks about his experiences in mental institutions for three years and how he recovered to talk about it. Beers believed he had crimes to pay for and saw everything that happened around him, especially how people treated him, in light of that belief. He described that the "benevolence" given to him, in particular from the many letters from his family, started to shed doubts in his mind that he had any crimes for which to pay. The very caring of his caregivers stopped feeling like manipulation to get his acknowledgement of a guilty plea. The kindness of the caregivers started to suggest to him that there had to be some truth to the letters he had received from family and friends.

In my understanding, Beers is saying that his belief that he had to pay for some crime served as a filter or a veil that did not allow him to see reality as it really was and created a paranoid vision of reality. But when he opened his eyes to the love from his family, the negative filter dissolved. He then remembered what happened during his hospital stay from the perspective of a healthy human being. From a psychological perspective, his personality was never affected by the mental illness, and the mental illness was not of a personality disorder. Instead, his mental health challenges were a natural consequence of his beliefs. And love was key in his recovery.

Beers went on to found the American Mental Health Hygiene movement. He wanted to help change the treatment of patients who suffered from mental illnesses. The story of how he went about it is a fascinating one because it shows how our perception of mental illness has changed very little despite all his efforts.

To me Beers is a key part of the history of psychotherapy and needs to have a more prominent place than he is given. He is remembered for his book, for the movement he created and founding the Connecticut Society for Mental Hygiene in 1908 that is known today as Mental Health America. And, although he became well known in America and in

Luc Watelet

Europe and received awards, what he had to offer was not fully received by his contemporaries who had the power to improve the care of the mentally ill. Later in life he felt like a failure.

Today, Beers may have been diagnosed with bipolar disorder with some schizophrenia prior to his institutionalization. But our culture seems to have very little notion that schizophrenia or bipolar disorders need not be personality disorders in that it may not be the brain that is ill, but there may simply be a fear serving as a distorting filter between the experience and the brain processing the experience. We have no idea as a culture that love may be key in helping people with such diagnoses be able to let go of the filter and therefore be free from the illness with which they were diagnosed.

Psychotherapists

Erich Fromm has written many books among them *The Art of Loving*.

McLeod, S. A. (2007) wrote about Carl Rogers:

> *Carl Rogers (1902-1987) was a humanistic psychologist who agreed with the main assumptions of Abraham Maslow, but added that for a person to "grow", they need an environment that provides them with genuineness (openness and self-disclosure), acceptance (being seen with unconditional positive regard), and empathy (being listened to and understood).*
> *Without these, relationships and healthy personalities will not develop as they should, much like a tree will not grow without sunlight and water.*[16]

Further along in the same article McLeod states:

> *Carl Rogers [...] viewed the child as having two basic needs: positive regard from other people and self-worth.*[17]

Virginia Satir (1916-1988) was an experiential family therapist for whom

---

[16] Retrieved September 19, 2014, and still active July 3, 2016, from http://www.simplypsychology.org/carl-rogers.html.
[17] Ibid.

self-esteem was the cornerstone of the healing of an individual. Here's her declaration of self-esteem:[18]

> I am me.
>
> In all the world, there is no one else exactly like me. There are persons who have some parts like me, but no one adds up exactly like me. Therefore, everything that comes out of me is authentically mine because I alone chose it.
>
> I own everything about me: my body, including everything it does; my mind, including all its thoughts and ideas; my eyes, including the images of all they behold; my feelings, whatever they may be: anger, joy, frustration, love disappointment, excitement; my mouth, and all the words that come out of it: polite, sweet or rough, correct or incorrect; my voice, loud or soft, and all my actions, whether they be to others or to myself.
>
> I own my fantasies, my dreams, my hopes, my fears.
>
> I own all of my triumphs and successes, all of my failures and mistakes.
>
> Because I own all of me, I can become intimately acquainted with me. By so doing, I can love me and be friendly with me. I can then make it possible for all of me to work in my best interests.
>
> I know there are aspects about myself that puzzle me, and other aspects that I do not know. But as long as I am friendly and loving to myself, I can courageously and hopefully look for the solution of the puzzles and ways to find out more about me.
>
> However I look and sound, whatever I say and do, and whatever I think and feel at a given moment in time, is mine. This is authentic and represents where I am at that moment in time. When I review later how I looked and sounded, what I said and did, and how I thought and felt, some parts may turn out to be unfit. I can discard that which is unfitting, and keep that which proved fitting, and invent something new for that which I discarded.
>
> I can see, hear, feel, think, say and do. I have the tools to survive, to be close to others, to be productive, and to make sense and order out of the world of people and things outside of me.
>
> I own me, and therefore, I can engineer me.
>
> I am me, and I am okay.

---

[18] V. Satir (1988). *The New Peoplemaking*, Science and Behavior Books, p. 28.

Luc Watelet

Further along in the same book, Virginia Satir uses the word love about the therapeutic process and provides a definition of this love:[19]

> I started a private practice over thirty five years ago. Because I was a woman and had nonmedical training, the people who were available to me were the "rejects" of other therapists and the very "high-risk" persons, those who had been abused, were alcoholic, "psychopathic," and generally seen as untreatable. But many of these people began to blossom as the treatment proceeded. I think now that this happened because I was working to contact their spirits, loving them as I went along.
> [...]
> It was as though I saw through to the inner core of each being. Seeing the shining light of the spirit trapped in a thick black cylinder of limitation and self-rejection. My effort was to enable the person to see what I saw.

These words by Virginia Satir, to me, are at the essence of the work of psychotherapy. It is not about fixing, it is about helping in the process of reconnection with oneself.

Ron Kurtz (1934-2011) talked about the role of loving presence and caring in the therapeutic process.

The Road Less Traveled, by M. Scott Peck (1936-2005) has the subtitle that is often left unmentioned: A new Psychology of Love, Traditional Values and Personal Growth.

He says,[20]

> Love is the will to extend one's self for the purpose of nurturing one's own or another's spiritual growth... Love is as love does. Love is an act of will – namely, both an intention and an action. Will also implies choice. We do not have to love. We choose to love.

---

[19] V. Satir (1988). The New Peoplemaking, Science and Behavior Books, pp. 340-341.
[20] M. Scott peck (2003). The Road Less Traveled: A new Psychology of Love, Traditional Values and Personal Growth, Touchstone, p. 81.

Heartwork Institute founder and author of *Heartwork: How to Get What You Really, Really Want*, Dale Goldstein (1945-present), saw through his own inner work "the need to combine psychological and spiritual work in one comprehensive system."[21] To him, and I fully agree, problems are resolved by opening the "heart of compassion."

Many therapists have embraced the inner world of their clients. If love is communicated by opening one's heart to someone, then listening for the inner world in a client is an act of love. The importance of this love exchange of energy between a therapist and a client was never mentioned in my mental health counseling coursework and yet it is essential and I wish it was acknowledged for the sake of what we pass on to our students and for the future of psychotherapy.

Love, Being in Love, and Mystics

A Meditation

Feeling in love with a person? Look deeper... If that person were gone, would your feelings of being in love disappear? If you think it disappeared, then rekindle its feeling in your heart; I bet you will find that what you feel in love with is Life, all of it, not just one person! Then you may feel in conflict between this love you feel for the one person and for all of Life... resolve that puzzle for yourself.... Wherever that leads you...

Mystics

Reading Rumi's love poems, and Khalil Gibran, and others, guides one out of darkness. Mystics know about the human heart and the human soul. I would love to see the field of psychotherapy embrace the knowledge of traditional healers and spiritual masters, including the mystics.

---

[21] D. Goldstein (2014). Retrieved September 19, 2014, and still active July 3, 2016, from http://awakentheheart.org/dale-goldstein-lcsw.

4 NATURE

In the Prologue, I state that *"Depression, as all "mental illnesses," is a disconnection from our soul and from nature."* So far, I have addressed the idea that mental illnesses are the result of a disconnection from our soul, our inner-self. I address here the relationship between mental illness and the disconnection from nature.

Camping Experiences

When I was finished with my dissertation in biostatistics, I had some time to myself. I was feeling at odds in my life and I wanted to explore what I would do next. I really wanted to understand myself better. I planned a bicycle camping trip to Whidbey Island, north of Seattle. I enjoyed using my own energy of riding my bicycle to a location I had never visited. After a few hours on the road, I took the ferry to the island. Then, I biked to a forest and found a spot for my tent. I had biked in the presence of cars on a road, with no bicycle lane, for four hours straight and was tired. I settled into my tent for the night.

In the early morning, when I zipped open my tent, I was greeted by a young fox's gaze from about 20 feet away. It felt like an apparition. We stared at each other gently for a while. Because of the duration of the connection, I felt I belonged there. After I stopped looking into the fox's eyes, the feeling of an apparition remained with me. This young fox was a messenger. It did not run away or show fear. It just stood its grounds gently. I felt I belonged and yet I felt I longed for something else than the woods.

I wanted to see the mountain. I packed up and continued riding my bicycle, following some inner sense of direction, and found a spot outside of people's view for my tent from where I could see a part of the Olympic Mountains. It rained a little and I danced naked in the rain. I started talking to the mountain. At a feeling level, I was communicating with the Universal Father. I don't remember what I said. Then I knew I wanted to visit with the ocean the next day. When I did, I talked to the ocean and it felt as though I was talking to the Universal Mother. Again, I don't remember what transpired. I just know that, in both instances, I felt a real connection with something bigger than myself. I felt welcome and I felt okay with myself and with the world. I then walked along the beach.

The young fox felt too much like me at the time. I longed for guidance. The fox had given me a reassurance that it was okay to be me, although I may not have been able to word it this way at the time. I only knew I was seeking clarity. Although, I longed to receive that clarity from the mountains and the oceans, not from something vulnerable and young, as I am writing this now, I am learning from this young fox to welcome and love my younger self. I had not recognized before that, because of my longing to be acknowledged by adults, I had distanced myself from my younger self. Thank you Young Fox!

In nature, I could connect with anything with which I chose to connect. I was not judged. I was not more or less than anything else. I was me, as everything else was simply itself.

The next day before returning home, I stopped at a local coffee shop and started talking with people. It is interesting how a little time alone, outside of my usual routine, leads me to want to be with people, with no other purpose than to get to know them. I love that feeling. A man asked what I was doing and I told him about biking and camping, following my own feelings of where to go next, and enjoying nature and being in it. He said he wished he could do the same.

From this experience with nature, I did not get any answers from what to do in my life. I think the gift I received was simply that it was enough to be. I had been looking for something else. Something dramatic and exciting. I found I felt more connected with nature than with the human world.

I made two more camping trips, one with a couple of friends to Sawtooth Mountain in Idaho and one alone to Arizona.

I loved my experience with friends at Sawtooth Mountain. While camping, we met South American men with two large dogs. They were herding sheep on State grounds along the highway. They baked bread in the ground and shared it with us and gave us the recipe. It was delicious. There was something serene about living simply, breathing, being, and connecting with others. Life felt very different from this perspective, relaxed, moment to moment, no hurry, no goals other than enjoying each moment.

In Arizona, I landed in Phoenix and rented a car at the airport. I was planning on driving a bit every day followed by setting up my tent, hiking some, sleeping, and eating when I was hungry. I was trying something new, and found something new about myself. In Sedona, for instance, I was mesmerized by the red color of the mountain. I planned to set up my tent in the sandy hills. When I arrived there, I was in my car and it had started to rain. I felt dejected. But suddenly I remembered what I was there for and rain or not I was going to hike! As I opened my car door, it immediately stopped raining and the sun came out. Just like that... as though with a flick of a magic wand. It did not rain after that for the rest of my trip. It was my first experience of feeling like my thoughts had something to do with my experience.

In nature, there was no expectation of me except to be me. I went skinny dipping. I hiked. I took photographs. I talked with people. I saw a shooting star. Life was to be lived and experienced and there was nothing to be ambitious about, nothing to achieve.

Bruno Gröning, German healer at the time of Hitler, describes nature as a place where, as a young boy, he could experience the love that he felt was missing from his family and from the human world. I might not have described my experience in those terms because I had not yet figured out the importance of love in my life. I know those experiences in nature felt rejuvenating and filled me with love.

Joseph Cornell says:

> *After spending many days in the wilderness, people notice that their problems and distractions have faded away. Everything they see, hear, and smell becomes extraordinarily beautiful, in their freed and focused attention. In this intensity of experience they may feel a deeper calmness, joy, and aliveness than ever before.*[22]

David Abram

In 2006, the Zen Center of Rochester celebrated its 40th anniversary. We had Jon Kabat Zinn and other impressive guest speakers I did not know. I remember Roshi Bodhin Kjolhede opened the symposium with comments on Buddhism to be more than an individual path to enlightenment, and needing to be actively engaged in the world. Jon Kabat Zinn talked beautifully about what he had come to be known for: healing with a mindfulness practice. Roshi Joan Halifax, the founder and Abbot of the Upaya Zen Center in Santa Fe was a welcome female voice among the men. The last speaker was Ken Kraft, Professor of Asian Religion at Lehigh University. The speaker before him was David Abram. I had never experienced a speaker as Mr. Abram before.

Each speaker was as eloquent as the next and said powerful things that were very spiritually meaningful. I was moved by each one to be more myself in the world. I felt uplifted at the end of each one's presentation. A great speaker is one who speaks simply from the mind with a heart wide open. They all did that.

When I started listening to and watching David Abram, it felt as though something else was present. Not just his mind and his heart, it felt as though all of nature was present and alive with him. He told us stories of being in nature with presence. I was captivated. I was alive. I bought his book: *The Spell of the Sensuous*. In it, he says that in his interaction with traditional medicine people from different cultures around the world, he'd learned that their key responsibility was not to heal the members of their community who fell sick, it was instead to preserve the balance between their community and nature. If that balance was

---

[22] J. Cornell (1987). Listening to Nature: How to Deepen Your Awareness of Nature, Dawn Publications (CA), p.10.

off in any way, people in the community would get sick and then they had to heal them as well as figure out how to help the community return to balance with nature. Sickness is seen as a symptom of a lack of balance with nature, including the spirit world.

A Direct Healing Experience with Nature

Around the same time, my friend D. worked as a nurse in a hospice. She often worked nights. I am rarely out at the early hours of the morning, but that particular night I was driving home around two in the morning. I had spent an incredible evening with new friends and we could not say goodbye.

On my way home, I called D., knowing she was on the night shift. I asked her how she was and she started talking about one of her patients being very difficult. This woman was in the throes of Lou Gehrig's disease (ALS) and was throwing her glass of orange juice at her bedroom window, could not sleep and kept everyone else awake. D., normally laughing everything off with grace, felt overwhelmed. I told her that I would meditate on her patient as soon as I was home and would call her after that. She asked me not to call in case her patients were asleep. She would call me after giving me about 15 minutes of meditation.

I knew I could not do mindfulness work, or help someone else do mindfulness work, with this patient due to the state of her mind that late in her experience with ALS. I had to find solutions that could be adapted to her specific situation. Thus, during my meditation, I tuned in to the inner space of D.'s patient. I felt it filled with fiery (dry and hot) and agitated energy. I felt how orange juice was exacerbating that experience which explained her being awake and aggressive. I asked myself what drinking water would feel like to her and I felt somewhat of a soothing experience, better even than not drinking orange juice. Then I asked myself what putting her bare feet on the grass would do to her experience and I felt even deeper soothing.

D., called and I explained all this to her and asked if she could pass on my message to the patient's family. I did not expect anyone would follow my suggestions but knew D. would start giving her water instead of juice. A week later, I had the lovely surprise to receive a call from D. Her voice was cheerful. She had the patient's daughter on the phone.

The daughter told me how grateful she was for my suggestions. For the past week, she had taken her mother out in her wheelchair, taken her shoes and socks off to help her experience her bare feet on the grass. D. told me her patient was no longer throwing her drink at the window and was now sleeping four hours a night and letting everybody else sleep at the hospice.

We are so disconnected from the effect nature has on us, that we don't even know how much we miss it!

War and the Destruction of the Environment

Julia Butterfly Hill is known for her two-year experience tree sitting on a 1,000 year old sequoia tree at the end of the 90s to save it from the tree logging company. That experience taught her what I was learning too that the problem is not war and the destruction of the environment, that's the symptom of the problem. The problem is our disconnection from the impact of what we do.[23]

To me it is the same disconnection that leads to addictions and mental health issues. Disconnection leads to the horrors of what humankind is doing, and reconnection leads to healing individuals and ultimately could lead to our own survival and that of the planet.

The Archetype of the Wild Man and the Wild Woman

A Healing Experience

I have had to wear low grade reading glasses for three years or so. I believe in spiritual healing. Yet, so far I have seen progress only once. It lasted a week of being able to read without glasses. But then it shifted back. I was wondering why and I asked a friend to help me. She uses a modality called the Emotional Freedom Technique (EFT). It is a method relying on connecting with what bothers you and reminding yourself that despite it you accept and love yourself while you use a specific sequence of tapping your fingers on parts of your head, your collar

---

[23] *"Disconnection"* by Julia Butterfly Hill, downloaded on January 9, 2016, and still active on July 3, 2016, from https://www.youtube.com/watch?v=HARZfLptcFQ.

Luc Watelet

bone, and the side of your rib cage.

I am not an expert at EFT; I just followed my friend's guidance. During the session, I remembered feeling bewitched by a woman on a street in Brussels. I had just come out of my grandmother's house. I was eight years old. I had taken a few steps on the sidewalk when a short and plump older woman dressed in grayish clothes looked at me with such intensity that I felt as though her eyes drilled into mine and hooked themselves there. I could not let go and I started to back up as she was walking toward me. She suddenly emotionally unhooked her eyes and apologized. I turned around ran back into my grandmother's house, walked up the stairs all the way to my bedroom on the third floor without talking to anyone, and lay on my bed, my heart pounding with fear. I did not share that story with anyone for decades. As we explored what went on for me then, I realized that my mother had used her eyes to control my behavior as a kid, especially when I wanted to express my joy when my father wanted to talk about work. The rule in our home was that adults had priority to express themselves over children.

During the healing session, I remembered the book *Iron John* by Robert Bly in which he describes the archetype of the Wild Man as a representation of what a boy needs to reclaim on his journey into manhood. One of the steps is to steal from under his mother's pillow the key to the cage where the Wild Man has been locked up. I did not quite know what to do with this knowledge at the time I read the book. But now I had a specific experience where I had allowed my inner wild joy to be locked up from me in a cage by my mother and I needed to find the key to free my joy. My friend continued by doing Reiki on me. She felt a lot of heat in her hands over my shoulders. I slowly experienced what it was like to allow my wild joy to be okay again and felt two distinct jolts of energy in my upper body that I described at the time as an upper body orgasm.

It became clear to me that the Wild Man, or Untamed Man as I prefer to call him, or Natural Man as others have also called him, is key to feeling whole. That Untamed Man or Woman is who we would be if we had not learned to behave properly, to be socially acceptable. S/he has qualities that we have learned to distrust, but that, at some point, become essential again to our growth. Entering the wild in nature, and truly letting ourselves experience it, is one way to re-access those parts of us.

This can also be done to some extent in meditation.

Robin's Experience in the Australian Rainforest

In her book *Naked in Eden*, my friend Robin Easton recounts, "Tears stung my eyes because living in the rainforest had turned my life 'real' very fast. I couldn't hide from myself in the same way I'd been able to in the outside world."[24]

A page further, the voice of the rainforest spoke directly to my friend's spirit: "Robin, the rainforest will teach you everything you missed and all you need to become a whole and complete woman. Be patient. Trust."

After some time in the Rainforest, Robin ponders:

> How much of our illness, physical or psychological, is a result of our disconnection and its manifestations? Are we so completely isolated that we no longer identify or empathize with other life forms, with our "Mother"? Ourselves? Maybe I'm not the only one who has lived in an autistic state. Could it be that "civilization" is autistic? And we don't even know it. If autism is being withdrawn or cut off from "Mother" or "Source," emotionally detached, unable to really feel or see or hear her presence, unable to interact or communicate, performing repetitive movements and compulsive routines, unable to be aware of other people's feelings, then our relationship to planet Earth has become an autistic one.[25]

I recommend this book for both men and women to understand the archetype and healing power of the Untamed Self from a real life account. There are other books about this archetype that can be found online. I suspect, like Robin, that, if more people reconnected with their Untamed Self, mental health challenges and other diseases would eventually decrease as a result.

---

[24] R. Easton (2010). *Naked in Eden: My Adventure and Awakening in the Australian Rainforest* (Kindle Locations 1437-1438). Kindle Edition.
[25] Ibid. (Kindle Locations 1969-1974). Kindle Edition.

Luc Watelet

Conclusion

The call of the wild is an essential piece to our human growth, personally and as a species. It is not a living room conversation, a discussion leading to a mental change of perspective or perception. It is not a transformation through activism. It is not an intellectual journey. It has more to do with experiencing. It is a journey to the very core of nature, face to face with the wild, outside of human self-centeredness and sense of superiority. For instance, how do we respond to predators and preys in the wild? Can we embrace the natural laws with an openness that breeds compassion and a celebration for the beauty of the dance between predators and preys? Can we find the humble space where we see our self as part of the whole, no longer separate from the streams, the rocks, the trees of the forest, or the six-foot, red bellied black snake staring at us a few inches away from our face, as Robin experienced? Can we let the judgment disappear and communicate with vulnerability and truth? There is no other way to communicate with nature. It uproots us from political correctness, the human discourse on economics, the corporate vision or any philosophy, and it grounds us into the very foundation of life, into the mystery of life – Life with a capital L. We start seeing with a clarity that makes us incorruptible to dogma and –isms.

Humanity has endeavored to conquer nature to make the experience of living more comfortable, but in the process we have ignored that in the end we cannot change the natural laws that govern the universe and us. The question is: What happens within when we open our self to accept these natural laws? Observing and being part of nature is one profound way I know to start answering that question for our self. It opens us to a very personal journey of self-discovery, healing and empowerment to the experience of who we really are. No one can make that journey for anyone else! But as a culture, we can make decisions to continue cutting ourselves off from this journey, or embrace it for our self and the sake of future generations.

5 LIFE ~ HUMAN NATURE

Everyone, whether a king or queen, pauper or beggar, lover or deserter, attorney or accused, is going to be challenged in life. One thing you cannot escape is challenge. Whether you challenge the challenge or you give in to the challenge, that is what decides your spirituality. Is your spirit higher than the challenge so you can face it? It is simple. If your face and your grace do not give in to the challenge, you are spiritual. Otherwise you are not. Period.[26]

~ Yogi Bhajan

Me and You, Me and God, and Back to Me and You

Me and You

First there was *Me*. I was born and I was the center of the universe. There was my mother and my father and then my brother... and then two cousins entered the picture. It was community heaven. My father could not find work in Belgium, or even in Europe; he found work in Canada instead. So we moved. I was five years old. I was curious, I always am. Yet, I lost my heaven. I lost the people I loved being with, the people who gave me a sense of who I was because I felt happy with them. I repressed some of my feelings at the time. I had taken *you*, that

---

[26] Yogi Bhajan, Exerpt from his Lecture on 12/31/1992, retrieved September 21, 2014, and still active July 3, 2016, from http://fateh.sikhnet.com/sikhnet/articles.nsf/9dee2aa6164e1d9b87256671004e06c7/97579da301f2a850872576fd007d177b!OpenDocument.

is, my cousins, and my brother, for granted because we were always around each other and I assumed *you* would always be a part of me. Suddenly, being apart from each other made me realize that *you,* that is, any other person, were separate from me. I became aware of *you,* outside of me.

I felt the pain, the loneliness, and did not know at first how to deal with it. Years later, after my first marriage had fallen apart, I met a woman, V., who was from Belgium and her mother had been to the same high school as one of my aunts. We lived in Georgia at the time. The chance of that! Naturally, I fell in love with her. With time it was clear that she did not feel about me the way I felt about her. Later, when faced with the prospect of another marriage, I became sick one weekend a month for six months in a row. I had a fever and threw up. With the last one, I understood I was sick over V. Before the last outburst, I had a meeting with V. and asked her one more time if we could have a relationship beyond friendship. She said she had been in this situation with another man who did not return her feelings for him. Thus, she was very understanding and supportive toward me. I finally realized it wasn't her I was in love with – it was what she represented: my lost heaven from childhood. It wasn't her unreturned love I was sick over, it was my lost childhood heaven. In that moment, I was finally able to let go of wanting my friend to be my lover and of my attachment to the loss of my childhood heaven. Instead, I realized that if I loved my childhood heaven so much it was because I loved community, I loved people, and I could create community wherever I was. I did not get sick over this again. I was free.

This all came together for me when I was living in an intentional community, at the Yoga Society. The experience of living with others gave me a sense of clarity about who I am.

Where My Relationship with God Comes into the Picture

I may not be talking about God in the way you believe in God. We all have a concept of God, even atheists, otherwise they could not make a decision about a world independent of God. More on the concept of God later.

The more people I meet, the more differences I learn to respect, engage with and accept, the more complete I become in my awareness of me, the more I am able to make peace within me, with the entire me. If you hold your space, respectfully acknowledging yours and mine, and I hold my space, respectfully acknowledging mine and yours, we transcend differences into a space of love. My community experience led me to become aware of the infinite nature of potential relationships I can have with all that is. What abundance!!! And, with each one, I have an opportunity to embrace more diversity and, therefore, more peace. Imagine if I made peace with all of the potential relationships, with all that is, then I would have complete peace with natural laws, or call it God. If I am at odds in one of my earthly relationships, I will feel that in my relationship with God. Conversely, if I am at odds with God, I am at odds in at least one of my earthly relationships.

In the *Bible*, Jesus is attributed as saying the following words (in one English translation) which point to the same idea: "Amen, I say to you, as much as you have done to one of these my little brothers, you have done that to me."[27]

The Concept of God

First, a parenthesis.

If we really knew how the universe works, we would no longer argue whether there is a God, whether there are many gods, or whether there is no God at all. Since we can only pretend to know how the universe really works or what the true nature of God is (or the true nature of gods are), why even argue at all?

Why put so much importance in beliefs? What if God were not separate from life? What if God were not separate from the universe? Do you ask yourself whether to believe in life or in the universe?

I think what we are actually doing is learning to cope with how to live not knowing the true nature of the universe. Some cope by believing in God/gods, others by being agnostic (not knowing what to believe) and yet others by being atheist (lack of belief in God/gods). Only a few can

---

[27] Matthew 25:40, retrieved on December 27, 2014, and still active on July 3, 2016, from http://biblehub.com/aramaic-plain-english/matthew/25.htm.

Luc Watelet

say they have really experienced God and, if they have, they most likely only have experienced a facet or two of God.

It is understandable that people who have had a beautiful experience that they attribute to believing in God or people who have experienced a facet of God, want to share that experience with others, wishing them the benefits of their own experience. But why get into an argument, why question someone's experience, or why impose one's experience on someone else once we feel resistance?

Often our conversations are less about experience and more about convincing. Whichever position we hold about God/gods has little to do with God/gods, it has little to do with an objective truth and more to do with our relationship with our self – unless we have an experience, and not just a belief, about something divine. In this world, if someone has an experience of something others have not experienced, that person may be thought of as crazy or having delusions. When I talk about my out-of-body experience, some people who haven't experienced one try to explain it away with an experience they have had such as a dream or a fantasy, as they cannot imagine that an out-of-body experience can be real. It can be hard for us human beings to allow ourselves to open up to the possibility of something we have not experienced.

If I am truly scientific about something I have not experienced then I have to open myself to the possibility that there is something I don't know and to open myself to experiencing it. In my life, when I am truly open to experiencing the truth, I eventually experience it.

End of parenthesis.

We all have a relationship with the concept of God. In order to decide whether one believes in, does not believe in, lacks a belief in, or isn't sure about the existence of God or gods, one has to have a concept of God or gods. One does not choose to lack a belief in God without having a concept of God. I do not know whether it is possible to know God completely. Each one of us has his own concept of God. Deepak Chopra explains in his book, *How to Know God: The Soul's Journey into the Mystery of Mysteries,* how our concept of God changes with our personal and spiritual growth. So instead of talking about God/gods with each other, it would be more accurate to acknowledge that we are only talking about our concept(s) of God/gods.

I would say that our concept of God is to our worldview what God is to universal laws. Our concept of God and our worldview are subjective, while God and universe laws are objective.

To me there is no difference between learning/seeking to live according to God (gods) and learning/seeking to live according to universal laws. Either quest brings ultimate healing or enlightenment. From this perspective, the difference between a believer, an agnostic and an atheist, is semantics. But these words make a huge difference in our experience.

Parallel Between Healing a Relationship on Earth and Healing our Relationship with our Concept of God

Imagine someone who lives in poverty and has stopped believing there is anything he can do to upgrade his life. That describes an aspect of his worldview. If he believes in God and believes God can upgrade his life, he would open up to the possibility, otherwise, it is as if he has started to believe that God does not want him to have a more affluent life. If he does not believe in God, he believes something is preventing him from being able to upgrade his life, something bigger or more powerful than himself. His worldview cannot conceive of a more affluent lifestyle for himself. That "something bigger or more powerful than himself" is a concept equivalent to the concept of God; it has the same effect as believing that God does not want him to have an affluent life. It is simply a different label. If he believes otherwise, he would still make an effort to change his life. Now imagine that a rich man, say Rich, meets Thomas, the poor man. Rich tells Thomas he can help him. Thomas is shocked at first, but, with time, he gives Rich a chance and opens up to learn from him, and it turns out that Thomas becomes more affluent. Something has shifted in Thomas's worldview and in his relationship with his concept of God or his concept of what had power over him.

Unless we are always honest with our self, and do not blame our limitations on anyone or anything else, we experience life like Thomas. This example shows how we limit ourselves and the role our relationship with God plays in our experience. Healing our earthly relationships with people and material things goes hand in hand with

Luc Watelet

healing our relationship with God, or our concept of God, which is learning to see Life as it really is.

Back to Me and You

That brings me back to Me and You. I could have been born African American, Indonesian, in the Middle East, with a different physical or mental ability, with a different hair color or eye color, with a different sexual orientation, with no sexual orientation, with no money or with huge amounts of money... My life would still be about learning to accept and love myself and learning to accept and love others – which comes to the same thing. By learning to love you, I love more about me.

Without love, there is no growth, no forward movement; it feels like we keep living the same day over and over as in the movie *Groundhog Day* (1993). Love comes first, despite what Abraham Maslow said in his hierarchy of needs. (Read more about Maslow's hierarchy of needs in Chapter 12.)

So, from my perspective, Life is about coming to terms with who we are and loving what we find. Everything and everyone around us contributes to this quest.

Life and God

To simplify, instead of saying "God or universal laws," I will now use the word God for both.

What astounded me most in my life is that I did not have to make it happen consciously, and with diligent planning, for it to go where I wanted. For one thing, I did not know completely consciously what it is I wanted. I only knew something about what I did not think I wanted.

Let us review some of the key steps, including some I have not mentioned yet. At 16, I was attracted to and read two books, one from Freud and one from Jung. At 17, I became aware that I wanted to be a psychotherapist. Once in college, I took a couple of psychology courses as electives and was completely turned off from studying psychology academically due to how it was presented. I went into mathematics and then biostatistics. Once in biostatistics, I felt I was in the wrong line of study and work, but had no thoughts of trying psychology again except for reading books from authors I enjoyed: M. Scott Peck, James Hillman, Viktor Frankl, and Arnold Mindell. Viktor Frankl appeared in my life when I found his book *Man's Search for Meaning* on the sidewalk by a bus stop. The book *Coma* by Arnold Mindell was introduced to me by a friend. And then a series of events led me to meditation, healing, and yoga. I had not planned any of these events; they just appeared to me and I said "Yes." It baffles my mind because these events brought me where I now know I want to be without knowing fully where I had wanted to be and, therefore, without planning any of it. All I knew was to follow my heart every single step of the way. I did not have a choice really because, having no conscious plan, I just said "Yes" or "No" to what presented itself to me according to what felt right at the time, according to my heart, not according to what I *should* do. The only thing I did is I kept a flame lit up inside about wanting to be me.

Again, this is not about believing in fate. It is about knowing I have a soul with dreams and a purpose and these dreams and purpose have an energy, whether I am aware of it or not, that attracts to itself what it needs. As I clear up the mud (my expression for what dims my soul's pure light) that has covered up my soul over time, its light becomes more palpable and attracts to itself even more of what it needs. We have free will in clearing up the mud or not. We have free will in relating to the light or not.

Earlier on in my life, the car accident of 1984 led to my out-of-body experience and is key to my understanding of myself and human nature. The synchronicity of such experiences started to feel like Life has a consciousness connected with mine, that I had a relationship with Life. The car accident of 1993 by Watertown, New York, was another unexpected piece to my guidance as it led to my move to upstate New York, the birthplace of living my spirituality, not just seeking it. I have come to see guidance as part of the natural result of seeking who I am. Guidance came from the very fabric of Life. Guidance was the same as synchronicity in Jung's language. But synchronicity was not only the experiences that I recognized to be meaningful because, even if I did not always see it, every single experience became meaningful if I meditated long enough to grasp meaning in it that corresponds to what my life is really about.

> *Synchronicity is an ever present reality for those who have eyes to see.*
>
> ~ *attributed to Carl Jung on the internet.*[28]

> *All things appear and disappear because of the concurrence of causes and conditions. Nothing ever exists entirely alone; everything is in relation to everything else.*[29]
>
> ~ *Siddhartha Gautama (Buddha).*

Living Consciously Is Being in Intimate Connection with Life/God

I had asked myself many questions but one of the most difficult ones to resolve was, "Why am I doing biostatistics when it does not feel like I belong here?" That led to, "Who am I?" Then I had many experiences, some of which, I described in Chapter 2, Life Lessons. Something happened when I started to engage with Life, when I started to ask questions, when I started to search for answers to questions that mattered to me. The experiences I received did not come from my conscious self as they brought me to new understandings. Some experiences were hard to understand and accept. I fought against being in biostatistics as I did not find it fulfilling. And I fought against getting divorced as I did not want to betray my commitment. I fought against foreclosure and bankruptcy. After all those experiences, it feels like I had little choice but to accept them and see what would happen when I did. In retrospect, I benefitted more from these experiences than by fighting against them. They became answers to questions that were deeper than I could have worded at the time. So my experience of Life is one of engagement, my understanding of God is not separate from my experience of engaging with Life.

In this experience, God is not responsible for wars and famines, or for

---

[28] I could not find the source of this quote. I love it though. The author deserves a proper reference. If someone knows the origin of this quote please contact me (see copyright page).

[29] D. Goddard (1934). *Buddha, Truth, and Brotherhood*, Chapter 2, section V, paragraph 4. Retrieved on June 10, 2016, and still active on July 4, 2016, from http://www.hinduwebsite.com/sacredscripts/buddhist_bible.asp.

resolving wars and famines, because we have free will. If we want to resolve these calamities, we need to put our human minds and hearts together to awaken to our own powers to resolve them. We have to find enough love/compassion for ourselves and our fellow human beings. We have to grow up emotionally.

You have noticed, I make a distinction between "life" with a lower case "l" when referring to what is alive, what is studied in biology, and "Life" with an upper case "L" when referring to the experience of living. Life, Nature, Universe, Universal Consciousness, or Love (and sometimes God) started to mean the same thing to me from different perspectives. Although, God is also the source of all of these and not separate from them.

The concept Jung called Universal Consciousness started to feel very real to me. It is in everything and everywhere, not just in human beings, not just in mammals. It is in plants and rocks and streams. Native Americans and aboriginal peoples around the world consider everything to have a spirit. This Universal Consciousness connects us to each other and to everything in nature and in the universe. Synchronicity comes from this force. Synchronicity is always there, but we often only notice it when we engage consciously with Life. We engage with Life by welcoming it, by surrendering to it (releasing control), by meditating, by opening our heart, by asking questions humbly or sometimes not so humbly, by being real with ourselves and others.

This consciousness is not independent from us. It is intimately engaged with our deepest nature, and our deepest desires. It is in synchronicity with everyone's and everything's deepest nature and desires. So everything in nature and in the universe, including us and all our relationships, works as clockwork – an organic living clockwork. This is an echo of the phrase "there are no accidents!" It also says that nothing is set in stone. Life changes as our consciousness does. And our consciousness changes as we learn from our experiences, that is, when we expand our worldview to be more compassionate toward ourselves and toward others, and also by releasing control over the outside world and instead see that our only control is over ourselves. This encourages us to live by engaging with love and creativity with the world.

Noticing more and more that everything is in instant synchronicity helps me feel like I am a part of everything. I am never and can never be separate from Life as it responds instantly to my inner deepest truths as well as my superficial most fleeting thoughts and feelings. That is why being in the present moment is so important. This leads me to try to use words to talk about the nature of God with the awareness that my words cannot replace the experience of being alive which is the true experience of God.

In that sense, Life on Earth is the most ingenious video game in which the consciousness of everyone is in instant connection to influence everyone's lives. It is infinite in time and space and creativity/generosity. The love that emanates from it is infinite. The creativity coming from it is infinite. God is infinite and eternal. What an awesome, awe-filled, Universe!

> How can the divine Oneness be seen?
> In beautiful forms, breathtaking wonders, awe-inspiring miracles?
> The Tao is not obliged to present itself in this way.
> [...]
> If you are willing to be lived by it, you will see it everywhere,
> even in the most ordinary things.[30]
> > ~ Lao Tzu

As I embrace my experience of being alive, I experience life, I experience God. After all, I started with a concept of God with all the limitations that I imposed on it. Yet, in the process of healing my relationship to it, in the process of healing myself, my concept of God becomes more infinite and more awesome than I knew. As I experience myself in synchronicity with the world, I learn to play with the universe. There is no separation. I am part of the universal dance. And everything that is part of this dance mirrors an aspect of myself. I am indistinguishable from this awesome universe! I am indistinguishable from God. As we all are.

It simply started with the question "Who am I?"

---

[30] Brian Walker (2009). *Hua Hu Ching: The Unknown Teachings of Lao Tzu.* HarperCollins Publishers, New York, NY. Passage 22, p. 26.

6 PSYCHOTHERAPY 101

There are different approaches to teach psychotherapy. One is to teach each step, one at a time. Practice listening, practice empathy, practice conversations and interviewing skills, practice multicultural awareness, practice different psychotherapy theories and models and see which one feels most natural to the student's personality style, and practice being a client, and so on. In the back of my mind, I would have a lingering question, "Why am I practicing all this?" Imagine that you wish to be a tennis professional, but you are not allowed to watch tennis at a level higher than your current skill. You never get to see how much better you could be. You would depend entirely on your coach to motivate you. Something would be missing.

From this tennis perspective, I want to present the basics of psychotherapy while keeping in mind the ideal we are aiming for, and how much better it can be. This chapter will give glimpses of psychotherapy 101 and beyond. The purpose is to reinforce the importance of basic skills, to motivate the desire to study, practice and learn, and to inspire to imagine the psychotherapist you wish to be, or the psychotherapist you wish to be helped by.

One golden rule, for the therapist, is to remember your client as a person, as a human being, as an equal from the perspective of the universe. I talk about therapists and clients, but I always know I am talking about human beings.

Luc Watelet

Medical doctors, and therefore psychiatrists, have patients and psychotherapists have clients. To simplify, for the rest of this chapter, I will use the word "client" for "client and/or patient," unless I am specifically referring to the work of a medical doctor doing psychotherapy and then I will use the term "patient."

Also, there is a difficulty in the written language when referring in general to one client or to one therapist. It is grammatically incorrect to say "they" when referring to one person, although it is tempting and common in conversations because it avoids the need to specify a gender. I have decided, in the rest of this book, to refer to a client or to a therapist by using the pronoun "he" or "she," interchangeably. I try to keep the same gender within a given context.

Being Present to Someone

One of my friends was wondering, as a new counselor, how to approach her clients. They suffered from a variety of problems, pain, medical conditions, addictions and mental health challenges... You name it! Where was she to start? The answer she was given is probably the best answer anyone could have given to her: "Connect with the humanity of the person."

What does connecting mean? And what does "connecting with someone's humanity" mean? The first thing to realize is that the client probably feels vulnerable or wounded in some way and, unless she is court ordered, or feels coerced to come see you, may come in with a mask of defiance. If the client feels wounded or vulnerable, one way to connect with her humanity is simply to acknowledge the wound or the vulnerability and not be scared of it, not be judgmental of it, and know that, no matter what, this person can be helped if she wants to. If the client wears a mask of protection, then one approach is to acknowledge what you see, not as a judgment, but as a way to empathize with someone who may not want to be there. You may say, with kindness, "It looks like you don't want to be here? Is that right?"

It may take a while to break the ice. I met a therapist who told me the policy at his office is to welcome the client anytime during the period assigned to him without repercussions for being late or not coming at all. They are charged for that session. One of his clients came in five minutes before the end of each session. He would sit there and say very little and then leave. He did this every week, for a year. The therapist was always pleasant and welcoming. Then, finally, the client started to arrive on time and fully participate in each session.

When you have broken the ice, you have the client's attention. There are several ways to continue the connection: reflection, being curious, asking a question with a specific positive intention, and being present. One of the best compliment I can receive from a client is "He gets me!" You want the client to feel understood and trusting. Underlying all of this is to listen well. We will explore listening in depth later in the chapter.

Reflection

Reflecting helps create a foundation of trust and understanding. There is no attempt here to treat a condition and find solutions.

Imagine that you are with someone who is telling you a story about a difficult situation. You listen with the intention to reflect back what you heard and noticed, and how it affected you, or what parts of the story affected you. You don't judge or try to help. You simply reflect back so what you are doing is accepting the person and yourself as she tells her story. You may ask if you heard her right. This usually encourages the client to be more precise or elaborate on what she previously said.

You may have noticed that she is experiencing difficult feelings she did not name while telling her story. For instance, she showed fear but may appear unaware of it. You may reflect back that while she mentioned a particular situation it looked like she was scared. You don't say, "It looked like you were overreacting!" No judgments. Or you may say, "When that happened, were you uncomfortable?" You want to ask a question that helps the client be more aware while keeping the question non-judgmental and as open as possible. Using the word "uncomfortable" is a little more open to possibilities than "scared." But sometimes naming the emotion correctly is really helpful.

At a more advanced level, when I am a really good listener, reflecting back in my own words what I heard or sensed, trying to be as accurate as I can, I may say things the client did not say explicitly. I may preface what I say by acknowledging that I may be going out on a limb and encourage the client to let me know if I hit the mark or not. So I may ask at the end of my comment, "Does this hit the mark for you?" This is a win-win, because I may be able to bring more awareness directly with my comment, or the client may be able to use what I say to improve on it and go deeper than she went on her own. I am not attached to being right. My intention is to help the client and it is often more healing if the client reaches her own conclusions.

Being Curious

After acknowledging what you heard, felt or noticed, pay attention to what you wished you understood more about the story. Look at what may be missing in it. Be patient and curious. For instance, the client may have mentioned a difficult situation with someone, but she does not say how it started, how long it had been going on, or that she had never trusted him from the start. You may want to ask enough questions that you get as true a picture as possible from her point of view, so she feels "you get her!"

Asking a Question with a Specific Positive Intention

It is possible to help without giving advice. A good way to avoid giving advice is to ask questions so you understand better and so the client understands himself better. An example of a positive intention is to help a client feel free from a burden. However, instead of knowing what would help, it is usually more effective to have this intention and ask questions.

For instance, if the story the client told concerns a bad experience with a horse, what question could be helpful? You may try, "Do you know how you would do it differently now?" or "What would you need in order to overcome the bad feelings you are left with?" Not every question will feel the same or open the same doors to the client, so you may ask, "Which of my questions felt the best to you?" or "Which of my questions helped you the most?" This teaches introspection by example and it helps the therapist understand the client.

In a non-therapeutic setting, I was listening on the phone to a friend who was complaining about her move. She really felt overwhelmed. I joyfully offered to come and help her. What happened was a complete surprise to me! She said she might call on me and stopped complaining. I saw her a few days later and she told me that my offer to help meant I was not overwhelmed. As a result, she saw what she had to do from a neutral place, the negativity had left her, and she realized she did not need my help.

In a therapeutic relationship, you would not offer to help. Instead, you would ask a different question such as, "Could a friend help you?" or "What if it was already done? What would it look like?"

Sometimes a client offers a lot of resistance. You may reflect that to her. You may say, "I hear you that you really think you are meant to be a victim the rest of your life. I don't think that is true though." You don't try to change her belief. You respect where she stands. You allow her to feel fully what she believes and it is okay to not agree. You simply let her know you believe she is more than what she thinks. One of the roles of a therapist is to believe in the client until she can believe in herself.

I had a client with this very belief. I describe this part of her story and call her E. in Chapter 8, Mindfulness Psychotherapy. This is an example of using an advance form of intention when I knew where I wanted to get and did not know how to approach it. I simply asked God (or the universe) to guide the conversation so she could heal. Then, I simply trusted that the conversation would guide us there.

Finding helpful questions, or intentions, is part of the creative fun of being a therapist.

Conversing with Presence

Since this is all about conversation and not about treating a condition, this approach to conversation can be used with anyone, a friend, a family member, a co-worker, and in a psychotherapeutic relationship. Of course, you always need to respect if the other person is not interested in the conversation you are offering. In the case where the other person welcomes the conversation, it is a very simple way to help someone feel supported and whole. It builds trust and helps the other person open up further. And you barely have any work to do to figure out what the source of the problem is. You just have to be present and caring to the other person and to yourself. You hold a heartfelt intention to be of service and trust the conversation to guide you to a better place.

Another part to being present is to feel what is going on in your body as you interact with your client. Your body is a radar that can perceive things about the client. For instance, as she is describing a difficult situation with her boyfriend, you may feel some constriction in your heart. Perhaps it is just you, but perhaps it is a pain she is feeling but not acknowledging to herself. You can say, "When you are talking about your boyfriend, I feel as though my heart is being pressured. It has no space! Do you feel that?" She may acknowledge that she is indeed. She may not feel the same thing but she may acknowledge a different discomfort that she became aware of thanks to your question. She will feel from such detail that you are really paying attention and she will trust you more. And it helps the client be less mental, and more grounded in her experience. The therapist needs to be real and genuine.

Mastering Psychotherapy

To understand what psychotherapy could be, or what one can expect from psychotherapy, it may help to ask what a master of psychotherapy would be able to do.

Starting with Freud, the interaction between a patient and a psychiatrist or psychoanalyst was supposed to be objective and clinical. It was believed that someone with an objective and clinical position would be best able to guide someone to some kind of normal. One problem with this view is that no one can know what is "normal" for someone else because, except for spiritual masters, no one can presume to know what someone else's life purpose is. Another problem with the objective clinical approach is that it is impossible to achieve because emotions flow freely from human being to human being. We are not separate islands. We might as well accept natural laws and work with them, not against them. A psychotherapist cannot hide from a client's subconscious what she is truly feeling. What we try to hide is part of what Jung called the shadow and, because it is energy, it takes a life of its own when it is suppressed. The subjective needs to be acknowledged so it does not act out in detrimental ways in the relationship. If a therapist has a negative thought about a client, it is best to let it go and replace it by a truer and positive thought. Similarly, if a therapist has an inappropriate thought about a client, it is best to find a way to let the energy of it go. Suppression will backfire.

Nevertheless, objectivity has its place in psychotherapy. Albert Ellis is the first therapist I believe to have expressed the idea that the problems from which we suffer come from the worldview we hold. I agree with this perspective. With this premise, the role of the therapist is to get a clear picture of the worldview that is causing the distress in the client, and help him become aware of the role of his worldview in his distress. In order to do that, the therapist needs to be able to navigate freely between worldviews without being attached to one. We need to be able to enter the subjective world of the client (walk in his shoes so to speak) as well as take on the position of an observer. We need to be able to navigate between the subjective of the client and our own and avoid the trappings of either one. We have to flow between the subjective and the objective. Now, the beauty of this work is that the therapist does not have to know the new paradigm that is best for the client as he already knows this at some level. The way to the new paradigm comes by having the client ask himself genuinely the key question, "Who am I?" Then the therapist only needs to know how to help guide him within his inner world.

To be able to walk in a client's shoes one first needs to refrain from trying to change the client and simply accept the client exactly as he is. Otherwise, how can one know how to really help? Carl Rogers, for instance, described his process as having "unconditional positive regard" for one's client. It is a perspective of no-judgment, acceptance and respect of the client. To get there, one needs to be a good listener and to genuinely care in order to reflect back what one hears and notices, and in order to ask helpful/healing questions.

I would say a master psychotherapist can see how to guide a client into his own world, into the inner workings of his world, so the client can see clearly what is leading him into trouble. The psychotherapist needs to become aware of which parts in the client need to speak to each other. The psychotherapist can also become intuitively aware of what the issues are or feel in her own body to know what needs to be addressed with the client. The inner exploration of the client's world may be done in many ways, questioning, guided visualization, exploring feelings, exploring sensations and pain (not intellectually but physically), experiencing, role play, art work, journaling, breath work and also music or even reading a story or watching a movie. There is no limit to what can be used as long as it respects a client's free will and his spirit.

An ideal for a therapist is for his behavior and words with clients to be in entire synchronicity with Life itself. Such a therapist no longer comes from personal ego or personal knowledge, but has become a humble and clear direct instrument of Life itself.

To Genuinely Care

Holding a space of no judgment and acceptance, a space of love, for someone else is the beginning of genuinely caring and of her healing.

People think they know how to care and dismiss the notion that sometimes this has to be learned. When I was a home health aide working for an agency, it became clear relatively quickly that only a few aides were requested over and over by clients. I was one of them, so I got curious about what I did that made clients want me back. The answer was that the kind of caring I provided helped clients feel dignity. This kind of caring comes from a place where the client is the focus of my attention. I am not with the client for myself, and I am not identifying the person with the disease, illness, or disability he suffers from. I am not with a client to make myself look good or to prove my credentials. I am there to be a human being relating with another human being.

My reason for bringing up examples from the world of home care is that if I brought examples from the psychotherapeutic world, it may be too close to home. It may be easier to look at the lack of caring from a distance, but my intention is that we use these examples to then reflect on whether we genuinely care in our psychotherapy interactions with clients.

Anyone who has had to work with an ailing parent or friend or has had to work with home health aides or with nurses know what "lack of caring" looks like. It is quite common. What I learned during my time as an aide is that a lot of aides came from self-centered perspectives that could be translated as: 1) "I will prove to you that I know my job well, so don't tell me what to do or how to do my job," 2) "I am just here to make money, so I'll do the minimum I need to do and get out of here," 3) "Because of your inability to help yourself, I'll just do as I damn well please," or 4) "I am so afraid of doing anything wrong that I will cover up my wrongs even if that means that it will inconvenience or even hurt you."

An example of 1) is an aide who acts very professionally, and does everything without asking a client's input on how they would like things done. They may even go above and beyond what is listed on the care plan, but with very little or no client input or interaction. It is as if they are there to prove that they know their job. When an aide asks how a client would like their dishes cleaned (left on the dish drainer or put away for instance) or how they would like their eggs prepared, suddenly a very different relationship is created. The client feels that his input and what he cares about are valued. He feels like a real person, not an objectified being that is identified and reduced to someone who needs home care.

An example of 2) is an aide who actually does what needs to be done but does it with little love and as little involvement as possible with the client. There is no warmth.

An example of 3) is an aide who ignores clients as if the client did not have preferences. For instance, a Christian aide at a Jewish client switches the TV channel to a Christian preacher while the client is also watching TV and without asking the client first.

An example of 4) is an aide whose client falls, for instance, and does not acknowledge the fall (or even denies it) to the family or the supervising nurse. So the client may have unexplained bruises or cuts. I met a family to whom it happened to their elderly father. I have a friend whose father had a cut on his face and the nursing home explained he did it to himself while shaving. But he only shaved with an electric razor. This also happens in simpler situations. I was with a client who had a non-working drawer in one of her dressers. I asked how it happened. The client said she suspected an aide did it but the aide denied it. I asked my supervisor if the company had money to cover something an aide had broken. There was. So I asked a woodworker to duplicate the broken piece which he did and the new piece fit perfectly so the drawer worked

Luc Watelet

again.

These may seem extreme cases, but they happen regularly.

It does not take much to care, and it is very rewarding. Learning to care means learning to see the real person you are working for and with, being curious about her, and being interested in what interests her. This is where engaging in conversations or some form of communication can be welcome (holding hands, reading a book, or listening to music, for instance). These forms of caring need to be adapted to the particular professional relationship you have.

Listening

The work of therapy is an interaction between human beings. The client in therapy is a storyteller and the therapist is a listener. Of course, sometimes, the therapist also becomes a teacher or a healer. Listening is multifaceted. I may describe some of what you already know in this section – after all, this chapter is titled psychotherapy 101! Nevertheless, I encourage you to read this section as I touch on aspects of listening important to the beginner therapist but are rarely discussed. Later in this chapter, I revisit listening at a more advanced level I have not seen discussed anywhere.

Storytellers who seek therapy want, consciously or unconsciously, to be heard because they seek to understand who they are. Therefore, the very first effort of a therapist is to learn everything about listening.

There is a lot about listening on the internet. It is known to be the number one quality of a good leader for instance.

Listening is not only listening to the content of what someone says, including the choice of words that person uses and the hesitations and where these hesitations fall. It is not only listening to the tone and emotions of the storyteller and reading them accurately or checking them with him. It is not only paying attention to the body language. It is also listening to what is not being said. It is listening to what is repeated often as it could be a sign of a deeply engrained and, perhaps, erroneous belief. It is about hearing what is unconscious in what is being said. It is about hearing the truth that is trying to express itself.

And it is about helping the storyteller hear what wants to be heard. Often, when people want to tell their story, it is precisely because there is something in it that wants to be heard. The storytellers would not need to tell their life stories if they had already really heard what they needed to hear from them.

Sometimes the truth is hidden in the muscles or the bones of the storyteller. In this case, the work is to listen to what is stuck in the muscles or the bones. We explore this by paying attention to the sensations. In doing so, we learn a new language, the language of sensations. We already know sensations as a language. How else would we know that we are upset, angry, sad, scared, or joyful? We may feel it in our chest, in our heart, in our stomach or, sometimes, everywhere. But there is so much more to sensations. I wish we would introduce children to the language of their sensations at an early age. We would raise the emotional intelligence of our entire culture!

Listening means to hear with ears, eyes, and our entire body! It matters to be aware of the sensations triggered in one's body, and especially to hear with one's heart. To hear with your whole body, not just with your mind, is called being present. Listening means to be present to the storyteller and to oneself simultaneously. Listening means to pay attention to and trust one's intuition and gut feelings. It also means to be silent sometimes in order to allow the storyteller to experience the energy of what is transpiring.

There is a golden truth in therapy: *People always learn better if they can see it or feel it for themselves.* It is less effective to change something, for instance losing weight, for some external reason than for personal ones. But the reason has to feel important enough that nothing will be distracting from losing weight, or whatever the objective is. Respecting a client's freewill will be more effective for the same reason. Hence, a good therapist guides a client to his own truth whenever possible, instead of giving an answer or advice – although sometimes giving an answer at the right time is just perfect! A good therapist allows a client to make his own mistakes as he may learn better from them than by avoiding them. A good therapist avoids at all costs playing the parent, unless it is role play, otherwise it is likely to create dependence. Dependence is likely to lead to tension, resistance and rebellion from the client.

Luc Watelet

Body-Oriented Listening

Amy came to our church for the very first time. We had started to offer healing services at the beginning and she came to me. I started by placing my hands about an inch over her head and then brought them over her shoulders while feeling the energy I could perceive from her in my body. I asked inwardly if there was anything I could help her with and the answer came in two words: "husband" and "death." I asked her if her husband had passed. She said, "No." So I asked if he had almost died. She said, "Yes, two weeks ago." She started to cry. I asked her if she wanted a hug and she said, "Yes." I gave her a heartfelt hug. Amy did not come for a therapy session. She came to find some peace and be heard at a subtle level. Acknowledging that we are not independent, disconnected vessels and that we communicate subtly all the time without words is very powerful and healing in our relationships with each other. This technique can and should be used in therapy interactions. Solutions depend on the professional context.

Beth came to my yoga studio for a healing session. I invited her to lie down on a large sheepskin and relax. I sat cross legged by her side and meditated, tuning in to her energy. I had sensations in my heart that felt like dry heat and reminded me of anger. I allowed that energy in me and gave it space. At some point it shifted. The new sensations were that of butterflies and also a sense of tightness in my belly. That reminded me of fear. I stayed with it and gave it space. Then it shifted again and I felt pain in my heart and that reminded me of emotional hurt. I almost had tears in my eyes. I could have stayed with it, as well, but instead I decided to ask my client what was happening in her heart. At that point she started to cry and told me about a difficult current experience. It is fascinating to experience first-hand Albert Ellis' theory of the order of feelings: anger-fear-hurt. After this experience, this is not a theory to me, it is human nature.

Cathy came to my yoga studio for a healing session. She started by saying that her husband had passed nine months earlier and grieving had become very difficult. She lay on my large sheep skin and I sat cross legged beside her. I tuned in to her energy and I felt nothing. There was no movement of energy in her heart as I would have expected from someone who is grieving. I realized it was not the grieving that had become difficult, but her attempt at blocking it. I asked myself what could prevent her from letting go of her husband and hypothesized to myself that she was scared for her future. At that point, I asked her about her future and she acknowledged she did not know what to do. We continued looking at what she likes and feels attracted to and at some point in the conversation I noticed tears in her eyes. I asked her what was going on and she said she was thinking about her husband. She was allowing the beginning of her grieving process. This is an example of listening to the presence of someone who is stuck and getting enough information from this "silence" to ask key questions without going through a whole life history.

Dani called in tears. She was divorcing her husband and he had just called her. She had initiated the divorce and felt nostalgic for their marriage. This had been a difficult decision for her. She knew she did not want the marriage back, so she felt conflicted about the nostalgia that was overwhelming her. After hearing her cry a bit, I asked her if she was ready to work. She agreed. I asked her where she felt the nostalgia in her body. She said she felt it in her chest. I guided her to forget her husband and the nostalgia and only focus on experiencing her sensations without labeling them. After what seemed like over a minute of silence (it can seem longer on the phone than in person), I asked her what was going on and she said it was like there was a party inside.

This is an example where a client's own experience of what is really taking place within her is so much more powerful than if a therapist had interpreted for her what was really going on. For instance, an experienced therapist might have said, "The nostalgia you experience is due to your fear of living without your husband's income, but inside I bet you are really happy." It also shows how important listening to our body is in order to understand who we are and what is going on in our life.

Paying attention, sensing, trying to understand, can happen very quickly without much input from the client or it can happen by guiding the client to experiencing themselves. In each of these examples, the listening is much less cognitive than in usual forms of therapy. This body-oriented listening cuts to the chase and leaves the client feeling deeply heard.

Luc Watelet

Helping the Storyteller Listen

A therapist's common dilemma is to be with a client who talks so much that it feels like regurgitation rather than therapy. Sometimes we have to listen until the very end because the client insists that this exercise is necessary. Sometimes we can interrupt to point out that some elements need more attention at this time of the therapy process. But what to do with the overwhelming amount of information that comes non-stop from a client who cannot stop talking? To ignore it may leave the therapist exhausted or agitated. One way I deal with it is to stop trying to grasp it with my mind and instead to let my body absorb all the energy that came with the storytelling. My body can process a whole lot more than my mind. When I allow my body to integrate the information simply by giving space within me to all that I feel, that is, by being present to myself, I get back to a place of calm. It feels magical because then, I also have some new clarity about the client. I may see something that was never spoken to directly, or I may have new questions.

I can also invite the storyteller into self-reflection. One way to do this is to say that I don't understand yet why the story is so important to her. When I have done this, it amazes me that the client may integrate self-reflection as a practice. Introspection can become a new habit for the client without my suggesting it as a practice.

Another approach is simply to let the storyteller know that all that talking left me overwhelmed and ask if he also feels overwhelmed. The risk is that the client may find his way back to non-stop talking. This is a time to encourage the client to feel the energy behind what is overwhelming.

I have a friend who will often stop her client from talking and tell him: "Listen, at this point, I need to take a deep breath. If you want to, you may take one with me. Would you like that?" She takes a deep breath and invites the client to take a couple of more breaths and then she asks the client how he feels.

To help a client truly listen to himself a therapist needs to be able to listen deeply, and in the process ask questions which will help the client understand himself. But to know what questions to ask, one needs to know what kinds of questions will help.

Who Am I?

The Importance of the Question, "Who Am I?"

The way through our difficulties comes by getting to know who we are. It seems obvious to me now that everything that has been happening in my life has helped me learn to be myself at deeper and deeper levels. A simple event like being punished for something as a kid may be a trigger to figure out why I did what I did, whether it actually mattered to me or whether I did it out of a negative impulse. Being bullied left me feeling I did not matter which, I realized, meant I had to find out how I mattered and, thus, it prompted me to know more about me.

More important than "Where do I come from?" and "Where am I going?" the most important question for us human beings is "Who am I?" Our lives start making sense when we get glimpses of answers to this question. The more you know who you are, the more clarity you have about the decisions you want to make. The more you know yourself, the less people can manipulate you or hurt you. The more you know who you are, the less likely you are to let yourself be distracted by addictive behaviors or outside concerns. The more you know yourself, the more you will notice how Life works with you for you to achieve your soul goals.

As therapists, we must be prepared to help our clients on the path to seek answers to this basic question as it will free them from the unbearable feelings when meeting struggles.

When I first started to work at an addiction recovery center and found my voice as a therapist, I told my clients at the beginning of our first session, following the intake, "I don't care about the addiction or the mental illness diagnosis, I care about you. So let's get through the questions the paying health insurance cares about and we'll then get to the real stuff." What I had learned is that people are not their behavior or their illness. Their personality is not broken. What is disrupted is the connection between their mind, their body, and their soul. By being interested in the disease or the addiction, we dismiss the real issue which is that our client's mind, body, and soul are not communicating with each other. The client may not be aware consciously that she is not the diagnosis, but she certainly feels ignored when the therapist only deals with the problems she faces and not with who she really is. That leads to rebellion and/or relapse! Instead of realizing that relapse is a product of the therapy approach that is based on treatment and not healing, most therapists have come to believe that relapse is part of the disease of addiction, and they pass that message on to their clients. A relapse is either simply that the addiction has never stopped or a choice has been made to re-engage in addiction.

As therapists, we need to learn how to help someone enter into a relationship between her mind, body and soul.

I Am Not My Mind

Examples

In conversations, we often say, "I think…" Have you ever asked yourself who is this "I"? Who is the thinker? Is it our mind? Did we ponder long enough on the thought before we decided that it is what we truly believe? Or are we repeating what we heard elsewhere without scrutiny? Or is it just something that went through our mind and we grabbed on to it, making it ours? Not all thoughts that we entertain are necessarily true or healthy.

For instance, a person thinks to himself, "I want a beer!" And when he has it in his hand, he suddenly has the thought, "I don't want to drink anymore!" This is a stage of transition in someone who is no longer interested in alcohol. It sounds like the two "I"s are two different parts of this person, right? Where does the first "I" come from and where does the second "I" come from?

I remember talking with a gentleman who made a statement that Jews killed Jesus. His tone was accusatory. I was wondering how to respond to that. He picked up on my hesitation and asked me if I did not think that way. I told him I was not a historian, but that I believed Jesus was born among the Jews and was probably therefore Jewish, and that there were no Christians yet when he was born. So to say that the Jews killed Jesus is like saying Americans killed Martin Luther King, Jr. It does not mean much. He replied "Oh! Right! I was just repeating what my mother used to say." He acknowledged to me and to himself that it was not his thought, even though he had spoken it as though it were.

So then who is this "I" that decides to believe or not what goes through my mind? Who is this "I" that decides to pay attention to my heart or my body, or chooses to listen to music or to someone talking? The 'I' that makes decisions is not my mind. Yet in daily practice the "I" I speak from also includes all of me, we make no distinction. Our language is confusing. Is it the same "I" that says "Jews killed Jesus!" compared to "I can see my mind struggling about committing to my girlfriend, while my heart isn't struggling at all!"? So for the purpose of clarity, let's think of my body as my vehicle on earth, my mind as a tool at my disposal, and the true "I" as my awareness.

Meditation

One of the key mistakes of beginner meditators is to think that the goal of meditating is to quiet the mind and, since they have tried and could not, they decided meditation was not for them. Meditation is not about quieting the mind. Quieting the mind is a side effect of meditation. Meditation is first about noticing through experience that I have an awareness that is separate from my mind. How can I quiet my mind if I think that my mind is who I really am? Once I make that realization, I can choose to engage or not with my mind. In meditation, I practice noticing what takes place in my body and mind and outside of my body/mind, and I choose and commit not to engage with any of it. I simply become aware every moment of what is taking place, and I let it go to pay attention to what comes next, and what comes next. The practice of not engaging with one's mind is what leads to the mind quieting down.

If I let my mind run the show, identifying with it, I become victim of my own mind. I am powerless. If I fight the thoughts in my mind, I become a bully. There is only one way to respond to my mind; I have to let it be and remain neutral toward it, choosing what I want to keep and what I want to discard. To be able to do that, I need to establish a relationship with my awareness.

Once I become strong in not identifying with my mind, knowing that when I say "I," I speak from a different perspective than that of my mind, I master my mind. That is, I choose with what to engage and what not to engage. I can choose to let go of reacting, with negativity, with

Luc Watelet

fantasies, with lust, greed, etc. and choose to engage by being positive, joyful, loving, solution oriented, etc.

This is the first step toward sanity.

My Body Holds Truths of Which My Mind Is Unaware

We react to outside situations with negative and positive emotions: anger, fear, jealousy, elation, etc. But what we forget is that we would not feel any of these emotions if they did not arise from sensations in our body. When was the last time you felt an emotion? Ask yourself how you knew what emotion it was. Ask yourself where it came from in you. Then forget the emotion you think you were experiencing and pay attention to the sensations that gave rise to it without interpreting these sensations automatically. Feel them by giving them space to flow freely in your body. You may be surprised that what you thought you were experiencing may actually be different. Our reactions often come from judging our experiences before truly experiencing them. And we then tend to blame others first. We react from habitual interpretations instead of from engaging with reality as it is. More on emotions in Chapter 7, Understanding Mental Illness.

Our emotions are often due to a misinterpretation of our own experience and the misinterpretation comes for habits of thoughts wired in our brain. This wiring can be changed. More on this in Chapter 8, Mindfulness Psychotherapy, and Chapter 10, Mental Health Outside the Western World.

Paying attention to one's sensations in response to what we say or to outside circumstances brings peace, self-understanding, and wisdom.

This is another step toward sanity.

Without these first two steps, we cannot know who we are.

The Heart

Knowing your heart means you know what you want, and you know what you don't want. This is not a decision of the mind. It is also where you choose to fear or to love.

The mind may tell you that you want a fancy car or a fancy house or a beautiful or handsome date, but your heart feels whether that fancy car, that fancy house, or that date are right for you. Your mind may want to compete with a neighbor, a sibling, or a parent but your heart wants what's right for you.

Furthermore, your heart is the doorway to your intuition. The heart center energetically closes down or opens up. When it opens up we are in a state of love, when it closes down we aren't. We cannot access intuition with a closed heart and we cannot access intuition with a chattering mind.

Intuition

Before working with one's intuition consciously, one needs to center oneself, to become calm. I start by taking a few deep breaths, by calming my physical heart, and by resisting the temptation to be distracted by my mind. I then bring my focus to my body and to what I sense. When I feel stable in my ability to pay attention to my body, when I feel calm, I ask a question inwardly and listen for an answer. I expect an answer without demanding an answer. I smile inwardly, content, unhurried.

The experience of asking for an answer is like expecting to connect with a dear friend. It is an experience of welcoming it with no fear, with a sense of loving expectancy, and we are in a state of openness that allows the answer to come exactly as it is meant to come, without controlling it. We may have to be patient. The answer may come in different ways: in words, as a movie, or as a physical experience. If it comes as a story it may be literal or it may be metaphorical. You have to figure out for yourself how you receive your answers. Sometimes they do not come right away. It depends on how you are meant to receive them, but they always come. They may come during a conversation with someone, for instance, or you may hear something on the radio, or they may be triggered by something you see in a movie. Or they may come as a feeling or a thought when you least expect it. If you ask yourself on your way home to your spouse and child or children, for instance, "What is the mood at home?" you can probably expect an answer immediately. If you ask yourself what is the score of a baseball game you were not able to watch, you could probably expect an immediate answer. But if you ask what you need to learn about love, you may or may not get an immediate answer. You may not even get an answer in words, or as a visual, instead it may come to you as an experience.

As therapists, we need to help our clients reconnect with their intuition and to learn to trust it.

Human Nature

If I did not know I have a soul or a consciousness, comfortable outside of my body and mind and, at the same time, needing my body/mind to manifest its dreams and purpose, I might think of a very different approach to psychotherapy. I might think of my body/mind the way I think of an automobile that needs regular checkups, that needs its own fuel, and that needs regular rest. But we are not just a vehicle; like Bruce Lipton says, we have a driver (see Prologue). This driver commands our body/mind. When it does so without a (healthy) sense of direction, our body/mind goes in unexpected directions that depend on the bumps in the road and the outside circumstances. When it has a healthy sense of direction, our body/mind moves through time and space with more ease.

What Gives Us a Sense of Direction?

I knew as a teenager that my dreams mattered more than anything. My dreams and what I love, that which gives meaning to my life, are what give me a sense of direction in life. I was puzzled by how many people had given up on their dreams by getting a job to pay for their homes, and their cars and their vacations. Sometimes people with whom I talk do not really know what I mean by "What are your dreams?" or by "What do you love?" Then I ask them, "What do you absolutely need to do before you die?" It can happen that this information is inaccessible at a given time for some reason. But it is worth keeping the question alive in one's heart and expecting to receive an answer, looking for it in our experiences.

What Is in the Way of Having a Sense of Direction?

Our body/mind holds joyful and painful memories. Our memories have something to do with how we respond to Life and what matters to us. *If*

I am hurt, that means something matters to me more than I gave it attention. Thus, blaming someone else for the hurt I feel prevents me from seeing what matters to me. And therefore not paying attention to what hurts me is bound to attract more of that hurt because I really need to pay attention to what matters to me. *Because hurt helps us remember what really matters to us, hurt is part of the journey to remember our soul's desires and who we are. And healing starts when we live from what matters to us.*

The desires of the soul have to do with what is truly satisfying to us; they have to do with a deep purpose we have to fulfill in this life. The desires of the body/mind have to do with safety, security, belonging, creativity, our sense of power, our need for love, and our need for communication, understanding, and recognition. In other words, our body/mind holds on to dreams that we learn we need from our family and from the culture in which we live, whereas our soul holds on to dreams that are deeply personal and are deeply related to the meaning we find in our lives.

Sometimes the desires of the body/mind are in direct conflict with those of the soul. The soul always wins because nothing will change in our life until the soul's desires, when they knock at the door of our awareness, have been acknowledged and satisfied. The soul's needs, when heard and embraced, help bring healing and peace to our body/mind, whereas the body/mind wants may not satisfy the soul's actual needs. It may be hard to believe that working toward our soul needs will also give us the safety, security, etc. that we need as human beings. Yet it is my experience that it works that way. I have met other people who have come to the same conclusion. We each have to test this for ourselves. In my case, I did not have much of a choice (see Chapter 2, Life lessons).

As human beings, whether we use our awareness or not, we are in continuous interaction with Universal Consciousness, and therefore with everything else in the universe. That is, we are always attracting through Universal Consciousness what we need in the moment. What our body/mind wants and what our soul needs may be in direct conflict and thus confuse the signal we are sending to ourselves and others, and delay the manifestation of what we want. This causes stress. There is no vacation for the need for communication between our soul and our body/mind!

When we don't pay attention to our body or our feelings, we disconnect our body from our mind. This causes stress. Our emotions need to be felt, heard accurately, and integrated. If they aren't, they get stored energetically somewhere in our body and that energy remains trapped. This creates pressures in our body which taxes the immune system which can lead to illnesses or cause physical strain or injuries.

When we don't pay attention to our soul, we make decisions in life without a true sense of direction. It is like sailing a boat by following the wind instead of a fixed point on the shore. At first, it may feel alright. We get to play. In the end, our boredom with this kind of playing will make us pay attention to the kind of playing that feels more satisfying. When that happens, we start paying attention to the soul. But, sometimes, it takes something profound to shake us out of our tracks: a relationship break-up, a car accident, a job loss, a theft or our house burning down, and so on.

The way physical or mental diseases happen is through stress left unaddressed for too long. Stress is the result of a lack of congruence between our body, our mind, and our soul desires or energies. If someone feels stressed at work, for instance, something is out of balance in the life of that person. Certain demands are put on that person at work, and may push the person in a direction that does not feel right. The person may continue to make the decision not to look at it because some other needs override the desire to solve the problem such has being committed to being the provider or being scared of what might happen if one looks more deeply into the situation. At any rate, not looking into the situation is bound to lead to further problems.

Reclaiming Our Sense of Direction

From this discussion, psychotherapy should really be about helping our clients reclaim their sense of direction and not depend on others for it. By treating diseases and pain, we ignore what matters to our consciousness or that of our clients.

Healing comes from connecting with love to what hurts. As a result, we learn our lessons. It is our personal gold. Psychotherapy, that seeks to heal, helps guide clients to glean this gold. When lessons are learned, they don't need to be learned again. The hurt that led to the lesson is no longer necessary. It leaves the body/mind.

When one stops seeing diseases and stresses as random, they become opportunities to embrace more of ourselves.

Identity Development

In psychology courses, we learn about identities such as Age, Disabilities (mental or physical), Religion or spirituality, Ethnicity, Socioeconomic status, Sexual orientation, Indigenous identity, National origin, and Gender.

The acronym is ADDRESSING (taking the first letter from the key words for each identity type). We have many other identities with groups we identify with such as vocation, hobby, and diet, which are not included here.

Looking into these identities helps start a more conscious inquiry process into who I am.

In class, we were asked to fill out our own ADDRESSING identities and I realized that if I answered factually, the resulting description did not feel like me. I realized I did not feel any association with being born in Belgium; I identified much more with the East Indian culture (food, spirituality, and, in particular, yoga and the teachings of the masters of the Far East). So I answered from a feeling perspective.

When I tried to answer the gender identity question, I realized I did not feel 100% male or female. I felt something like 60% male vs. 40% female. Being forced to specify the percentages still felt uncomfortable. I talked with a transgender professor and she said that a lot of trans feel that way and that they do not force the percentage of male-female to add up to 100%; it can add up to anything we feel is right for us. That was a new opening in my thinking. I could then say I feel 70% male and 40% female, for instance.

Then I realized I really have more than one perception of myself. I have the perception of the human being for instance and the perception of that part of me that is pure awareness. My awareness, as I experience it, has none of the identities, no gender, no sexual identity, etc. Yet it feels more real than my human body and my mind because it is indestructible; it cannot die and cannot get sick or hurt. As a human being, I sometimes transcend identities.

I asked myself about the purpose of these identities because my awareness/soul does not experience any of them. I realized my human identities help me see the world from one potential viewpoint, I have to make peace with this set of identities and how it is perceived in the culture around me. And I have to make peace with other sets of identities around me.

Therefore, from this perspective, sexual orientation has less to do with sex and more with learning to accept and love oneself in the context of the culture where we are born and where we live.

As I meet other people with different identities from my own, I have an opportunity to develop compassion toward them. Dr. Weiss gives the example of a client who was stuck in life deeply angry toward a particular culture. Using past life therapy, Dr. Weiss helped her see that she had a history of acting with anger toward other cultures, only to reincarnate in the culture she was fighting in the previous lifetime. As she became aware of this, she learned she had to make peace with all cultures. Only then was she free to move on in her life.[31]

So it appears that our human mission is to learn to have compassion toward everyone, everything and every situation. This may help the reader understand the importance behind the invitation by Jesus, and other spiritual teachers, to love our enemy. I suppose that when we are as compassionate as is possible and there is no longer a need to experience an identity to learn more compassion, we can drop our human form. We are then ready for lessons that are beyond what is offered on earth.

Hence, it is not surprising that, as a species, we are going through an

---

[31] B. L. Weiss (2004). *Same Soul, Many Bodies: Discover the Healing Power of Future Lives Through Progression Therapy*, Free Press, A division of Simon & Schluster, Inc.

explosion in the diversity of identities. *As a species, we are learning about compassion in all its forms!*

Interface Between Human Being and Life

Illusion versus Reality

I wrote a letter to the Universe in an effort to understand why reality is not as real as it appears and in an effort to help others understand the confusing nature of reality.

To the Universe,

I thought I was being realistic by looking at life as it happens: a war here and a famine there, global warming and rainforest destruction, political and legal abuses of power, and, more individually, rape, cancer, mental health challenges. And also recognizing all the wonderful people working toward healing all that. Please wait while I reprogram my brain worldview as I did not realize that the previous programming which I thought was realistic, was perceived to be negative thinking by you.

Although there is some truth to this realistic worldview, I understand now that what I see currently in the world around me is a combination of an old paradigm still running its course, blended with a new paradigm which is only in budding form. It is like watching a movie playing the old worldview that has not finished running its course, while the current paradigm is not fully hitting the screen yet. So "being realistic" is being behind in time from what is really taking roots in the world today. "Being realistic" is believing what is already gone because the true reality is not completely perceptible yet.

It is not that we should ignore what we see, but it is not as real as it appears. It may just be the last breath of something dying, so we may be giving it more power, by thinking it is real, than it really has and thereby keeping it alive instead of simply letting it go.

That is why dreaming what I really want is infinitely more real than what reality looks like!

In psychotherapy, we can work with the material from dreams or from life in the same manner. Life is very much like a dream. Nothing is real, everything changes. Even the experience of rape can change with time as one reevaluates it during the healing process. I don't mean to minimize the horror of the experience. But the soul cannot be raped, only one's body and one's mind, until we learn to value who we are so much that others' abusive behaviors no longer hurt. Instead, we see their pain and we willingly let them express their abuse with compassion so they learn how hurt they are. This is expressed for example in the lives of Jesus, Gandhi, Martin Luther King, Jr., and Bruno Gröning.

When we heal, we experience a new reality, that of the heart. Then, we see that only pure love is real. The rest is illusion; all the pain, all the horrible things people do to themselves, to each other and to the planet. Love helps us see through the veil of the dream-illusion (drama) that life presents to us. It is a play that we need to participate in by contributing to it, or withdrawing from it, with the purpose of bringing healing.

Lessons and Purpose

On the one hand, we have the life before us, the point in time in which we live as part of the evolution of humanity. This includes all extremes of wealth and all extremes of poverty and everything in between. It includes difficult diseases, mental and physical, and famines, and military as well as economic wars. It includes the most daring acts of creativity and generosity to the most obscene acts of greed and oppression. We can each feel the depth of elation and pain of all these human experiences.

On the other hand, we have a soul with a specific purpose, a gift we each have to offer this human world. So we have a choice before us. We can ignore our gift; we can ignore what we are meant to share with others to uplift humanity and, instead, feel powerless by the depth of despair and misery experienced by our fellow human beings. Or we can respond each day by sharing our gift with others.

I had a yoga student who shared her feelings of powerlessness that overcame her when she thought of wars and famines and widespread greed in the world. She could not shake it off. It made her feel like she had a hard time moving forward. I started by explaining to her that not all of humanity is at the same level of spiritual growth. That some people still need to experience abuse of power or being abused in order to learn their lessons. This did not help her. So I talked about the part in each of us that still clings to anger or blame, and when that adds up over an entire group of people, that can lead to outbursts toward other groups. So in effect we are each responsible for everything still happening in the world. By taking responsibility for our own feelings, they are not passed on to others or against others. This, again, was not enough to help her. She wanted to clean up her own life, free herself from anger and greed and blame. Still, the misery of the many affected her deeply. So I let her talk for a while. When she stopped, I asked her, "Where is your joy?" She replied, "Yes, but ..." and added some more justifications to explain herself. When the next moment of silence came, I asked her "Where is *your* joy?' "Yes, but ..." came her answer. I don't remember how many times I asked the same question to each of her justifications. I continued asking until she stopped arguing. At the next class, a week later, as she entered the classroom she told me "I was really angry at you at the end of class last week." I smiled. "But then," she continued, "I got it!"

We have a gift to share with humanity and if we don't share it, we feel miserable or get sick.

Everyday Life gives us experiences with which we can choose to feed our hurt, or to embrace our gifts. The more we embrace our gifts the more radiance we have and the more we attract opportunities to share them. My teacher Yogi Bhajan said:

Patience pays. Wait. Let the hand of God work for you. The One who has created you, let Him create all the environments, circumstances, and facilities and faculties.
Too kaahay doleh paraanee-aa tudh raakhaigaa sirjanhaar.
Jin paidaa-is too kee-aa so-ee day-ay aadhaar. [Spoken in Punjabi.]
Oh individual, why you are in a very doubtful state?
The One who has made you will take care of you. [Yogi Bhajan's translation.]
The One who has created this Universe, all the planets, planetary faculties and facilities on Earth, He is the One who has created you. Wait. Have patience. Lean on him. And all best things will come to you.

> *Dwell in God. Dwell in God. Dwell in God. Befriend your soul. Dwell in God and befriend your soul. Dwell in God and befriend your soul. Dwell in God and befriend your soul. All the faculties and facilities of the Creation, which are in your best interest shall be at your feet. You need million things. Million things will reach you if you are stable, established, firm, patient. Remember, Creator watches over you and Creation is ready to serve you, if you just be you.*
> *So please take away the ghost of your life and stop chasing round. Consolidate. Concentrate. Be you. And may all the peace and peaceful environments, prosperity approach you forever. Sat Nam.*[32]

Sat Nam is the Punjabi equivalent of *Namaste* in Sanskrit. Literally *Sat* means *truth* and *Nam* means *name*. It is a way of acknowledging our inner truth, our unique fragrance. It is one of the ways Sikhs and also Kundalini yoga practitioners greet each other.

This, in essence, summarizes our human experience and purpose. We have hurt with which to deal and we have a purpose in the form of a gift to share with humanity. In addition, we have to learn trust and develop faith that Life will sustain us and give us everything we need to fulfill this purpose while helping us heal. A lot can go wrong in a person who ignores her hurt and ignores her purpose.

In sports, athletes can only improve in the beginning if they measure themselves against better athletes. And at some point, in order to be the best of the best, they need to measure themselves against an imagined ideal for themselves. It is the same for all of us human beings on the spiritual path. In order to be truly ourselves, we come to a place where there is no one to measure oneself to, not even to the Buddha. There is a Zen Buddhist saying, "If you meet the Buddha on the road, kill him!" In effect, it is saying to stop being a follower, and to find one's own path. The only way I know is to imagine my ideal self. In this way, I see more clearly my shortcomings and also how much more I can shine.

The Role of the Therapist

I started this chapter by describing the master psychotherapist as

[32] Yogi Bhajan. *Patience Pays*, retrieved on September 28, 2014, and still active July 5, 2016, from https://www.3ho.org/articles/patience-pays-affirmation.

someone who is able to navigate, without attachment to one's own paradigm and one's client's, in order to help the client move out of the worldview construct that is the source of his current problems. One of the key tools to see clearly what one's client is going through is by deeply listening. That opens the door to the question "To what am I really listening?" And the answer to that is that there really are infinitely many details one can perceive. So then we need some guidelines to help with the process of therapy. One of them is that there is a key question with which we, as therapists, need to help our clients. The question is "Who am I?" That question led me to what I describe in this chapter. It is the result of a journey of exploration of the relationship between my mind, my body, and my heart/intuition/soul. I discussed here notions of human nature, our core identities and our soul identity. I also discussed our relationship as human beings with Life.

With this understanding, I have a clearer picture of the nature of my client and the playground in which my client is trying to play. My role as a therapist is to help my client play more freely and with more joy in this playground. In order to do that, I don't use objectives, as in traditional therapy, because I do not want to guide my clients away from their own souls' objectives. Instead, I work with intentions. If a client is in his mind, I have the intention in my mind and heart to help my client reconnect with his body and heart. I don't have to know how to do that. I have to trust my instincts once I am clear of what my intention is. If my client is in pain, I hold the intention in my mind and heart that my client finds healing and that I find the process to help him get there. I work with intention during the therapy process and outside of the therapy process. I work on being clear with my intentions and trust that Life will guide me and my clients accordingly. I don't have to work within a theory or a model which would likely be limiting that process. I also help my client become clear of his intentions. These intentions need to be freeing. So if a client says he wants out of a relationship, that decision may not be a truly freeing intention. Intentions that are more freeing may be, "I want peace in my heart," "I want love in my heart," " I want to heal any relationship in which I am involved." These intentions may very well lead to the initial desire to be out of the relationship, but not necessarily. We need to help our clients get to the core of their soul's real fulfilling desires.

Luc Watelet

Listening Skills Revisited

From my perspective, there are different layers of listening: direct and literal, metaphorical, and also spiritual.
The direct and literal listening has to do with what the client says and does not say. This includes clients' choice of words, the senses they use in describing their story, the feelings they use, their self-awareness, etc. Sometimes a client repeats a certain word, or omits some senses, or avoids certain feelings. It may be important to explore what is behind their choice of words, and their omissions.

The metaphorical listening comes from becoming aware of what the story represents in the client's life. It is seeing the story as if the client was sharing a dream. It asks the question, "Why is this story important to my client, in his life, right now?"

Let's look at a case both literally and metaphorically. For instance, a client has been working on no longer having affairs. He has been working on remembering the love for his wife. But all of a sudden, she discovers his latest affair before he has a chance to come to her first and apologize. The question the therapist may be wondering is, "Wouldn't it have been more healing to have been in a situation where the client could have come clean to his wife before her finding out about the affair?" After all, her client has been working so hard for several months to be an honorable husband. There can be a difference between what we might assume is better and what Life presents instead. Why is it better for that client that his wife became aware of the affair before he came clean to her?

Looking at this case literally, the questioning might go something like this. Perhaps the client's ego was taking too much importance and even thinking of being some kind of hero for the work done, and the client needed a reality check. Or perhaps the client's guilt was becoming overwhelming and his wife's discovery made him aware that he had not fully dealt with the guilt as he thought he had. Perhaps his wife needed to find out first for her own self-esteem. If she had not found out before the apology, she might always ask herself why she never sensed it and always suspect he is cheating on her because she could not tell that he was in the past.

Looking at this case metaphorically, the questioning might go something like this. We start off by looking at the story as if the affair were only a dream, and, in the dream, the client's wife found out. What would such a dream represent in the client's life? Perhaps he is feeling some boredom that he has wrongly blamed on the relationship. Perhaps he has a secret dream that feels forbidden to him and he is afraid his wife would find out. The affair would not represent something sexual, but something forbidden in the client's mind. Perhaps the affair represents something related to his purpose in life that he feels extremely frightened to acknowledge or pursue.

You see that the literal approach leads to a behavioral change, but may be missing something important that the metaphorical approach brings to the surface. The literal approach could leave the client dejected because he has not learned what the affair was meant to teach him and so his wife needed to find out about the affair so he could start facing his truth from a new perspective.

And then there is the spiritual listening level which asks, "How does the experience described by the client fit in his lessons and his gift to the world?" This is the most obvious question following the metaphorical inquiry. Now, we are addressing why life happens the way it did from the perspective that everything happens to support us on our spiritual path. In the case above, the question becomes, "What is the actual dream or purpose the client feels is so forbidden?" And, "What is at the source of the forbidding feeling?" Because once the trauma that expresses itself as the forbidding feeling is released, the client will finally feel the love he really has for his purpose. Now, we are tapping into the life story as part of the synchronicity of Life. Of course, a parallel inquiry is also possible for the client's wife's spiritual journey.

Our experiences can inform our spiritual journey and, in doing so, we can truly apologize for our wrong doings because we know the healing truth behind them. The apology is real and feels real by the receiver because full responsibility has been taken for actions that resulted in painful experiences and lessons have been learned.

As therapists, we have to listen behind the story and behind the perspective of the client, and see how the experience is presenting an opportunity to raise our client's awareness. In order to understand how to begin to address the spiritual aspect of listening, one needs practice with one's own life experiences and seeing them through the lens of how these helped with one's personal and spiritual growth. One also needs to know the client reasonably well and notice patterns between all the stories shared in the course of therapy by the client.

Also, as described above, in order to help clients get a more accurate picture of their story, it is often important to ask them where they feel their story in their body and to engage them in releasing tension around the story using their breath and an attitude of non-judgment. This can bring people to a place of new freedom on their journey.

The psychotherapy I envision is to help our clients play as freely as possible in their own playground. This freedom can be thought of as infinite in its divine nature. This goal I set out as a therapist is so that I do not impose on my clients personal goals that could be limiting. From this perspective, psychotherapy is deeply entwined with the discipline of spiritual growth.

7 UNDERSTANDING MENTAL ILLNESS

AUTOBIOGRAPHY IN FIVE SHORT CHAPTERS[33]

by *Portia Nelson*

CHAPTER ONE
I walk down the street.
There is a deep hole in the sidewalk
I fall in.
I am lost ... I am hopeless.
It isn't my fault.
It takes forever to find a way out.

CHAPTER TWO
I walk down the same street.
There is a deep hole in the sidewalk.
I pretend I don't see it.
I fall in again.
I can't believe I am in the same place.
But it isn't my fault.
It still takes a long time to get out.

---

[33] P. Nelson (1988), excerpt from *There's a Hole in My Sidewalk*. Simon & Schuster, Inc.

CHAPTER THREE
I walk down the same street.
There is a deep hole in the sidewalk.
I *see* it is there.
I still fall in ... it's a habit ... but,
My eyes are open.
I know where I am;
It is *my* fault.
I get out immediately.

CHAPTER FOUR
I walk down the same street.
There is a deep hole in the sidewalk.
I walk around it.

CHAPTER FIVE
I walk down another street.

Mental Illness

When I first started to work with people in a recovery program for addiction (and dual diagnoses: addiction and mental illness), I had no experience helping people with such challenges. All I knew was what I had learned from our psychology manuals in school.

I mentioned Clifford W. Beers in Chapter 3, Love. Beers' book, *A Mind that Found Itself,* moved me to believe that recovery and healing from mental illness was possible. I read this book as part of a project I elected to do during my program in mental health counseling. Beers believed he had crimes to pay for. This belief colored every one of his experiences and he acted with paranoia and delusions. This led him to be in institutions for three years. He started questioning his belief due to the benevolence he felt from his family and friends as well as the kindness from some caregivers.

Today, Beers may have received a diagnosis of bipolar disorder or schizophrenia or a combination. According to his own account, his personality was never affected by the mental illness, and the mental illness was not a personality disorder. Instead, his mental health challenges were a natural consequence of a belief that he had a crime to pay for and people were after him to get him to admit it. But he could not remember having committed a crime. That tortured him. This account led me to question the idea of personality disorders and I started to believe that there could be a solution to help people heal from mental health challenges. I was starting to believe like Albert Ellis that the problem is in the worldview of the client.

But to me it went even further; I saw it as part of a spiritual journey. Just like the narrator in the song *Amazing Grace*, Beers was lost and he was found. His journey through and out of mental illness was like Dante's journey from darkness to light. From that perspective, it is the journey of all human beings. Each human being simply creates his or her own hell. The key is to learn how to separate from it and let it go by embracing the light.

Beers' book gave me some hope that I could relate to the people seeking help from mental health challenges. Also, my out-of-body experience gave me the experience that my consciousness was not affected by the car accident that had my body/mind out of commission for 20 to 30 minutes (my estimation given where I was and where the hospital was). If I have a consciousness that can separate itself from my body/mind and is not affected by an accident, why can't this also be true for all human beings? If my consciousness is not affected by an accident, why should it be affected by physical or mental illness?

After a couple of weeks of internship interacting with clients and leading groups, I recognized that even though I did not care for drugs and alcohol and even though I did not have a mental illness diagnosis, we spoke the same language of thoughts and feelings. We all had darkness with which to grapple and beautiful dreams to share with each other. I could understand their humanity.

There is a common expectation in our culture that only an addict can understand an addict and only a person with depression can understand another, and so on. So how could I understand them? When a person in a group asked me if I ever struggled with addiction, I had an answer ready. I told her, "Every human being struggles with one addiction or another, if it is not alcohol or drugs, it is with sex or anger or victimization or money or something. Show me someone with no addiction, no compulsion, no obsession, I will show you a saint. I have had my struggles with feeling victimized and I know something about the effort it takes to stop seeing myself that way." I was never asked again whether I could help or not.

If a person with a mental illness had asked me the equivalent question about mental illness instead of addiction, I would have answered that every human being struggles with mental illness to some degree – except for spiritual masters, perhaps. Do you know any human being, who is not a saint, who never loses hope if only momentarily, or who never doubts herself? We all fall. The only difference is how we respond to it.

And here is why I could understand them...

*A **definition of mental illness:** The problems my clients face always fall in a combination of two categories: 1) They believe their mind without making sure the thoughts are congruent with who they are and want to be, and 2) They don't pay attention to, or don't trust, their feelings whether emotional or intuitive. Behind this is a lack of proper boundaries, lack of self-esteem, and lack of self-love, which is all programmed in their belief system.*

This is a clear description of mental illness, but also of every human problem. It is simply a question of degree and the ability to find a way out. The difference is simply that some people have the ability to remain functional and being functional in our society is enough. In a culture where being authentic is the "norm," anyone with a career that does not match his purpose would be considered inauthentic and, therefore, mentally ill. It would not matter how lucrative one's career is.

I suggest we forget the labeling of mental illnesses because labeling points to a fundamental problem in a person. Instead, we need to figure out how to help them love themselves, help them sort out their thoughts and help them learn to trust their feelings. How can we do that if at the same time we put them down with a label that is a cultural stigma and points to them as being defective in some way?

How We Think of Mental Illness May Contribute to the Problem

In summary, the first misconception about mental illness is that it is a personality disorder. The second one, which leads to a similar conclusion, is that it is genetic or due to a chemical imbalance. These assertions may be true sometimes, but 1) they are at the very least an overgeneralization, and are disempowering, and 2) I have not met any case that supports them so far. To me, there is no such thing as a mental illness that is different from a normal consequence of how a person deals with thoughts and feelings. Therefore, working on overcoming mental illness is an exercise in personal and spiritual growth and can be done using mindfulness. There is a scientific basis for this which I will get to in the next chapter.

I have interacted with people with many diagnoses such as addictions to alcohol or drugs of all kinds, major depressive disorder, anxiety disorder, bipolar disorder, childhood Post Traumatic Stress Disorder (PTSD), antisocial personality disorder, paranoia schizoaffective disorder, traumatic brain injury, avoidant personality disorder, and others. In all cases, with the proper medication and sometimes none at all, it was very easy to have a coherent conversation with the people experiencing these diagnoses. The only difficulty I encountered that prevented any progress was with people who refused to explore their feelings and thoughts genuinely. Anyone who was willing to speak earnestly about who they were and about what bothered them was able to get better.

There is one critical question: Is the person who is struggling willing to make the journey to his consciousness? Because when one is, there is no turning back. Once a person sees it from the healed perspective, he finally sees that he had a choice and therefore the perception of disability, mental or physical, was an illusion, something he had attached to and held on to because of a habit of seeing himself and the world in a specific limiting way. The choice may appear irrational, but it brings some benefits, otherwise people would not, consciously or unconsciously, make it and therefore it is rational, albeit based on a limited perception of reality.

In the same way, spiritual healing from cancer or a leg shorter than the other may appear to be magical thinking to some. That is part of their worldview. It is a limiting view (not a scientific one) in the light of such healings being documented by medical doctors.

Luc Watelet

I am not saying that it is easy to get out of a long time worldview and I am not blaming anyone for experiencing mental health challenges. God knows I have had my own difficulties embracing my consciousness. I have too often chosen darkness over light, not recognizing that I had a choice or perhaps not wanting to see my choices out of a rebellious fit. The truth is, for the longest time, I could not and did not believe it was that simple because when in darkness, it seems and feels as though there are no possible solutions and no one could possibly understand me. For a long time, I did not see that I felt powerless and therefore had given up. I had to recognize when I felt powerless to give up that self-defeating perception and embrace the possibility of receiving what I really wished. Imagine an athlete who does not believe she can win. What will be the likely outcome of her next race? The way we think about our problems matters and affects the outcome.

Remember my story of feeling increasingly disgusted, so much so that my brain turned itself off and I ended up sleeping for two hours? As soon as I woke up and I was given the simple truth that "disgust is fear of love," I was able to shift my focus. I was positive and my eagerness to live and love had come back. As long as my focus was on figuring out the negative, I was in a downward spiral into a darker and darker abyss. I have found myself in various situations of despair in my life and not seeing my way out. Sometimes, when pressed by outside circumstances such as being invited to a party I really wanted to go to or a class I needed to teach, I would pray to God for help. Then something would happen that helped shift my state of mind, sometimes even instantly. Once, after I asked God for help, I got a phone call within seconds from a friend who, without knowing the mental state I was in, asked me to help her translate a poem. I was amazed I could let go so easily of the dark space I was in. That space felt so overwhelming, so unbearable, so impossible to get out of, and yet a simple phone call, a focus on a lovely poem, a task I love to do with a good friend, and I was free again. She told me she was going to call later but she heard inwardly, "Luc is ready now!" During that phone call two more friends called me. Life had heard my prayer. I felt supported.

Autobiography in Five Short Chapters

I have come to see mental illness and any disease as a hole into which we fall, as described by the poem above by Portia Nelson. I think of it as a Zen poem by its simplicity, its clarity and its universality. It describes our human condition so clearly and with such a delightful lightheartedness that it is healing to read. It speaks the truth. Anyone with some experience has experienced what this poem describes. First, you get stuck and you blame the world for it. You may fall over and over again and not take responsibility. Then, one day, you decide to take responsibility because no one can help you out if you don't decide you want to get out. And if you can learn to get out of one hole, no matter how shallow, shake yourself off, and learn from your experience, you can learn to get out of any hole, no matter how deep, because the depth of a hole is only a matter of perception, it is not real. We make the problems we face our own and then take them way too seriously. We have no idea how our thoughts make it even more difficult to see the light at the end of the tunnel, a light that is always present, but we have covered it with dark overwhelming clouds.

One way out of the hole is to reconnect body, mind, and soul, by recognizing where our thinking and emotions fell apart and take responsibility for our ability to think and to feel.

Next time you find yourself in a negative frame of mind, notice that your mind is preoccupied with dark thoughts. Remember that we can only think one thing at any given time. So give yourself permission to stop paying attention to the brooding thoughts and, instead, allow yourself to think of something beautiful. Give yourself permission to be grateful for being alive and having an opportunity to learn something new, be grateful for an opportunity to respond to the call to embrace happiness.

This may not be easy; you may find resistance, as if you could die. The part that might die is that negative part... so trust... it will be alright. Notice how attached you are to the brooding thoughts. Why this attachment? So tell yourself you can come back to these thoughts later if you really want to, just give your mind a vacation from them. Imagine a beach, a safe place by a stream, or watching the world from high up on a mountain. Imagine swimming with a dolphin or going on a walk with your favorite pet. Practice a mantra for joy, sing a song, or say a prayer. Now feel what happens in your body as a response to the shift of focus in your mind. If you stay in this beautiful space long enough, do you still want to go back to the brooding thoughts you left behind? You become aware that while in the brooding space, you can't seem to imagine a solution: You are possessed. It is like an addiction to darkness. But once out, it is amazing how simple it was to shift perspective. It is a realization that the darkness had no strength of its own, that it is only an illusion.

Emotions

When there is no resistance to the emotions we experience, they flow. If we are stuck in an emotion it is because there is a fear somewhere. For instance, being stuck in sadness, grief, or nostalgia indicates a fear of the future and, instead of looking at it, we focus on what we miss from the past. Being worried is also a fear of the future but instead of retreating into the past, we focus negatively on the future. Anger "protects" fear which "protects" emotional hurt. Hatred and disgust are forms of fear of love.

For example, I was working with a client who struggled with a relationship, leaving it, then coming back to it, then leaving it again, several times. She finally decided enough was enough and asked him to leave. She promised herself she would not go back to him this time. But after a while, she started talking about grieving the relationship and talking about really loving the guy even though she knew he was not good for her. I listened for a while. Then I asked her, "Have you noticed that when you asked him to leave, you took some of your power back?" She thought a little and agreed with me. "So," I suggested, "look at what you are learning instead of what you are missing. What do you see?" "I have never taken my power before!" she said. "So it is like entering a new world, right?" "You got that right! This is new to me! I want to learn more about my power!" she said. "What is the level of your grieving for this man now, same as before, lower, higher?" "I see what you mean," she said, "the grief is much lower now!"

Similarly, what we call mental illness starts with a fear, usually fairly big. Depression can be an expression of giving up on something that matters. I have had clients who forget what they really love. They experience a disconnection from their passion. It has helped to look into the source of the block. Delusion can be an expression of avoiding something about reality that brings up intense fears. Paranoia is a way to protect ourselves from repeated trauma by being very alert, but to the point where we start looking for things that justify the trauma.

During a hike going up a mountain, I realized that what I thought was a fear of heights was actually a fear of abandonment. A while later, it suddenly occurred to me to ask myself, "What is behind this fear of abandonment for me?" I could then feel that it was more than fear of abandonment, it was fear of being made fun of, despised, and even crushed, tortured, and killed. It felt powerful, like it came from God himself. Every now and again, when I felt it coming to the surface. I reacted with anger because I did not know where it was coming from and how to respond to it and I certainly did not want to be passive and/or depressed about it.

This time I stopped being afraid of it. I looked at it, I felt its energy while remaining at peace, strong yet humble, centered. I had an attitude of, "Tell me who you are, tell me what you really want?" I was willing to be tortured and die if it came to that. It wasn't God, of course. It seemed much less powerful now. I waited until the tension dissipated. I started to see all of my self-defeating devices gathered into this one inner demon that presented itself as if it represented the world. As I stopped reacting to it and allowed it to think whatever it wanted of me, as I stopped giving it my attention, I smiled inwardly that this demon no longer mattered to me and I started to feel that I have power. Not a forced power. Instead it was a natural power. I saw that it had always been there. When I felt powerless, I really believed I had no power. There is a desire then to seek force to get revenge, or to give up. But it was the wrong interpretation. I had power, but I was giving it away. Viktor Frankl said in *Man's Search for Meaning* how he survived, and helped others survive, the concentration camp. The solution was to reconnect with something you love, something you have to accomplish and hang on to it for dear life. But I had to rediscover it for myself. So feeling rejected or abandoned was just a warning sign that I was giving my power away. I had to become aware of how I gave it away, through which belief, and change that belief. And then I just needed to feel the energy of rejection or abandonment and give that away knowing it was an illusion, not ignore it, but simply not attaching my identity to it. And slowly remember my joy, simply remember my joy. My feeling of abandonment was from abandoning my own joy!

Examples of Mental Health Challenges

In the following examples, the therapists' names are real. All other names have been changed unless explicitly stated to be the real name.

Depression

Joe

Here is Joe's story provided by Tonya Girard, LMFT:[34]

> I met Joe soon after his break-up with his fiancée. He expressed clinically significant symptoms of depression including hopelessness, anhedonia [inability to experience pleasure], psychomotor retardation, hypersomnia [excessive need to sleep] and negative rumination, increased irritability with angry outbursts, passive suicidal ideation and low self-esteem.
>
> I asked Joe to close his eyes and describe his experience to me as if the feelings that were holding him back were a character from a story. Joe began describing a young man sitting in the corner hiding his head while thick black smoke from a dragon cloaked the room. He explained that he was the young defeated man, his experience of depression was the thick black smoke while the dragon represented his past.
>
> As we worked toward increased personal awareness through investigation of his family of origin and his dominant narrative, Joe began to envision the young man standing up and swinging a sword to defeat the dragon. Soon, as the smoke cleared, Joe could look out over a vast landscape and communicate to me the direction we needed to travel to address the root of his self-sabotage. We mapped out the landscape together and decided on a path through a forest and up a mountain to the cabin at the top. We explored Joe's life long struggle with impulsive angry outbursts, his sense of entitlement and insecurity.
>
> As we continue our journey toward increased personal awareness,

---

[34] Published with Tonya Girard's permission.

Joe reports increased control over his behaviors and a decrease in his experience of depressive symptomatology. He continues to find new lands on his map to explore as he strives to become the man he knows he is.

This is the case of a man who can reflect about his life using the language of metaphor, not just staying in metaphor, but use the metaphorical language to know what he needs to explore in his real life, address it and see how it shifts his narrative.

The language of storytelling fits Joe very well. This account demonstrates how Joe has the answers within and part of the psychotherapist's expertise is in guiding Joe to explore his inner world so he can get to his answers.

Depression for 30 Years

I mentioned someone in the Prologue who had been living with a diagnosis of major depressive disorder for over 30 years. She had been in therapy for at least that long. I was wondering if I could help her in any way. It turned out it was very easy. One of the first things she told me was that she had no sense of self. Each time we met, it took less than half an hour to bring her spirits up. The reason her depression had lasted so long was that no one had paid attention to her distress as a result of how she lived her life and she herself did not know how to pay attention to it. All I did was ask her when she last felt a bump in her depression. We discovered she was giving up on her wants a little every day thinking it was the normal thing to do. The problem was hidden under giving up a small want that seemed so petty it was not even worth paying attention to. For instance, one small want was: *not wanting to prepare her husband's cup of coffee in the morning*. With a mindfulness technique I will describe in the next chapter, she discovered there was a deeper issue: an interaction with her father when she was three years old which led her to dismiss her wants and more profoundly, a big part of her creativity, what she loved. The day after she remembered and felt the pain (if only partially) of her long time forgotten secret, she said "No" to her husband for the first time in thirty years in a direct manner, that is, without being passive-aggressive about it.

We had not discussed how to deal with her husband and we had never practiced being assertive. I simply guided her to a buried experience that had contributed to making her believe she did not matter. It came naturally. She had come out of her shell. She was learning she had a self and that her self mattered. Working on self-awareness together for a little under two years led to her decision to have her daily dose of anti-depressant gradually lowered from three pills to one. She was writing e-mails to her mother regularly, but for the first time, she wrote to her that she felt happy.

The length of time someone struggles with a problem is not an indication that the person's problem is genetic or that it stems from a personality disorder. It may just mean the right questions were never asked.

Hints on the Path

After my first separation, I had been feeling low and forced myself out of the house for a walk. I was really feeling out of sorts and with no purpose. On the sidewalk, at a bus stop, I came across the book: *Man's Search for Meaning* by Viktor Frankl. I read it and it became a source of inspiration as I had felt in a prison of sorts. Viktor Frankl had survived the Holocaust, never giving in to the feeling of being in a prison. It put things in perspective for me.

Apathy and lethargy are aspects of depression. I remember feeling apathy one day. I forced myself outside for a bike ride to get my energy going. During my ride, I noticed a porn magazine on the side of the trail. I was puzzled by this porn magazine on my path. Would Life condone pornography? Was I to stop and indulge in porn? And suddenly I heard my thoughts, "You're disconnected from your passion, your creative juices!" It made me smile. It was as if Life made no judgments and pushed me gently to reconnect with myself, even using porn on my path. I did not have to indulge in it, I just needed to remember my passion.

Indifference

In counseling school, we were asked to acknowledge with which kinds of clients we would have the hardest time. I thought that I would have the hardest time with people who had no passion for anything, no drive, completely indifferent to everything. To help them find the switch within to something they are passionate about would be almost impossible. I know for myself when I touch that space, I shock myself out of it by being angry at my state of being. My anger connects me back to my passion for being alive and alert, and being in love with Life. To help clients out of indifference, I suspect we need to find something that triggers their anger and, thus, helps them see what they are willing to fight for.

Anxiety

As a student, I had panic attacks during exams. I calmed myself down by rationalizing that I was a good student and that if I could not finish all the questions, I was probably still going to be able to complete more questions than most other students. Thus, if we were graded on a sliding scale I'd still come out with a decent grade. My heart calmed down, I stopped sweating profusely, and I was able to focus on my exam, one question at a time.

Often when someone has a panic attack, the thinking has gone into a fear of what might happen even before that person is able to articulate what it is that might frighten him or her. Because of this, the person barely breathes. So the first step is to become conscious of one's breath and start breathing deeply. The second step is to do a reality check: Am I in immediate danger? Is my thinking factual? What positive scenarios might also possibly be true?

With practice, one can notice the negative thinking, and become aware that at the base of the negative thinking is a lack of trust in life. So the work out of anxiety is to open up to and practice having faith in life.

Here is the story of Lucy provided by Tonya Girard, LMFT.[35]

I met Lucy following her victorious battle with cervical cancer. She reported that following her surgery she began experiencing an alarming increase in symptoms (previously managed on her own) including severe and frequent panic attacks which would often

---

[35] Published with Tonya Girard's permission.

consist of dissociation, increased heart rate, chest pain, and intense fear, flashbacks related to her life-long relationship with trauma and feelings of being overwhelmed. This prompted her to seek professional treatment. Lucy explained that she has always been the one to solve the problems, to care for those who could not care for themselves, almost a lynch pin holding her friends' and family's lives together. Lucy was adamant that she did not want pharmacological intervention to treat her symptoms; if she was capable of helping others, she would be capable of helping herself. This is where my work began with her. Throughout our assessment period together, I learned of her relationship with trauma and anxiety. I also began to notice an interpersonal pattern which entailed Lucy being drained of her personal energy by those around her. Lucy explained that some days she would have 70 or more calls from friends and family seeking her attention or advice.

Together we decided that although her history of trauma was clearly impacting her experience of anxiety (i.e., flashbacks and dissociation), it was not going to be our area of focus. Instead, we would look towards the here and now to decrease her experience of current symptoms and prevent new symptoms from developing. We began conversations about the accumulation of stress over time and how this accumulation can impact mental and physical health. We also discussed the transference of energy from one being to another and how to create healthy boundaries to protect oneself from being drained. We talked at great length about prayer/meditation to ground oneself when panic threatens to catch us in a whirlwind. We practiced meditation, deep breathing, appropriate use of language and affirmations in session together. We explored how these themes run through families, society as a whole and our part in making the changes on a personal level to help those around us including the ones we love. Lucy quickly began to realize how her 'helping' behavior of always being available to anyone who reportedly needed her was harming her and created barriers in other areas of her life. She recognized how her relationship with severe trauma informed her sense of duty to those being victimized or in need of help. Slowly she began to redefine what it meant to be helpful. She began to recognize how power and control had been dancing through her life story and developed a new definition of what being a powerful woman meant to her. She learned what power she had to control her actions/behaviors which would, in turn, influence her thoughts and feelings. Lucy began applying what she learned from our conversations to her life and reported a decrease in the frequency, duration, and severity of her panic attacks.

Lucy and I continue to meet regularly as she hones her personal awareness and practices the techniques discussed in our sessions. She reflects on the changes she has made and how they have impacted those around her for the better, noting a deep appreciation for finding a clinician who is willing to explore treatments that do not include medications but rather focus on personal awareness, strengths, and empowerment.

Schizophrenia with Delusions and Paranoia

Schizophrenia can be a daunting experience. Once a person starts saying things as if they were true that appear delusional to others, she is labeled and her community often starts ostracizing her. That's what happened to Joy. After seven years of therapy, disconnected from her community, and resisting taking her medication, she finally heard in a meditation that she should take her meds. Her therapist had repeated many times that not taking her medication was part of the disease, and pleaded with her to take it. When I started talking to Joy, I heard her talk about schizophrenia as if it controlled her: it made her say things that pushed people she cared for away from her, and it made her not take her medication.

I asked her if she remembered a time when she did not take her medication. "Sure!" she said. I asked her, "What happened in you that you did not take your meds?" She said, "No one ever asked me that before. I... I preferred delusion. I never knew that..." She was startled by the realization. "Why did you prefer delusion?" I asked. She explained that she feared she could not live without a person gone from her life.

She now knew she was choosing delusion because of an intense fear. She also, as a result, knew that she could choose to face that fear.

Bipolar disorder

Havalynn (real name with permission) is considering writing her own story, therefore I will only give a brief account of it.

Around three years old, Havalynn started to be abused physically by her mother. By five, she was suicidal. After being beaten one day, at the age of five, crying and wishing she was dead, she saw a vision of Jesus and heard the words, "Everything is going to be okay." An immediate sense of peace washed over her. When she told her mom what she'd just seen and heard, she was not believed, even though she was raised Catholic and taught to believe in Jesus. At nine, she wrote in her diary things she would not do to her own children, like abusing them physically, and things she would do instead, like talking to them about why they were acting a certain way. Havalynn ended up using drugs. She also ended up getting pregnant at a young age. She had two daughters who she started abusing physically when they were around three years old, the same age as she was when she was first abused. She realized what she was doing, but could not stop at first.

When Havalynn was diagnosed with bipolar disorder, she was put on medication. In time, she found her diary and when she read what she had said she would and wouldn't do to her own children, she had to accept she was not succeeding. It took some time. She had a third daughter.

At some point, she found herself using words that put people down as part of a game she and some of her friends played together. And she had another drug experience which turned out differently from before. This time, she went into some kind of spiritual place where she was shown the impact of mean words on herself and on others. At the end, she was asked if she understood. She did. After that, she used all her courage to stop her behavior. She began therapy. Then she gathered her daughters and told them to tell her everything they wanted her to know such as what she did that hurt them. She did not want to interrupt them and did not want to tell them they were wrong. As she listened to her daughters, she could feel the urge to deny what they were sharing, just as her own mother did with her. But she listened until the end. She thanked them for being so honest with her. She apologized and promised to do better. And they cried and hugged. This began the journey of healing for herself and her family.

Havalynn made a courageous effort to feel the pain of the words directed at her when it happened, instead of letting herself feel powerless by them. During the high phase of the bipolar cycles, instead of thinking it was wrong, she learned to appreciate feeling so awesome. She stopped judging herself so much. Little by little she weaned herself off of medication. She developed what she calls "a self-validating, positive, uplifting and elevating inner dialogue" and encouraged herself by saying "Yay me!" for each positive step she noticed.

She now enjoys life with gusto, continues to meditate, and uses mindfulness as a way to approach anything in life. Havalynn shares her experience in public presentations and in private sessions to help people understand mental health challenges. She teaches people her "self-validating, positive, uplifting and elevating inner dialogue" method and teaches others to celebrate each of their positive steps with "Yay me!"

Antisocial Personality Disorder

James was diagnosed with antisocial personality disorder when he was 11 years old and was placed in a juvenile detention center until he was 18. After he was released, he used and sold marijuana. It did not take long before he was caught and asked to clean up his act. He had no intention to and couldn't care less what anybody said. He had become a rebel.

I only saw him three times. During our sessions, James drew graffiti in a notebook. He had talent. I let him. I wanted to get to know him. I asked how his childhood was. Around the age of seven, his parents separated. He was then spending time with each parent separately. But when he was with his dad, his dad disappeared and James did not know where his dad was. So he called his mom in tears and she came to pick him up. This happened over and over. Later he learned that his dad was shooting heroin in the bathroom.

When he was eleven, he stabbed a school teacher in her hand with a pencil. I don't know how often he had acted with some violence in school, but I cannot imagine this was the first incident. After this incident, he was diagnosed as having antisocial personality disorder and sent to the juvenile detention ("juvie") center.

As we talked, he shared that he was convinced he was born bad, and he also hated a system that would just not leave him alone.

Given this information, I was wondering why he was diagnosed with an antisocial personality disorder and not with childhood PTSD. I was wondering what made him feel he was born bad. Something had gone terribly wrong. As a society, we should do better.

I knew he could be belligerent and rebellious... but I would be frightened for James if, as a kid, he had not reacted in some way to ask for help. Rebellion is the natural result of not being heard for who you really are inside, and not being given kindness.

My job with him, in the little time we had, was to help him see he was not naturally bad and to try and relate to the part of him that cared to live and was as beautiful as his graffiti artwork. I planted the seeds in him that he could overcome not only what he had experienced in his family of origin, but also the effect of the label our society's mental health system had given him starting at eleven and continued to give him for at least nine more years.

James became curious to learn more about childhood PTSD.

Addiction

Knowing Who You Are

When I was working at an addiction recovery center, I used to tell groups: "Can you imagine Jesus, Martin Luther King Jr., Mother Teresa or Gandhi drunk, or using drugs? Why do you think they weren't interested?" I continued, "The only difference between you and them is that you don't know your purpose, you don't know who you are; if you did, you'd be interested in something more important to you than drugs."

I am not saying that it is not difficult to get out of an addictive behavior. What I am saying is that the traditional approaches to recovery need to include a self-discovery program. Simply monitoring addictive behaviors and behavior changes is not enough. Furthermore, monitoring behavior change may be perceived as parental monitoring which does not build trust, but rebellion. The 12-step program is very helpful and works very well for many. But it is not for everyone. I had clients who weren't interested in it. They graduated nevertheless from our program using my self-discovery approach.

What works best for me to get out of passivity about giving up an addictive behavior is to find a spiritual motivation, something that will last me forever. If I cannot see a spiritual motivation, any other motivation is likely to only work temporarily for me.

Meaningful Communication

One of the most important papers about addiction I discovered during my coursework in mental health counseling states that it is the lack of bonding between family members and the lack of social support that leads adolescents from alcoholic families to abuse substances.[36] The people with addiction issues, I worked with or met, experienced little or no meaningful communication in their families. This, to me, means addiction therapy needs to be based on real and healthy communication so that clients can learn to communicate with themselves. Communicating with our self is one of the most important skills one can develop. How else can we learn what we want and how to deal with experiences of being out of balance emotionally or otherwise?

The Rat and Cocaine Experiment

In the American, and perhaps Western, psyche, we have started to believe that a rat in a cage given the option of two water bottles, one with pure water and one laced with cocaine or an opiate, will choose the drug-laced water bottle until it overdoses if its consumption is not limited. This picture is not complete. It misses a key piece of information discovered in the 70s by Bruce Alexander and his team at Simon Fraser University.[37] What Alexander suspected was that the rat experiment described above constricted the rat to a small and solitary cage that did

---

[36] A. Orenstein & A. Ullman (1996), *Characteristics of Alcoholic Families and Adolescent Substance Use*, Journal of Alcohol & Drug Education, 41(3), 86.
[37] B. Alexander (2010), retrieved on May 24, 2015, and still active on July 6, 2016, from http://www.brucekalexander.com/articles-speeches/rat-park/148-addiction-the-view-from-rat-park.

not resemble a natural environment for rats. When he created, with his team, an environment that is pleasant to rats, an environment where rats could reproduce and play, they no longer chose the drug-laced water bottle over the pure water bottle. They called this environment Rat Park, which gave the name to the experiment.

This suggests a very different picture of addiction, one where drugs do not create addictions, and instead the lack of a suitable environment is responsible for an addictive behavior. Bruce Alexander wanted to understand how human beings end up consuming large amounts of drugs even though their physical space was not restricted like the rat in the first cage experiment. He assembled the documentation he needed and published his books: The Globalisation of Addiction: A study in Poverty of the Spirit (Oxford University Press, 2008 and 2010).

Conclusion

In essence, my view of mental illness is that it stems from a lack of a healthy positive relationship with our thoughts and feelings, and a lack of relationship between our mind, our body and our soul. In that sense, we all suffer from this to one degree or another. The darkness we face shows us where we need to grow. Contrary to common belief, our true identity is still whole, we simply need to reconnect with it; that is, we need to take responsibility *for falling in the hole in the sidewalk and getting out of it, back to the light.* Our true identity is being in complete connection with the light, with love. If we don't feel that connection, we have strayed away from our true self. How is it possible to stray away from our true self? Because, like the rat experiment demonstrates, we have free will, and if we don't find what we need in our environment, and our mind, body, and soul are not communicating with each other, we may seek a solution to the dark feelings in the wrong places: addiction for instance, or be overwhelmed with stress that we don't know how to handle. Unlike the rat, we do not depend on the environment if we don't allow it. We can look within for answers, for a deeper connection. This is far from a new idea and it may not necessarily be easy to put in practice: Socrates used to say, "Know thyself." This leads to a mindfulness approach to psychotherapy and to healing.

8 MINDFULNESS PSYCHOTHERAPY

I will be silent on the meaning of yoga for India, because I cannot presume to pass judgment on something I do not know from personal experience. I can, however, say something about what it means to the West. Our lack of direction borders on psychic anarchy. Therefore any religious or philosophical practice amounts to a <u>psychological discipline</u>, and therefore <u>a method of psychic hygiene</u>.[38] *(Highlighted by the author.)*

~ *Carl G. Jung*

[W]hatsoever the meditation, it has to fill this requirement: that the body, mind, consciousness [soul] – all three should function in unity. Then suddenly one day the fourth has arrived: witnessing. Or if you want to, call it God; call it God or nirvana or Tao or whatsoever you will.[39]

~ *Osho*

What if there were no such thing as abnormal psychology? What would psychology look like then? If people's problems were the natural consequences of something, what would that something be?

---

[38] C. G. Jung. *Yoga and the West* in Jung's Collected Works, Vol. 11. Quoted from the Introduction of *C. G. Jung, The Psychology of Kundalini Yoga*. Princeton University Press. Edited by Sonu Shamdasani. 1996. p. xxviii.
[39] Osho (2000). *The Book of Wisdom: The Heart of Tibetan Buddhism*, Talk #23. Element Books Ltd.

Luc Watelet

Self, Inner-Self

Stress: One Way to Begin to Experience a Self and an Inner-Self

When we get stressed, something happens that we did not expect. It may be being overworked or burned out, it may come as an illness, it may come as tension in a relationship or a break up... something does not fit our Self anymore. Machines get stressed with time and parts break down. For human beings, it is different; when we get stressed, we get emotional, agitated, scared, anxious, angry, or disempowered and lethargic. If the stress is mild, it can stimulate our creative survival or well-being drives; if it is too high, we may not respond to it with the most creative attitude and, as a result, create more problems. We would not be stressed out if there weren't a part of us that wants something different from what we are experiencing.

Let's look at a simple example. Let's say that I love being around Sally. The more I talk with her, the more attracted I feel to her. As we talk, it becomes obvious that she is from an upper class family whereas I am from a middle class family. She is attached to the upper class lifestyle. At that revelation, I may hear a message in my head, "She's not for me!" Now I have a conflict to resolve.

I may choose to ignore that message as a way to resolve the conflict and invite her on a date and hope that the relationship will work out. I may choose to believe the message without further exploration and never seek a deeper relationship with Sally. Either way, whether I rebel against or obey my inner voice, neither approach will help it go away. It'll come back at the next opportunity. Reacting does not resolve anything.

I may also choose to look more carefully at what just happened in me; that message could have come from different parts of me. It could be that I don't feel good enough. I may have self-esteem issues. The relationship with Sally is giving me an opportunity to challenge how I feel about myself. Or, I could have received the message that I'll never be accepted by the upper class due to my family's worldview that has been passed down for generations. By interacting with Sally, I may become aware that my family's worldview does not define me. Before Sally, I believed that part of my family's worldview defined me. After the proper inner work, a new awareness arises in me, I am free from the old script. After this experience and release, if the same situation arises again, that voice would not have any effect on me. I become free to live the upper class lifestyle. I am freer with Sally than if I kept trying to push down the feeling that she is not for me.

On the other hand, that message could come from a place in me that realizes that I don't want to be limited by the upper class lifestyle. It is not that I don't feel good enough. I am free to enjoy Sally's lifestyle. But I may also want to walk with ease with people of any social status. I may not want to separate myself from my fellow humans just to be with the woman to whom I find myself attracted. I may have to talk with Sally to check how flexible we might be with each other's lifestyles. If it mattered to me, for instance, to work in Africa or South America, would she follow me there?

In the latter case, the inner voice would not have come from an inner tape, but from an inner knowing of who I really am in this moment. That place in me that this kind of inner knowing, my truth, comes from, I call my inner-self. It can also be called my soul or my consciousness.

Of course, the truth may be a combination of these options. I may need to open up to wealth in my life and/or not look down on the upper class lifestyle, while remaining available to people of any social status.

A similar message sometimes comes from both an inner tape and from my inner-self. That can either be comforting or very confusing. An example where it was confusing to me but could have been reassuring is the following. When I went to graduate school to study biostatistics, I experienced a deep conflict. It was tearing me apart. I did not feel I belonged there, not because I was not good at it, but because it did not make my heart sing like I felt when I had begun studying and playing with math. Something was missing. I felt strongly that I would disappoint my father if I did not finish my Ph.D. When we talked about my doubts, my father tried to convince me to finish what I had started. But I could not tell if it was coming from him seeing my best interest or whether it was coming from his dream to have a son with a Ph.D. That conflict was very stressful. I had symptoms for which I went to see a doctor, then a psychiatrist, and then a social worker, as I described in Chapter 2, Life Lessons. In the end, it turned out biostatistics was a gift in my life, something I was good at, providing me with material security, an experience with teamwork on something that mattered to other human beings, and a sense of accomplishment, while I was getting experiences leading me toward my life's purpose. There did not need to be any conflict. My conflict was generated by the belief that I was at odds with my purpose and by my mistrust of authority. My inner tape was playing the tune that I could not trust my father's opinion to continue my Ph.D. My inner-self was encouraging me to continue with my Ph.D. as my father was suggesting. Had I understood this clearly then, there would have been no conflicts.

I may not know the distinction between an inner knowing and an inner tape for sure until I do the introspective work to sort it out. And as long as I don't do this work, I remain in a state of conflict and, thus, I put my life on hold. Furthermore, in a relationship like that with Sally, if I don't do the work necessary to find clarity, I may keep her hostage of my desire to be with her out of my own ignorance. If I pursue a relationship with Sally, wouldn't it be respectful to let her know of my inner truth, whichever it is? As human beings, we don't always do this and yet the truth is likely to come back to haunt us and create strain in the relationship at some point in the future if it is not acknowledged.

We need to sort out these different parts of ourselves in order to get clearer about our motivations and our desires: inner tape, inner-self, and ego. Historically, our language is complicated here. Freud used the terms ego, id, and superego. I use a different language as I wish to be less conceptual and describe more directly our experience. In the yoga culture, the term ego comes from Eastern teachings and is different from Freud's definition of ego. I use the self and the inner-self. The self includes our socially acceptable self, our hurt, our ambitions, and our inner tapes. The inner-self is what holds our truth and our dreams. The self and the inner-self have conscious and unconscious components.

Congruence Between Self and Inner-Self

The cornerstone of mindfulness psychotherapy is that we have an inner-self and a self and a problem arises when the two aren't congruent with each other. In my experience, it is our self that decides, for instance, to take alcohol or drugs, or that gets stuck in misery, experiences injuries, pains or sickness, or mental health challenges; it is never our inner-self. I agree with Jerry Hicks' quote of Abraham: "We feel wonderful when we are in congruence with our inner-self and miserable when we are not."[40] But these experiences of misery, injuries, pains, sickness, or mental health challenges are not negative if we use them to understand how we got there and, therefore, reconnect with who we are thanks to them.

An example of getting my self and inner-self in congruence: I was coming down with the flu one day when I was living at the Yoga Society. I did not want to get sick. I wondered what bothered me. I remembered reading on the refrigerator door, where we left community news on a white board, that we were each supposed to contribute money for a cause. I did not have much money then and felt angry because I was not part of the meeting during which my housemates decided to contribute to this cause. Then I realized I did not have to be passive about it, I could talk to my housemate whose idea it was and let him know I felt in a bind. He had no problems with me not contributing. I had misunderstood the note to mean I *had* to contribute, but it was simply an invitation to contribute. The symptoms of illness immediately disappeared and I did not get sick.

The same is true if I hit my toe against a piece of furniture or get a cut or a burn while cooking... all these little things that happen regularly in life are little warnings that something is off. Sometimes when we don't pay attention to little warnings, we get bigger warnings, and eventually they may become chronic diseases. In the end, it is always time to pay attention to these warnings, no matter how long we have been ignoring them. If we look deeply enough into them, we will inevitably notice that each body pain is an expression of anger or fear we have ignored.

I was helping a woman to look into possible sources for the multiple sclerosis (MS) she had been experiencing for many years. I heard from my intuition the word "adultery." I had never heard that word for anyone else I had worked on so I chose to inquire. Indeed, there was adultery in her life some 20 years earlier, before the symptoms of MS started.

---

[40] J. Hicks (2007). From: *The Astonishing Power of Emotions: Let Your Feelings Be Your Guide*, Hay House.

Luc Watelet

Louise Hay describes in more detail the emotional map of physical pains or injuries (e.g., http://journeysministry.yolasite.com/resources/Heal%20Your%20Body.pdf). For instance, Louise Hay describes knee problems as related to pride and inflexibility. For my part, in my experience, knee pains and injuries have to do with relationship imbalances. The left side is our feminine side, and the right side is our masculine side. So a left knee weakness, or injury, even sustained as a sport's accident, could indicate a tension with a woman in our life, or with the inner feminine.

I have met many people who tell me that their injury was just an accident. Why did the accident affect that particular part of their body and not another? You don't have to believe the mapping by Louise Hay or my suggestion that knee problems have to do with relationships. But you can still inquire, when you or your friends have pains or injuries, if the suggestions by Louise Hay seem to make sense to you or not.

If a client hurts a body part, I find it useful to ask what was triggered emotionally when it happened or what might still trigger them about it emotionally. Inevitably there is fear or anger. And, behind these, is some emotional hurt that was already there prior to the injury.

Look at the history of athletes who hurt a left (or right) knee and then search what happened between this athlete and an important female (or male) relationship around the time of the injury or before.

Trust

Trusting Clients and Trusting Life (Synchronicity)

I want to start with a story Jung tells in his book *Synchronicity*:

> *My example concerns a young woman patient who, in spite of efforts made on both sides, proved to be psychologically inaccessible. The difficulty lay in the fact that she always knew better about everything. Her excellent education had provided her with a weapon ideally suited to this purpose, namely a highly polished Cartesian rationalism with an impeccably "geometrical" idea of reality. After several fruitless attempts to sweeten her rationalism with a somewhat more human understanding, I had to*

confine myself to the hope that something unexpected and irrational would turn up, something that would burst the intellectual retort into which she had sealed herself. Well, I was sitting opposite her one day, with my back to the window, listening to her flow of rhetoric. She had an impressive dream the night before, in which someone had given her a golden scarab — a costly piece of jewelry. While she was still telling me this dream, I heard something behind me gently tapping on the window. I turned round and saw that it was a fairly large flying insect that was knocking against the window-pane from outside in the obvious effort to get into the dark room. This seemed to me very strange. I opened the window immediately and caught the insect in the air as it flew in. It was a scarabaeid beetle, or common rose-chafer (Cetonia aurata), whose gold-green colour most nearly resembles that of a golden scarab. I handed the beetle to my patient with the words, "Here is your scarab." This experience punctured the desired hole in her rationalism and broke the ice of her intellectual resistance. The treatment could now be continued with satisfactory results.[41]

Notice that Jung said he was left to hope something unexpected or irrational would happen. So he was asking for Life to contribute the right experience for his patient to be able to progress. He consciously engaged synchronicity to help with the psychotherapeutic process.

Substance abuse treatment centers have a culture and the clients come from their own as well. There is sometimes a clash between the two. Many counselors have experiences of clients who sound earnest, but relapse, or lie. I was taught in school that building trust is essential in a successful therapeutic relationship. How could I resolve this apparent conflict? Instead of trusting the client unconditionally, I trusted in Life to support the client. That made a big difference in my understanding of building trust.

Jack

Jack could hold his alcohol so well I did not know he was drunk. At the request of an experienced counselor, I gave him a breathalyzer test. He

---

[41] C. G. Jung (1969). *Synchronicity: An Acausal Connecting Principle*. Princeton University Press. pp. 109–110.

came out with 0.40, a level that can be lethal for some people or at the very least affect their memory. Yet when I met him later, and he was sober, he remembered our conversation perfectly.

This story is less about alcoholism than learning to trust Life in helping my client. When I saw him the first time, he was clear that he wanted to be sober. But he had a girlfriend who drank with him and he could not stay sober with her. He knew he would have to leave her if he wanted to succeed. The next time I saw him, he tested positive for alcohol. I had to tell him we could not have a session due to insurance policy and had to dismiss him. He got a ride home. When I told what happened to my supervisor during our next regular meeting, she wanted to send him to an inpatient clinic to get him detoxed, so she wanted to have a meeting to announce her plan to him and his parents.

Jack was 40 years old and already felt humiliated to have to stay with his parents. I knew he would not want his parents involved in this decision. I did not think involving his parents was right in this situation and I did not think the inpatient clinic was the correct first move because we had not given him a chance to prove to himself that he could get sober on his own. I preferred to give Jack an opportunity to take responsibility in changing his life on his own because then he would build self-confidence and self-esteem, rather than imposing a change on him from the outside, which would take his initiative away and may push him into rebellion.

Nevertheless, my supervisor was experienced and believed in her approach. She asked me to call him and set up an appointment with his parents. I did not tell him about the reason for the appointment, just that my supervisor wanted to talk with them as a family. As I suspected, he did not want his mother involved. His father would not come. I left it as, "Just trust, we have to do what my supervisor says, and we will see what happens, okay?" He either trusted me enough or he did not feel he had a choice, so he agreed.

What happened was worthy of a Hollywood movie! Before the appointment, a snow storm started of the likes we had not seen yet that winter and made it impossible for anyone to come to our center. We had to cancel the appointment. My supervisor then said that I should just have my regular appointment with Jack the following week, give him the breathalyzer test and take it from there.

When he came to our regular appointment, the breathalyzer test came back negative. He told me he spent the weekend at his girlfriend's drinking as always and then she pulled a knife at him and drew blood on his chest. He called the police and asked to be driven back home. He had preferred to be with her rather than be with his parents to keep a sense of personal freedom, but now he was done with her. He'd been sober since. I was afraid that for his health he should not stop so abruptly given the quantity of alcohol he'd gotten accustomed to drinking regularly. His response was that he'd done it before. He knew himself. He could do it. I tested him at each of our sessions per protocol. The tests remained negative for the next six months until he graduated successfully from our program.

Jeremy

At the center, there was a gentleman who was in a group I had led a few times, so I knew him a little. I never had a private session with him. Jeremy seemed honest and genuine in his desire to be and remain sober, and to turn his life around. He was happy with his progress. I have met many people who appear genuine, but are not; they just know how to play the system. I did not have that feeling from him, although I was open to being wrong.

Like any other client in his situation, he had signed a contract with the center before starting his program that he would not use opiate-based drugs, including prescribed medication, during his time at the center. Many pain medicines are opiate-based. One day, he was caught using opiate-based medication after a routine drug test. It was his first mistake in the program after being an active and model client for at least a year.

I talked to Jeremy privately to ask him what truly happened. He explained that it was an honest mistake. He had trusted the doctor to prescribe what was okay for him and did not double check. He knew the counselors felt he was trying to fool the system and was pretending innocence. He felt wrongly accused. He really did not want to go to the inpatient clinic because he had given it all he had for his recovery up to then and did not want to start from the beginning as if all the work he had done was worth nothing. I could sense his feeling of powerlessness in the face of authority not trusting him. I could also sense that sending him to an inpatient clinic would reawaken a deep feeling of rebellion in him. I encouraged him to tell his truth, as he had spoken it to me, to the director of the center. But he felt too embarrassed and untrusting of the system to do so.

We discussed Jeremy's case at a counselors' meeting and everyone believed that Jeremy needed proper consequences for his behavior. For the reader who does not know substance abuse treatment centers, you have to understand the pressure counselors are under, not only the workload, but also the responsibility to the insurance companies. People who are in active addiction can play a really good game to get their fix. It is easy to be fooled and it does not look good for a center to be played by a client. Despite this, I thought I should speak up. I asked if anyone had heard Jeremy's version of the situation. No one had. I shared my private conversation with him and urged someone to speak to him, to hear his views before sending him to an inpatient clinic and possibly pushing him into rebellion. I had done what I could but I did not think anyone thought much of what I said. If Jeremy did not speak up for himself and change his attitude toward authority, he could pay the consequences.

Someone in a position of authority decided to have a private conversation with Jeremy as a result of what I said during the meeting. She came out of their meeting agreeing with me and he did not have to go to the inpatient clinic. I spoke with him afterwards to check whether he understood the risks he took in not trusting authority and avoiding to speak up for himself. He understood.

Jill

Jill was a model client in recovery. She had started using drugs around the age of 11 and had learned to survive the street drug scene. She approached life as a no nonsense leader and let no one make decisions for her until she realized she needed to attend our recovery program. Then she learned to rely on the counselors' advice and experience.

Among our clients, she continued to be a gentle leader by her presence. She was not authoritative. She was not judgmental. She led from her determination to be sober and from her experience on the street. She had a beautiful light about her.

One day Jill disappeared. When she came back, I learned that she had relapsed. I noticed her light had dimmed. She was carrying a lot of shame from what she had done. I took a moment with her alone to ask her what happened. What I got from her was that she had started to use drugs again with an old boyfriend and he would not come off of it with her. I reflected back to her what I understood: "So you had a boyfriend who was still using drugs. You thought you could help him out by using drugs with him again as before, but this time by encouraging him to stop with you at some point and it did not work. He still wanted to use when you offered him an out." "Yes, that's pretty much it," she said still defeated. I told her: "The way I see it, you tried saving someone you care deeply about! It failed. I don't think you'll want to try this method, again, right? But didn't you think it was worth trying?" She smiled and thanked me. She'd never heard anyone at substance abuse treatment centers talk this way. She could now forgive herself and move on. Her natural and beautiful light came back.

Later she said in group that I should work with women because I was an example of a man who they could trust after so many experiences with men they could not trust.

Jude

Jude had a history of bending the truth. He was married. He was having a hard time at work and tried to use an *Attention Deficit Hyperactivity Disorder* (ADHD) type drug to give him the mindset to accomplish his responsibilities. But one thing led to another and he was tempted by heavier drugs. His wife was a strong woman who knew not to be an enabler (someone who supports consciously or unconsciously someone's poor behavior). She loved him and was determined to get him off drugs and save their marriage.

The way Jude spoke, one could not tell if he was being secretive in order to manipulate or from lack of self-awareness. Though when you asked him a question he had not thought about, he really thought about it and gave you an answer that felt honest. I started with some suspicion about his real motivation for being at the center. He did not want to lose his marriage, but felt in a bind at work. He needed a healthy solution for his feelings of being ineffective at work. I learned to trust him as we worked together.

We had a new wrench in our relationship when the doctor who prescribed him a drug to help him off opiates started to feel suspicious because Jude was asking for more of it sooner than he should have. Jude told him he had lost part of a bottle he was prescribed. But in explaining what happened he seemed evasive. The doctor wondered if Jude was reselling some on the street. Since I was the responsible counselor, the doctor spoke to me. His lack of trust in Jude led him to consider terminating his role as Jude's prescribing doctor. I told him to hold off on making a decision until I spoke with Jude but that in my experience the evasiveness did not come from a lack of commitment toward his recovery but from a lack of clarity about himself. My trust in Jude was a little shaken up because there was a small voice in me that suspected exactly what the doctor expressed. So I promised I would look into it. Jude never failed a drug test during his recovery under my guidance, and he did not fail at his next visit.

I told him I had a conversation with his prescribing doctor and asked him if he was aware the doctor felt he was being evasive. He was aware he was being evasive. It was because he was embarrassed at what happened that led him to ask for extra help from the doctor. We talked about the perception of honesty in the way we give information. He understood and promised to be more direct.

The doctor was not completely convinced from my account and told me he wanted to have a meeting with Jude and his wife to have a clearer picture of what was really going on. I welcomed that. The result was that the doctor ended up seeing it my way. He was completely convinced by Jude's wife and her directness, and ended up trusting Jude from then on.

Jude continued to pass his drug tests without a glitch and graduated from our program.

It is harder to talk about cases where you really don't trust a client. Perhaps someone is in danger depending on your talking about it. Not everyone I dealt with was trustworthy. Sometimes you are lucky to hear from someone who wishes to speak on the condition of anonymity because they were threatened not to share what they know. In such cases, you may have to call the police. I always trust that Life can guide me and all parties involved get to the best decisions.

I hope these examples show the difference between trusting blindly someone and trusting that by keeping an open line of communication and an open mind and heart about Life, that the most supportive outcome can become clear even if it is a group decision.

Jean

This is a different story. It is an interesting account of how Life creates situations that become positive learning experiences.

Jean just lost her husband. She had always been a wife and mother and had never thought of her own life. Jean was in a state of shock and perhaps depression, not having any further goals in life that she was aware of and not wanting to draw attention to herself. One day, her caregiver and daughter A. called her to tell her she was going to the food store before coming over to visit her and would she want anything? The mother answered casually that she was okay but she was on the floor and couldn't get up. She had dragged herself to her bedroom hoping she could more easily grab onto something to help herself up, but could not. "Hang on mom!" A. told her, "I am coming over immediately!"

A. drove so fast that a trooper stopped her and asked her why she was driving so fast. A. was a little annoyed at the delay, explained the situation and the trooper seemed not to believe her. A. got her mother on the phone and handed her phone to him to prove she wasn't lying. The trooper told her he would send the medics and the police to her mom's address and her mother better be as she stated to him when they find her. "Fine!" A. said, "Thank you!" "And drive at the speed limit," the police continued, "they will be there when you arrive home."

When she got to her mother's home, the medics and the police were there and they found Jean on the floor. The medics checked for any damage to her body and brain. They did everything that A. could not have done. So it was a blessing that A. was stopped by a trooper who sent in the medics. Jean was lucky that she had nothing hurt.

The funny thing is Jean had an emergency bracelet and she could have called the medics herself all along, but instead had chosen to remain on the floor for a couple of hours instead of "making a fuss." So A. pointed out to her that instead she ended up with a bigger fuss! The mother promised that next time she would press her emergency button.

When a therapist trusts Life, her clients learn their lessons from their experiences, and the therapist is present to help them through, if needed. The therapist then works with Life and the client as a team. The cognitive work alone can only go so far, compared to experience. In turn, Life experiences that are understood and integrated help clients trust themselves and, in turn, helps them trust their therapist. This nurtures further healing.

Earning the Trust of Clients / Holding One's Space

If, as therapists, we trust our trustworthy clients, we earn their trust. It is important to earn their trust because often people who seek therapy have been or have felt abused or betrayed. Their suspicion level is high and they may be on constant alert. I have a client who trusts so few people that I am amazed she keeps on trusting me. *I asked her what makes her continue to trust me, even when I argue with her. She told me that my body language, my eyes, and my words are always in congruence. She does not trust people who show any sign of incongruence.*

As a therapist, you have to be clear about which side you are on. Clients have different parts to them. If their ego feels bruised, are you taking the side of their soul without telling them, or a societal or parental side? If you do couple therapy after having met only with one member of the couple, your original client, you may suddenly discover that the partner is not the demon you were led to believe. You may then see that your client has a distorted perception of reality. They may both have distorted views of each other. So when you talk to each of them in front of the other, you may give the impression that you are taking sides with one or the other. Or they may both have the impression you are taking side with the other. You need to be clear with yourself about the position you are coming from. I side with the truth, which is often hidden from all parties. This allows me to not take side with a person against another, but to seek the truth together.

With one couple, I really liked having the feedback in therapy from the one who wasn't my original client because that person's viewpoint was forcing my client to face issues I did not know how to help her face without triggering deep resistance in her. When I approached the issues, my client could not see there were different realities and that her perception of reality was only one perception. She believed her perception was the only truth. I knew her perception was rarely the truth because I knew other people who experienced being judged wrongly by her. I ended up telling my client, when I was welcoming feedback from her partner, that I was taking the side of her soul and it just happened that her partner represented that side at that time. I was the only person from whom she sought advice who defended her partner. But I was also the only person who had talked with him. That made my position delicate because everyone else who was giving advice, and was also in a position of authority to her, was telling her she was being abused and she should leave him. And it is true that he was abusive in some ways, but this did not mean that what he had to say should be ignored. Negotiating land mines like this is not unusual in therapy.

Part of what I do, aside from being congruent with myself, is that I hold my space. The concept of holding one's space is important. When someone is upset with you about something you have done or said, you need to ask yourself if you owe an apology to that person, if you did what you did to the best of your ability, or both. If you decide to stick to your deed or words, then you need not feel guilty about it no matter how much the other person blames you. You simply fill yourself with the knowing that you did the best you could. You love yourself for what you did and wait for the other person to take responsibility for his feelings. If you do not hold your space, if you bend under the feeling of shame or guilt, you become a victim of manipulation and you dilute the responsibility the other person needs to face.

This is especially confusing in families with alcoholism or drugs. Say the husband is an alcoholic and the wife is not. If she does not hold her space, she will either become an enabler or a nagging wife. Either behavior will not get the husband to take responsibility for his behavior.

169

Instead, she needs to be clear in her heart what she wants and does not want in her life. If she does not mind that he drinks, then there is nothing to do. If she is clear she wants a sober husband to be able to have clear conversations with, then she needs to hold that dream in her heart and not let anything disturb it, not his behavior, not what she believed about him in the past, not what other people say. And she needs to stop trying to get him to change as well. She gives him total freedom, but she holds her space in her heart with love toward herself and his choices. Only then does he come to feel his responsibility and then can make up his own mind about how he wants to live.

Psychotherapy

Freud is the founder of talk therapy. Our gratitude to him cannot be measured, whether we agree with his therapy legacy or not. Two of the most famous students of Freud, Adler and Jung, both physicians as well, have a place in today's mainstream psychology courses and have had deep influences on the evolution of psychotherapy. Both Adler and Jung had profound disagreements with Freud and separated themselves from Freud's influence creating their own psychotherapeutic systems.

According to Jung, all three created a vision of psychotherapy according to their personality types (which Myers Briggs popularized from Jung's work). Jung was less driven by theory than by experiencing and discovering. His theories come from experience and not in trying to explain experience. Adler's legacy is profound as well as he was focused on the reality of the circumstances in a person's life. From the three, I prefer Jung's inquiry, because it is the most freeing to me and the most compatible with my personality. I also know that all three brought important legacies which we may be able to integrate, if not in their details, at least in their spirit.

I am a truth seeker – the healing truth. I want total freedom as a therapist. I want to be informed by my colleagues, yet I don't want to be bound by the limitations of the medical and scientific paradigms. Jung had already warned about being too constricted by science:

> Anyone who wants to know the human psyche will learn next to nothing from experimental psychology. He would be better advised to abandon exact science, put away his scholar's gown, bid farewell

to his study, and wander with human heart through the world. There in the horrors of prisons, lunatic asylums and hospitals, in drab suburban pubs, in brothels and gambling-hells, in the salons of the elegant, the Stock Exchanges, socialist meetings, churches, revivalist gatherings and ecstatic sects, through love and hate, through the experience of passion in every form in his own body, he would reap richer stores of knowledge than text-books a foot thick could give him, and he will know how to doctor the sick with a real knowledge of the human soul.[42]

~ Carl G. Jung

Jung asks us to learn about the human heart and feel the world with the heart. One problem with science is that, through it, we look for a method that can be applied to a large group of people. Science becomes a filter between the therapist and the client. The solutions I find come from exploring the subjective, what makes the client unique and to help the client love himself as he is. Furthermore, I believe each client has his own life to live that has to do with his inner-self. The discordance between the life to be lived (related to the inner-self true wants and needs) and the life being lived is reflected in the out of control feeling experienced by the client. Since the solution is inside the client, I need the freedom to explore that inside with my clients. I need a client-driven approach to therapy. If science can make space to explore the subjective and not impose a solution from the outside, then we will make progress.

I want more for my clients than be guided by the ethics of: 1) Do no harm and 2) Do not create dependence. Instead, I want to be inspired by the intention to: 1) Heal and 2) Free. I want my clients to be better when they meet with me, and to be able to continue their work by themselves when they are ready. I am not here to create clients, but to help people be ten times better at healing themselves than I am at healing myself or than I am at guiding their healing. (This is in a true spirit of freedom. My yoga teacher Yogi Bhajan always said he was not here to create students, he was here to create teachers, and he wished for all of us teachers to be ten times better teachers than he was.)

---

[42] C. G. Jung (1992). *Two Essays on Analytical Psychology*, Appendix I: New Paths in Psychology, Collected Works of C.G. Jung, Vol. 7, London: Routledge, Psychology Press, pp. 246-7.

Therefore, I am not relying on psychology alone. I study healing from both traditional healers and from spiritual masters to understand human nature and the healing process.

I dream of a humanity where my work as a psychotherapist is no longer necessary because, in that world, everyone knows how to do this work for themselves and/or with their friends.

Mindfulness and Introspection

I had a client in addiction recovery who was upset with me because I asked him questions about his life unrelated to the problem of addiction. I told him: "If you don't discover and establish a relationship with a part of you that is not interested in addiction, how will you ever find a reason, which comes from you and not from the outside world, to leave addiction behind?"

Mindfulness is being in the present with me, my mind, my feelings, and my body. It is about getting to know me now without the filter of someone else's judgment or idea about me. I pay attention to and accept me, what motivates me, what triggers me, what I love, and what I don't love, without judgment and without reaction. And if I have a judgment or a reaction, I notice it and accept that as well.

For instance, a mindfulness practice could be simply about feeling all the sensations about my breathing, in and out. Being aware of how long I inhale and how long I exhale. Being aware of which parts of my body are receiving my breaths and how my breathing affects my body, my mind, and how I feel. Cleaning my house mindfully (karma yoga) means to do each task, such as sweeping, vacuuming, doing the dishes, or cooking, etc., by being totally present to that task and, if my mind is distracted, to bring my awareness back to the task at hand. Being mindful is a practice.

In comparison, an introspective practice is a specific inquiry into something I don't have a good grasp on about my experience/life. It is using mindfulness in a very specific way for a specific outcome: understanding oneself in a particular situation. Introspection is never about looking at the past or the future; it is looking at the present experience of memories or stories about the past or the future. For instance, a woman may reflect on a rape experience that happened 50 years ago and cry about the experience as if she were still there. A day or two later, she may reflect on how that experience helps her appreciate and honor her feminine nature in a way she would have never thought possible before. Introspection is a specific way to use mindfulness.

With clients, I use introspection and mindfulness with inquiry and experiencing what is going on in the body in relation to specific emotional concerns, with guided visualizations and playing with shifts of perspectives or worldviews. I might also encourage my clients to be creative with a specific focus such as "What is self-love for you?", using poetry, painting, dance, etc., depending on my client's natural interests.

Metaphor

Looking for the metaphor a disease or mental health challenge represents in one's life is one method of inquiry that is very powerful. It may not always be the right approach for someone. But if it were right for a client, it would work something like this. For instance, someone struggling with an auto-immune disease might reflect that her body's defense system is not protecting her against external attacks. What could this be a metaphor for in her life? One possible metaphor is that she is allowing other people's thinking to overrule her own thoughts, or she is allowing external negativity to control her mood. We have to look for the right metaphor for the person with whom we are working and given the symptoms she is experiencing. Sometimes we have to find very specific words which hit the mark just right and only then will a shift occur in the client.

Someone with cancer may reflect that the cancer cells are growing without control and drawing the life out of him. What could be the metaphor in this man's life? Perhaps some brooding thoughts are gnawing at him and he cannot control how these thoughts grow in his psyche, literally having a life of their own and taking the life out of him.

Someone with a chronic cough may be trying to cough a secret off his chest his family had always kept.

For someone with major depressive disorder the image "depressed" is very descriptive. The obvious question is, "What is stealing the joy/passion away?"

Someone in delusion is escaping something from reality. The obvious question is, "What could that be?"

Instead of thinking that something is wrong with the person because there is a disease or a mental health challenge, the metaphor work assumes everything is exactly right as it is in response to the current circumstances and to use the disease or mental health challenge as a metaphorical clue to figure out what the real problem is. That problem usually has solutions. And when the solution is found, the problem disappears.

Mindlessness

There is a kind of meditation called mindlessness. It simply means to leave all thoughts behind. This is not "trying or practicing to have no thoughts," or "trying or practicing to have a blank mind." It is recognizing that there are other things in life than our thoughts and we choose to pay attention to these other things, as a result we stop paying attention to and engaging with our mind and any thought going through our mind. We can, instead, pay attention to a beautiful image of nature, listen to a calming piece of music (Note to musicians: without analyzing it!), open our heart to beauty and peace and joy and harmony, and practice remaining stable with that feeling. Taking a walk in nature and choosing to appreciate what surrounds us, really leaving all other concerns behind, is entering mindlessness. We give our self a chance to separate our mind from the problem.

When one is able to do this, one feels refreshed and is able to look at a previously distressing situation with more calm, from a fresh perspective.

With clients, I might encourage walks in nature, and also creative adventures, but without a specific inquiry, simply for the fun of being fully in the moment. I might encourage also being creative just for fun and being curious at what comes out. It is a return to the child's approach to living, removing the burden of practicality and productivity and financial return on one's investment.

Neuroscience

In a recent article,[43] Deborah Becker discusses meditation in the treatment of people in addiction recovery. A seven year sober practitioner said, "When I take the time to be mindful, I am improving my conscious contact with something bigger than myself, and I'm able to really see why I'm here, [...] I've connected to a purpose. For me, that's recovery." The article goes on to say that scientists are now attempting to demonstrate this statement

This article supports my claim about the importance of connecting with our genuine self in addiction recovery. It is not surprising to me that the area of the brain involved in addictive behavior, that the article refers to as the "brain default network" (neuroscience terminology), is also involved in many mental illness disorders such as autism, schizophrenia, and Alzheimer's disease.[44] This last article mentions that depression, obsessional disorders, attention-deficit/hyperactivity disorder, and post-traumatic stress disorder have also been found by researchers to have links to the brain default network. Given the role of the brain default network in both addiction and mental health challenges, I would not be surprised if it were shown scientifically that meditation has a positive effect for people who suffer from mental illnesses, as well.

In overcoming overwhelming anxiety from childhood, Buddhist monk Yongey Mingyur Rinpoche writes:

Through the patient tutoring of experts in the fields of psychology and neuroscience, like Francisco Varela, Richard Davidson, Dan Coleman, and Tara Bennett-Coleman, I've begun to recognize why, from an objective scientific perspective, the [Buddhist] practices actually work: that feelings of limitation, anxiety, fear, and so on are just so much neuronal gossip. They are, in essence, habits. And

---

[43] D. Becker, July, 2014, reported by 90.0 WBUR Boston's NPR radio station, retrieved on July 7, 2016, from
http://www.wbur.org/commonhealth/2014/07/10/addiction-brain.
[44] Buckner, Andrews-Hannah, and Schacter (2008). *The Brain's Default Network,* Annals of the N. Y. Academy of Sciences, 1124: 1-38.

habits can be unlearned.[45]

In conclusion, what neuroscience tells us is that part of our brain default network is wired with neuron connections that are triggered by certain situations in life that are still painful to us. Those responses may lead us into darkness and addictions or mental health challenges. These parts of our brain default network act as an inner government to which we have given our power. Our work is to reclaim our power and consciously choose our inner government to replace the default one. With myself, my clients and students, I work on an inner government based on joy, love, peace and harmony. It is a moment to moment work that can only be taken on with awareness and mindfulness. At a conceptual level, self-love is this commitment to our self to choosing the inner government of our choice, and happiness is the name of that government. Not a happiness that ignores everything that does not feel happy, not an autocratic happiness, a happiness based on a commitment to being true to oneself with awareness, wisdom, patience, and honesty.

Self-Love Revisited

What Is Self-Love? How Do You Pass it on?

Loving Myself

What is self-love in practice? The best way to know if I grasp something is if I can teach it to someone else. It took me a while to understand how to do that with self-love. The first time I became aware of the concept of self-love was when a friend asked me to look into a mirror and tell myself, "I love you!" At the time, it felt extremely uncomfortable to me and trite. I did not feel tears or sadness. I did not feel that I did not love myself and needed to learn something. I was blind to what I was missing. I was disconnected from self-love. But I knew how to love others with kindness and acceptance and no judgment. So I taught by example; by showing how I love the person who wanted to learn self-love from me. But it wasn't enough because then people relied on me to feel loved, but not on themselves.

---

[45] Y. M. Rinpoche (2008). *The Joy of Living: Unlocking the Secret and Science of Happiness*, Harmony Books, p. 47.

Furthermore, because I mistrusted other people's love, I needed to learn to love myself and, in the process, learn to trust being loved. Experience would help me find the words to pass it on.

The second time I was hit by the concept of self-love was at a time when very little money was coming into my life. That led to a divorce, foreclosure, bankruptcy, and not being able to live close to my son. I felt unsupported and scared and terribly lonely. I did not trust anything or anyone. I kept trying to create businesses without success. Not knowing where to turn for help, I did a labyrinth walk trying to get some clarity about my financial affairs. Before the walk, the facilitator had us draw a card at random. Each card had a different word on it. We were to think deeply about what we wished an answer to and draw a card. The card I drew had the word LOVE on it. I did not understand. I needed money. I needed to be able to afford a roof over my head and pay for food and child support. I was crying for help inside. I did not know where to turn. And this is all the universe could give me, a card with the word LOVE on it! It ended up being the perfect word for me... as I figured out later.

At some point, I decided that instead of being concerned about my material needs, I would give myself time to experience joy. I had to let go of the fear that leaving behind material need concerns would lead to a disaster and trust that I was always protected and safe. I had to let go of my concerns for the outside world and care about me.

An Experience of Teaching Self-Love

A client was in a relationship in which he had put a lot of hope, but now he felt manipulated and trapped in it. He had tried to get out of it but kept staying in it. At some point I told him, "It is not about her, it is not about the rest of the world, it is about you!" He looked puzzled. "It is about loving yourself!" I said. Again it seems those words did not mean anything to him. "But she is the one making my life miserable!" He said incredulous. "Give it a chance!" I said, "Just take a moment to love yourself!" "When I love myself, I don't want her in my life!" he said. "You are angry, right?" I said. "Damn, right!" he said. "Ok! But that's still being concerned with how she does not love you!" I said, "Let go of her, let go of needing her, let go of not needing her!" "Ok," he said. "Now let nature love you (he was not particularly a believer in God)!" I said, "Is there a person, a being, you can allow to love you?" "No, not now..." he

177

said. "So then remember when was the first time that you felt unloved," I said, "How old were you?" "Really young, four or five," he said. "So love the boy you were then, can you do that?" "Oh! I can hug him!" he said. "How does that feel?" I asked. "Real good!" he said, "I have never felt that before." "Good, in that space, can you let anyone else love you, like animals in the wild or a being you feel inspired by like Gandhi, or the Buddha, or Mother Teresa?" I asked. "I feel loved in nature," he said. "So how do you feel about your lady friend now?" I asked. "It isn't about her," he said. "That's self-love!" I said.

Self-Love: Naked to Oneself

Self-love is about learning to be true to our self no matter what others might say, or what others' reactions might be. Self-love is about risking to tell one's truth in a relationship, even if it means potentially feeling, or even being, rejected. Holding one's space and loving our self for it. Learning about self-love requires time alone outside of social pressures to learn what is natural and spontaneous to us, and also to learn what it is like to live with our self – with our mind and thoughts, and with our body – to learn to love who we are because no one else is there to love us. Self-love is learning to turn loneliness (fear) into aloneness (contentment).

Self-love can only happen if we let go completely of the need to be loved by others. This need feels like neediness to others and puts people off or leads them to shy away from us. That need limits us, consciously or unconsciously, to receiving only love in the way that we think we want, not in all its abundant and exuberant fragrances. Without self-love, we control and constrict the way Life flows in us. We create lack and misery. By letting go of that need, we free others to love us, in their own ways, without expectations on how that should look. In turn, we allow the world to give us infinitely more than we knew was possible.

I put together a few stories that show the diversity that self-love work takes for different people. Some of these stories are about a deep self-love lifetime quest and others are steps toward self-love.

From Worry to Joy

My personal quest was about overcoming worrying and embracing joy. It was interesting how working on joy shifted things. I did not understand how at first. I realized, I also had to consciously stop the inner worrying as soon as I became aware of it. Then I started to understand how I experienced freedom. Cutting off worrying and opening to joy may be intertwined, but are not quite the same. I think it is because worrying was in my brain default neuron connections, and they had to be undone. My mind was falling back on those connections spontaneously without my noticing it.

Letting Go of the Victim

E. had a history of childhood abuse and, as an adult, chose partners who were abusive to her. She behaved, she thought, as a dutiful wife. When I saw her she thought of herself as though God had meant for her to be abused all her life. She could not see herself any differently. Aside from exploring her attraction toward abuse, I wanted to help her connect with something beautiful in her. I saw in her the talents of an artist and inquired about her exploring that. She did, and although I noticed her developing an interest in her creative abilities, her adventure with art did not seem to awaken her out of the abusive scene. She kept relationships with people who could be kind, but could also be hurtful.

I had heard of experiments to help women with a history of abuse in which they were brought together with men with no abusive history. The men were trained to listen with their hearts to these women telling their stories and to offer a genuine apology, as if they had been the perpetrators. According to the account, these apologies were heartfelt and had a profoundly healing effect on the women. I thought I would like to offer an apology to E. for the abuse she had received in her life. But I wanted to be in my heart when I did it. I did not want to be a detached observer offering an intellectual apology. I knew I had possibly only one shot at this because if my attempt failed, a second attempt would trigger her as not being sincere. I asked Life to guide the process and expected an opportunity would come but I did not know how.

The next time I saw E., I asked her a question about her past and she responded with her typical detachment about some of the abuse to

Luc Watelet

which she had been subjected, but then she shifted to saying with some energy that she can't trust anyone. And, she added: "Not even you!" I understood where she was coming from. If she trusted anyone, she was at risk of being betrayed, which would be worse than just being abused and expecting it. So I said that I understood. But she repeated it: "Not even you!" And she said it again. By then I started to hear it differently. I was no longer in my mind, compassionately understanding, I was in my heart and I felt the pain of not being able to trust anyone. I had tears in my eyes. And I said: "If I ever said or did anything that felt hurtful to you, I am sorry, I would never want to hurt you!" She was listening very deeply. "And," I continued, "I want to apologize for all the people who have ever hurt you!" She was a little taken aback, "No one has ever said that to me..." she said, very moved. Then, as though forcing herself back to reality, she readjusted herself, "but I still cannot trust anyone." A couple of days later, I received a phone call from E. She had decided she wanted my help, she was ready to let go of the victim in her. I was thrilled. But then, at our next meeting, she was back to her former self believing that there was no way out of being a martyr for the rest of her life.

So I wondered what else I could do. I decided to try something against the code of ethics we were taught. According to our code, we are not supposed to socialize with our clients. I decided to invite her to a party with many of my friends.

I had been inspired by an intervention by Caesar Millan during an episode of the TV series: *The Dog Whisperer*. In that particular story, there was a dog who was aggressive toward the boyfriend of the woman who owned it. The boyfriend was ready to bail on the relationship. The dog was never allowed in the presence of other dogs and never left to sniff other dogs. Caesar decided to introduce the aggressive dog to his pack of dogs. The idea was that the aggressive dog no longer knew what it was to be a dog, whereas his pack of dogs knew how to be dogs. The pack of dogs, in a way, retrained the aggressive dog by establishing hierarchy the way dogs do including sniffing each other. After a while, Caesar took the woman's dog out of his pack and reacquainted him with his owner and her boyfriend. The dog was transformed.

I thought that by introducing E. to my friends, who are not abusive, something would shift in her and she would be able to see that she could belong among people who know how to be kind and respectful. It worked. Soon after that, E. started to be involved with groups of people who were respectful of her and with whom she was able to discover other parts of herself. And my code of ethics was respected again as she did not end up being a part of my social life.

For E., self-love involved feeling that she could belong with people who know how to respect others, and also with people who did not see her as a victim.

Rich and Poor

A Catholic priest friend of mine told me this story. Early on in his career, he was assigned to a parish and he soon realized that rich people came to one of his Sunday services and poor people to the other. He decided to hold only one service followed by a reception where he invited rich and poor to mingle. Within two months, every poor person from his parish who did not yet have a job ended up with a job. And this remained true for the years that he remained responsible for that parish.

From this example, the solution to poverty is simple. It needs to start at a community level by consciously breaking the cycle of social stigma of poverty and the schism between rich and poor. Once we solve poverty locally in enough communities, it will soon be solved at a state level and then at the country level. It wouldn't take too long to solve it worldwide.

Racial, Sexist, and Sexual Orientation Stigmas

There is a similar issue that needs to be addressed between races, between men and women, and between people of different sexual orientations. As long as we focus on past grudges, we can't see the real person. *We need to get off script, our own and the one inherited culturally, to be alive to each other.* The day we will come together to play, to allow ourselves to meet each other genuinely, and not to focus on fixing problems, that day we will start loving each other.

Luc Watelet

Self-Acceptance

S. asked me to help her with self-acceptance. She knew she was a people pleaser and that had led her into decades of hardship, including addictions. By the time I met her, she had been sober for over two years. For over two years of therapy, she did not understand that she interpreted others through a filter of paranoia. She interpreted people's words and deeds in ways that justified her suspicion that they could not be trusted. She grew enough to allow a man in her life. He helped her see that her suspicions were not always real. But mainly she did not feel loved the way she was hoping to feel in that relationship and that led her to understand that she had to take responsibility for herself and her life in a way she had not been able to see before. She was able to start letting go of her need to be a people pleaser because she finally saw that it was not giving her what she really wanted. People simply took advantage of her people pleasing approach to life.

For S., self-love came as an awareness that she can't wait for others to give her what she really wants, that she is the only one who can give herself what she really wants.

Hating Oneself

When I asked M. what she thought of self-love, she immediately said that her problem was that she hated parts of herself and that she spent her whole time trying to fix them. We become aware of the parts in us we dislike by the way we don't feel loved or accepted by others. We can only really change if we learn to accept ourselves first exactly as we are.

For M., relaxing into self-acceptance of those parts by truly feeling them was part of learning about self-love.

Alcoholic Father

W. had an alcoholic father. She made the decision to keep her distance from him. Despite that she felt uncomfortable around people who drink. Distinguishing what aspects of her father's alcoholic behavior felt painful to her, and not just blaming it all on alcohol use, became an aspect of the process of self-love.

Using Jung's Personality Types as a Tool to Self-Love

Q. had trouble with one man in her life and thinking of him brought her to tears. After a few questions, Q. said that during a conversation they had in which she opened up to him about feeling misunderstood by him, he also acknowledged that she did not get him. I spoke to her about Jung's personality types popularized by Myers and Briggs as MBTI. I suspected that their personality types were opposites of each other. My assumption was correct.

A little background about personality types: Jung found that we have rational functions (thinking (T) and feeling (F)) and a-rational functions (intuition (N) and sensing (S)). Thinking is the ability to play with logic; feeling is the ability to evaluate feelings, or art, or how colors or patterns look together. Intuition is about having an ease with abstract notions and sensing is about being down to earth and practical. Aside from these functions we can also be introvert or extravert, and judging (having things decided) or perceiving (open to the process). What Jung discovered is that one cannot simultaneously use the two rational functions together or the two a-rational functions together. For instance, one cannot evaluate how different clothes colors and styles work together while being in logic mode. Or one cannot juggle with abstract notions while learning to fix a car. One has to choose between the two functions within the rational ones or the a-rational ones. But we can use a rational and an a-rational function together, actually it is impossible not to. For instance, using N (intuition) and T (thinking) together is useful to a scientist, using S (sensing) and F (feeling) is useful at a party or doing interior decorating, using N (intuition) and F (feeling) is useful when studying mythology or writing fiction, and using S (sensing) and T (thinking) is useful to a lawyer, a historian, or a journalist. We also each have a dominant function, and the opposite, the inferior function, is typically one we have some difficulty accessing. With our inferior function, at least in the beginning, we tend to be in or out, we are less subtle about it than with our other functions. The other two functions are usually relatively easy to access and may be more or less balanced.

Not only do people have a personality type, but cultures do as well. I see the USA as an ST culture, Germany as an NT culture, and France as an NF culture. The French part of Belgium and Quebec are SF cultures.

Luc Watelet

Cultures are also extraverted like the USA, or Quebec, or introverted like Germany. You might notice that the USA is also known for Hollywood which has a strong NF/SF side. Each of us has its opposite within as well. For instance, a natural ST may have exhilarating NF moments.

Back to Q. Not only did she have the opposite personality type from the gentleman with whom she felt at odds, but her type is also opposite to that of the culture in which she lived. She was already feeling oppressed or not fully accepted in her culture, so when she faced the gentlemen with whom she felt at odds, he represented to her that very culture and she feared not being liked by him.

For her, self-love was helped by understanding that she was perfectly fine, even if her personality did not fit the ideal of the culture in which she lived. Two weeks after our conversation about personality types she told me with a big smile there was no more tension in her relationship with the gentleman.

In each case, an inner government based on love was offered to replace an inner government that led to an experience of misery.

The Inner Government Named Happiness

Happiness is not a feeling you wait for. It is a choice, no matter how you feel, to be grateful for being alive, to be grateful for experiencing whatever it is that is coming to you and learning from it, to be grateful for the ability to overcome challenges, and to be passionate about something especially about life and to share that passion.

Mindfulness Psychotherapy

To me, mindfulness psychotherapy is a blend of learning self-love, mindfulness, and mindlessness in order to access one's truth, essence, and soul.

But therapy is a two-way street: 1) helping clients become mindful of their experiences and motivations, and 2) being aware of my own experiences and motivations in relation to the therapeutic process and therapeutic relationship(s).

In the previous chapter and in this one, I describe with many stories how Life is a multi-dimensional representation of who we are and that by paying attention to it, by establishing a relationship and engaging with it, we heal and grow; that is, we live more fully, with more awareness and more joy. In mindfulness therapy, the role of the therapist is not to label and treat as that would ignore all the gifts provided by Life in support of our clients' healing process and our own. Instead, the role of the therapist is twofold: 1) to help clients understand why Life is operating as it is in their lives and, 2) to understand why we, as therapists, need the experience of this particular client with his particular struggle.

Therefore, to be in therapy mode I have to be present to my client and to myself. To find the right questions, I start with natural questions; I follow my instincts and natural curiosity to get to know the person who seeks my help. I ask questions by trying to avoid making assumptions, by following the conversation closely, and by making sure I correctly understand what is shared.

I often think the conversation has a consciousness of its own. I start with intention and then let the conversation unfold. The first intention is to get to the crux of the problem, usually where there is a misalignment between outer desires and inner desires. The second intention might be to find a way for the client to receive the information or experience required for a healing shift in perception. Another source that guides my questions is the quest to understand my client's soul and deepest dreams. If the difficulties in life are the result of a disconnection between one's outer and one's inner life, life's experiences are a clue as to what people are or are not paying attention to that matters in order to reconnect with their inner life.

I follow the conversation by paying attention to my client as much as I pay attention to what is happening within me. A pain in my heart may mean my client is in pain or it may mean I need to pay attention to something in me. A sensation of a hit in my belly may be sudden fear in me or in my client. I may also remember situations from my life that help me understand my client's story. Sometimes I share what I experienced, or am experiencing in the moment, if I think it might be helpful. Sometimes I ask the client to acknowledge her emotions, and then experience where in her body she feels these emotions and then shift to paying attention to the sensations at the source of the emotions. Then I encourage her to give space to the world of sensations enfolding inside her and to forget the emotions. We cannot change our emotions, but we can free ourselves from difficult sensations as they are an experience of energy stuck. By freeing the energy flow, the emotions change.

"Tension and pain are symptoms of energy trapped," I might say, "so give it all the space in the world. Don't be scared of it! Let it invade your entire being!" I encourage her to keep describing what is happening as a way to keep her alert and mindful of her own process.

At some point in mindfulness work, it becomes important to find a way to a good question. The question always comes. I never worry. I just trust my gut about where to go. And when I don't know, I take a moment of silence and feel everything about the conversation of the session and let the sensations in my body settle and, when they settle, I know what to say.

I might simply summarize what I understand or I might have a new direction because, all of a sudden, I feel that something was missing from our conversation. I always find a thread that is worth exploring. Sometimes it seems magical to my clients. "How did you think to ask that question? I have looked at this countless times and missed that angle!" or " I did not know I felt this way!"

In mindfulness therapy you trust that Life works to bring congruence between you and your inner-self, or between your client and his inner-self. So if an experience does not make sense, it is worth exploring its role in re-establishing congruence. How would a rape help bring congruence in a person's life, for instance? How would losing a job or a relationship help bring congruence in a person's life? One has to ask these questions at the proper time to get out of victimization.

I now describe two examples of asking key questions.

I explored a childhood series of rapes for some time with a client. Then a sudden car accident made her feel as though everyone was out to hurt her, just the same way her father was running after her to catch her as a child. I let her explore that for a while and, at some point, I said, "June, your father has not run after you in a long, long time to catch you... Now you fear people are after you to catch you and you feel you want to run away. What are you really running away from?" She felt her body and thought a moment and she looked at me with her eyes wide open, "I am running away from the void inside." "Okay, I said, so you see we are no longer dealing with the rape anymore... What's so scary about the void?"

With a friend who had shared much with me about her self-healing journey, I asked, "So what was the trigger for you losing control of yourself?" She said, "Money was. When I had money all was fine and when I ran out... it was hell!" I could relate to that and yet something was missing for me, so I said, "Where does that reaction to money come from?" "Well," she said, "when I was a child, everything was fine around my birthday and around Christmas." "So you mean that's the only time when your parents had money to spend on you and the rest of the year was poverty?" "Oh! No! My parents had money, but that's when they wanted me to be happy." "And the rest of the year you did not feel that they wanted you to be happy." "That's right! The rest of the year they were telling me I was always doing something wrong or being stupid." "So," I said, "I guess it was not about money really, it was about your parents opening or closing their hearts to you, and you associated that with money." "Wow!" she said, "I love that."

The Therapist's Experience

People often ask me: "Don't you need to debrief after a heavy session with a client?" "Don't you need to seek counseling yourself?"

The short answer to the first question is that I rarely need to debrief because I don't hold on to people's negative energies, I don't attach to it because it is not the real person. I always seek the real person. Part of my therapeutic practice requires that I remain aware of the impact of a client's energy on me because that gives me information about my client. And I use how I feel to guide the therapy process, unless I know it is my stuff to deal with. If I feel agitated, I stop therapy to feel it and resolve it on the spot. The resolution in me leads to the next phase in therapy. At the end of a session I do not carry over any extra energy – at least not the client's energy.

That brings me to the second question. I may need to look at myself because some of the issues brought up by the client mirrors issues I still need to resolve. After seeing seven therapists, I learned to resolve my own issues using meditation to recognize my issues and resolve them myself. I will sometimes ask friends who work in the healing field to help me heal something I have a hard time getting at on my own.

Remember that mindfulness therapy deals with seeking the truth. It is not about giving a treatment or advice. Giving a treatment makes the client dependent on you, giving advice may make you upset if the client chooses not to follow it. We, as therapists, need to help clients learn to find their own solutions and learn to trust themselves. We need to respect their free will and help them transition from powerlessness to empowerment by noticing the choices they have.

Another perspective that helps me not carry over negative energy is that I know there is a positive outcome for any negative life situation. For my part, it is simply about finding the right question to help shift the negative perspective. There is never a negative energy with which to be concerned. There are only clients who are not always ready to change their perspective. I don't have to be worried about that because I see myself as a presence in their life to support them, not to change them. I don't have an attachment to their recovery or to the speed of their recovery. It is a celebratory moment when a milestone is achieved, but it is not defeat if a milestone is not achieved. There is a sense of joy shared by just being in the presence of another soul and being given a chance to help and serve, whether or not that service is received or accepted. There is a celebration in having had an opportunity to serve.

Knowing that, in all cases, there is a potentially beautiful resolution, even while we don't see it yet, keeps me from thinking negatively about negative experiences.

Reflections

1. Psychotherapy can become a wonderful adventure of working together with others to make peace in our lives, heal, find our truth by feeling and integrating our experiences and engaging with Life, trust, have faith, love more compassionately, and manifest our dreams. If therapists do this with their clients, I bet therapists will

enjoy their work more fully, feel less burnout, if any, and have more success with their clients than by using the diagnosis and treatment approach.

2. Because the role of a mindfulness therapist is to help clients find their truth, couple or family therapy should never come to a place where one person feels that the therapist is taking someone's side against someone else's. When we experience truth, we realize that the truths of each individual in a group are all compatible at a soul level. That is, if someone's truth is to leave the relationship with a group, this also matches the truth for the remaining members of that group. As long as there are conflicts we have not reached the place of truth. If a member of a group needs to experience something from a place of truth, that experience is also beneficial for all the other members of that group as a whole. The same is true when someone dies suddenly. At a soul level, it is the right time for everyone who knew that person to allow that transition in their lives.

3. The Health Insurance Portability and Accountability Act of 1996 (HIPAA) are privacy standards meant to protect individuals' medical and psychotherapy records. These privacy standards should prevent professionals from telling stories about their patients/clients in a gossiping way and should prevent health insurances from using our records against us. The other side of this is that letting the world know who we are is freeing because we no longer need to spend energy hiding it, fearing that it be discovered. We may realize that, when the world knows it, the very thing we wanted to hide due to shame or something else, no longer hurts us. In that sense, privacy is over-rated and can prevent healing. Yet, I do believe people need to know the therapy conversations will remain private and it is essential that therapists honor their privacy, as this allows most people to be more open during therapy and to trust the therapist.

We have a strong reaction as a culture about the intrusion in our individual privacy from the FBI, the CIA, other governmental agencies, and the corporate world. We should, as it is disturbing and obscene to have our money spent against us and that human beings should dedicate their lives to such activities. Another side to this, from a spiritual and healing perspective, is that if I stop fearing that who I am can be held against me, if I start loving myself with all my gifts and all my wounds and mistakes, then no one can use anything against me in a way that is hurtful. I am free.

The privacy act serves to prevent gossiping, and to me, we should extend that to stop *inner gossiping*, that is to stop inner judgments about our self and our clients. Ultimately, therapy is about helping our clients be free from suffering and to be infinitely creative and happy, while honoring their free will, so they can start playing with their gifts and share them with the world. Honoring their free will is not simply in how we talk to them and what we say to them or about them, it is also how we think of them. If we have a judgment about them or if we hold them to a specific outcome, unless it is unlimited, our thinking is controlling and not honoring their free will.

4. And a final point, in any conversations we have with others, if there is a misunderstanding, it is often that there is inner confusion in the person trying to convey the point. If a client is not getting a concept a therapist is trying to convey or is not progressing, it may be that the client is not ready for it. It may also be that the therapist has something to learn about that particular issue. In my experience, if I take the stand that I have something to learn when the client is stuck, and I make the effort to understand my side of the issue, at the next opportunity, the client is usually able to grasp more and heal more.

9 WESTERN PSYCHOTHERAPY BASED ON A HEALING PARADIGM

A common theme among the psychotherapy practices that are overlooked by the mainstream is a focus on healing and wellbeing rather than treating. As you read through this chapter, you may be struck that the future I envision for psychotherapy is already moving toward supporting people on their spiritual journey; it is no longer about treating diseases.

While this chapter is meant to show what is already available in the Western culture, it is not meant to be an exhaustive account of everything available.

Body-Oriented Psychotherapy

This very interesting practice of psychology was completely absent from my mental health counseling program. This psychotherapy practice can be used to align mind, body, and soul. As early as in the 1930s, Wilhelm Reich suggested that trauma can be stored in muscular tension. To place this psychology perspective on a historical timeline, the European Association of Body Psychotherapy was founded in 1988 and the US Association of Body Psychotherapy was founded in 1996.

I feel a kinship with two psychotherapists who have contributed to body psychotherapy, Ron Kurtz and Arnold Mindell.

Luc Watelet

Kurtz received a lifetime achievement award from the US Association of Body Psychotherapy in 2008 in recognition of the work he called the Hakomi Method (first created in the late 1970s) and later the Refined Hakomi Method. Peter Levine, author of *Waking the Tiger: Healing Trauma* (1997), and other books on releasing trauma, received that same award in 2010.

Arnold Mindell's work on the Dreambody is recognized as part of body-oriented psychotherapy. He was one of five people honored with the Pioneer Award from the US Association of Body Psychotherapy in 2012. Mindell is originally a Jungian psychotherapist who founded Process Oriented Psychology (POP). He and his wife, Amy Mindell, have many fascinating books with a wide range of topics. The following quote from psychotherapist Linda Hartley shows the closeness of my view of human nature to Mindell's and this view is part of my purpose in writing this book. It is my heartfelt wish that our culture embraces this paradigm as part of our future in psychotherapy.

> [POP]… most explicitly seeks encounter with the unknown and the irrational side of life. Process theory views what bubbles up from the unconscious as meaningful and appreciates symptoms and disturbances of any sort, not as pathologies to be healed or transcended or somehow got rid of, but as expressions of the very thing we need for our further growth, happiness, or enlightenment.[46]
> ~ Linda Hartley

For more information about POP, I recommend starting with reading *Riding the Horse Backwards: Process Work in Theory and Practice* (the first edition was in 1992) by Arnold Mindell.

Eye Movement Desensitization and Reprocessing (EMDR) is described as a mind-body therapy and appears to me as a part of Body Psychotherapy.

Transpersonal Psychology

Transpersonal psychology was created in response to the need for

---

[46] L. Hartley (2004). *Somatic Psychology*. London: Whurr Publishers Ltc. p. 213. This book is now published by Wiley.

psychology to acknowledge spiritual experiences.

In 1967, a small working group, including Abraham Maslow, Anthony Sutich, Stanislav Grof, James Fadiman, Miles Vich, and Sonya Margulies met in Menlo Park, California, with the purpose of creating a new psychology that would honor the entire spectrum of human experience, including various non-ordinary states of consciousness. During these discussions, Maslow and Sutich accepted Grof's suggestion and named the new discipline "transpersonal psychology."[47]

~ Stanislav Grof

The Journal of Transpersonal Psychology was created in 1969 and the Association for Transpersonal Psychology was founded in 1971.

Mindfulness-Based Stress Reduction

Jon Kabat-Zinn, a medical doctor, studied Buddhism and yoga and brought a mindfulness practice in 1979 to the University of Massachusetts medical school. His first book, *Full Catastrophe Living: Using the Wisdom of Your Body and Mind to Face Stress, Pain, and Illness,* published in 1990, describes his *Mindfulness-Based Stress Reduction* (MBSR) program and provides scientific evidence for it. Kabat-Zinn is a Western pioneer in bringing an Eastern approach to stress reduction to the Western culture, and has done much to change the perspective from which medicine and psychology can be practiced. MBSR has been used successfully in reducing anxiety and depression.

In our Western world becoming more holistic in its approach to health and well-being, there is a merging of all health related and spiritual disciplines. Healing, be it physical, mental, emotional, or spiritual, leads to a greater spiritual awareness and a deeper sense of compassion.

---

[47] S. Grof, *A Brief History of Transpersonal Psychology*, p. 3, retrieved on September 3, 2015, and still active on July 8, 2016, from
http://www.stanislavgrof.com/wp-content/uploads/pdf/A Brief History of Transpersonal Psychology Grof.pdf.

Luc Watelet

Past Life Therapy

Past life therapy was discovered by psychiatrist Brian Weiss. He describes his discovery in his book *Many Lives, Many Masters (1988)*. Weiss was not a believer in God or in past lives when, quite by accident, a Catholic client, who did not believe in past lives either, went spontaneously into a past life during a hypnosis session. That incident eventually led to the healing of the client in three months who had made no progress for a whole year prior to the introduction of hypnosis in her therapy. Past life therapy deals with much more than actual past lives. It really taps into our unconscious narrative which may or may not actually be past lives. These stories can lock us in paradigms that imprison us in ways that can be quite painful. The practice of past life therapy can also be used to explore future lives, as Weiss discovered. This practice is useful in exploring the progress made by a client or patient when a future life shows whether painful issues remain or have been dealt with (*Same Soul, Many Bodies, 2004*).

Internal Family Systems

I discovered Richard Schwartz by reading one of his articles in the magazine *Psychotherapy Networker*.[48] In this article, Schwartz describes the therapeutic process in which he engaged with a client struggling with anorexia. Instead of figuring out a treatment approach and helping the girl follow that treatment, he simply engaged the girl in thinking about herself as having different voices. This is the basis of internal family systems. The anorexia is not her, but it is a voice in her that controls her behavior. So he asked the girl to talk with the anorexia, to ask it what it is trying to do. The girl was ashamed of it and angry at it, so initially, the last thing she wanted to do was to talk with it. But Schwartz helped her feel safe. When she did talk to the anorexia, she realized that it was trying to protect her. This form of protection was actually hurting her. But she understood and she could then choose a healthy approach to protecting herself.

Schwartz was fascinated by the discovery that, as therapists, we do not need to know what the answers are; the clients have the answers. The

---

[48] R. Schwartz (2004). *The larger self: Discovering the core within our multiplicity.* Psychotherapy Networker, May/June, 37-43.

problem is that they don't know how to access them. The therapist's role is simply to help them find the path to themselves.

The Emotional Freedom Techniques

Gary Craig, a graduate engineer, came up with the Emotional Freedom Techniques (EFT) in the early 1990s. The method involves a mixture of finding the right words to describe a difficult emotional issue and tapping with one's finger tips on various parts of the face, upper body, and hand. The technique is more and more commonly used in some US addiction treatment centers and at some US veterans affairs (VA) centers.

Tom Porpiglia, LMHC, EFT-ADV, says the following about EFT (personal communication based on an unpublished article):[49]

> *Emotional Freedom Technique or EFT has proven to be the most effective technique for treating trauma of any type. I know this from both a personal and professional standpoint in my private practice, along with a research project I have been involved with for the last five years. I spent a small part of my time as an EFT coach for the Veterans Stress Project, documenting the outcomes of using EFT on combat PTSD, hoping that the Veterans Administration would take note of the research and start to use it in their treatment facilities. The only other technique that holds a candle to EFT is Eye Movement Desensitization Reprocessing (EMDR). There are two main differences between the two: 1) EFT can be self-applied, and EMDR cannot and 2) The EMDR practitioner has to be highly trained and skilled to apply EMDR to someone who dissociates.*

Case Study from the Same Article by Tom Porpiglia: An Afghanistan/Iraq Veteran[50]

Dan was a sniper in the Army for 12 years. He is an Afghanistan: Operation Enduring Freedom (OEF) / Iraq: Operation Iraqi Freedom (OIF) veteran. When he arrived in my office, his PCL-M (PTSD self-report check list) score was 70 out of a possible 85. Any score over 50 is

---

[49] Published for the first time, with Tom Porpiglia's permission.
[50] Ibid.

Luc Watelet

considered clinically positive for PTSD. He had been through nine different treatment modalities with very little success. He recalls that his original PCL-M score was over 80 before those treatments. He had tried Cognitive Behavioral Therapy (CBT), Cognitive Processing Therapy (CPT), massage, and nutrition, mindfulness processes in a Buddhist monastery, hypnotherapy, medications, exposure therapy, and Reiki. He attempted police assisted suicide and thought about suicide daily. He would get angry with very little provocation. He and his wife were at their wits' end, and the VA was of little help to them.

We had 15 minutes at the end of our first meeting to apply EFT to a traumatic memory that had a SUDS (Subjective Units of Distress) level of 10 (out of 10). We collapsed the SUDS level of that memory and some of its aspects to 1 or 2 in those 15 minutes. When Dan came back for his first full session, he related something very profound and powerful. He told me that typically, when he started working with a new counselor, therapist, or doctor, and had to recount some of these memories, he would end up in the hospital, and this time he did not. This pleased both him and his wife and gave them hope that there was a way out of this. When we finished his six sessions, his PCL-M score was 24, and remained at that level well past six months. In addition, if he keeps using EFT on any remaining or hidden traumatic memories, it is quite possible that his score could drop even more.

Wayne Muller

I mentioned Wayne Muller, a minister and psychotherapist, in Chapter 3, Love. His first book *Legacy of the Heart: The Spiritual Advantages of a Painful Childhood* was published in 1993. It describes how we can choose to view painful experiences from childhood, not from a place of suffering, but from a place of opening to something we were not aware of that we needed all along. Pain becomes the birth of something that gives us more life, more aliveness. This is true of all pain, including mental health challenges. And that is just the starting point of Muller's work which serves as guidance into our personal spiritual journey.

Equine Assisted Psychotherapy

Karen Frewin and Brent Gardiner quote a 1988 paper by M. R. Riede: "The seeds of EAP [Equine Assisted Psychotherapy] were sown more than two centuries ago. German physicians advised horseback riding to reduce attacks of hypochondria and hysteria related to mental illness."[51]

From the same review paper, the professional development of equine assisted psychotherapy started "[i]n 1996, [when] the North American Riding for the Handicapped Association (NARHA) formalised a specialised section of its organisation as the Equine Facilitated Mental Health Association (EFMHA)." And "[i]n 1999, another professional body, the Equine Assisted Growth and Learning Association (EAGALA) was founded."

There is also the Eponaquest® method developed by Linda Kohanov author of *The Tao of Equus* (2001).

The natural ability some horses have to connect at the level the vulnerable person needs is a branch of therapy with fascinating stories of healing that could not be obtained with traditional therapy. I encourage the reader to start with *The Tao of Equus*.

Although I have experienced basic elements of EAP at a local horse farm with the psychiatrist owner, I do not know the differences between the various organizations and would not be able to advise one over another.

Heartwork

I mentioned Dale Golstein, LCSW-R, in Chapter 3, Love. His book *Heartwork: How to Get What You Really, Really Want* was published in 2006. His work includes one-on-one therapy sessions, as well as group work. It is about introducing people to a spiritual discipline and practice of being with oneself.

The work of Dale Goldstein is relatively new within the framework of psychotherapy and continues the work of Kabat-Zinn from a psychotherapeutic perspective while going beyond stress-reduction to embrace self-discovery. It is part of the long tradition of the work of spiritual teachers. I asked my friend Dale for a couple of case studies to

---

[51] K. Frewin and B. Gardiner (2015). *New Age or Old Sage? A Review of Equine Assisted Psychotherapy*, retrieved July 8, 2016, from http://www.marleysmission.com/pdf/new_age.pdf

describe his work with his clients. As a result, I interviewed two of his clients and their stories are published here for the first time.

Case Study 1 ~ An Interview[52]

1) What was your life like before therapy (symptoms, problems, diagnosis if any, and medication prescription, if any)?

I first entered therapy with Dale in 1998 after becoming physically and emotionally sucked dry by a deeply troubled person I had been trying to help over the course of the previous six years. When I saw Dale, I was still feeling a high level of anxiety, depletion, and disconnection from myself. I was not on any medication.

Before 1998, I didn't realize I was trapped or incomplete. I felt I was functioning at a high level and believed I had opened my heart and soul after having grown up highly emotionally defended and "cerebral."

Over the course of six years, the troubled person I was in a helping relationship with manifested multiple personalities and became increasingly dependent, manipulative, suicidal, and threatening if I didn't give her the huge amounts of time and attention she seemed to need to keep her from melting down or being self-destructive. Little by little I gave up my autonomy and power, and became very emotionally entangled in her pathology as I tried to keep her from becoming destructive to herself, others, or me. I was perpetually highly stressed, never knowing when the next emergency call would come, and having repeatedly sacrificed my life with my wife and children. I was going through the motions of being basically functional in my work, but felt like a mere shell with great turbulence, anxiety, and powerlessness going on underneath.

When I finally found the courage to end this relationship, no matter the cost, I was still a wreck on the inside. That situation had been a "perfect" re-enactment of my childhood dilemma, of swallowing myself and my needs and autonomy to please my parents and not upset

---

[52] These two case studies are published with Dale Goldstein's permission and each of the two clients, respectively. The clients preferred their names not to be mentioned.

anyone. Working with Dale enabled me to not only open my heart and release the pain, but also to open to my belly, my repressed power, and to find my sense of "I am-ness." Then, once that separation was healed, I was able to grow and unfold spiritually as well as emotionally as a whole person.

2) Your experience with therapy before meeting Dale Goldstein.

Immediately before working with Dale, I had been seeing a psycho-dynamic oriented therapist weekly for two to three months. It was somewhat helpful, but not deeply healing.

3) The approach of therapy with Dale Goldstein: How was it different from what you tried before? What worked for you and how did it help you find a way toward healing?

Though I have seen Dale individually off and on since 1998, the most powerful healing and growth have come through the three to five day intensives and retreats, of which I have probably attended 10 or so. Though a variety of tools are used, the process has been one of opening my awareness more and more deeply and trustingly to the wounds or stuck emotions, releasing them or creating the spaciousness of awareness around them, and letting them dissolve or resolve. Tools have included deep breathing, music, physical unwinding, group support, inquiry, repeating questions, meditation, a soft belly exercise, awareness exercises, etc.

In individual sessions, I open to what is going on under the surface (usually lying down), and open into it through awareness as fully as I can. I have the option of working in his "process room," a dark, sound-insulated padded cell where any type of expression is possible. At times, I have worked in there for several hours at a time with Dale briefly checking in on an hourly basis (between clients).

About a year ago, I became physically and emotionally depleted, and went into an extreme anxiety state. I had weekly sessions with Dale, but much of the work was at home, opening and releasing, opening and releasing for long periods of time, with daily e-mail or sometimes telephone check-ins and guidance.

Luc Watelet

This depletion came about by a "perfect storm" of extra demands on my time and energy and a case of bronchitis, while simultaneously dealing with a conflict with a woman that triggered my aversion to standing up to or hurting my mother. It was some of the same emotional dilemma presenting itself in a different way. Beginning on a Thursday, I felt like I was going through the motions, doing what I knew I needed to do, but feeling kind of "not there" – an unfamiliar feeling for me. I spent a couple hours working with Dale the next day, getting in touch with my inner scared little boy and also with my anger and power. He said to be very gentle with myself and rest as much as possible. But on Saturday, when I had to prepare a sermon for Sunday, for the first time, I couldn't write a single word. Nothing came. I called in a substitute preacher, thinking I could at least help with the rest of the worship service. But when I went to do that, I became dizzy and had to leave. An anxiety reaction ensued – not from worry about being incapacitated, but the anxiety seemed to be a physiological reaction to the depletion and was very incapacitating. I felt totally unable to focus or concentrate, and my primary care physician (PCP) prescribed Citalopram (Alexa), supplemented by Xanax, as needed.

Dale guided me in opening as fully to every feeling and sensation as I could. I did this for hours at a time each day. I also let go of all attachments, expectations, need for approval, and fear of disappointing people. This was very hard, but also very freeing.

It took about six weeks to be able to begin being able to focus on work and begin ramping back up to a full schedule. By Fall, I felt pretty much like myself, but have continued to gradually increase in my sense of openness and groundedness beyond what I had before this episode started.

I have also participated in Dale's inner work groups of six to eight people, where participants may choose to open their issues in the group setting, while Dale guides them to resolution and the others vicariously experience the process. But the intensives, retreats, and individual work is where I did my deeper work.

The benefits of this whole work are that it opens up the trapped emotions that interfere with the fullness of living, and it allows the emergence of the essential self – open, whole, free, grateful, loving, and powerful. But we open, we close, we open, we close. It's ongoing and ever-deepening.

4) How long was the process of therapy with Dale Goldstein?

I have attended an intensive or retreat every year or two and have had countless sessions over the past 17 years. It isn't as much treatment for a condition (other than the human condition!) as it is a way of life that goes ever deeper.

5) Your life now: symptoms or problems left, if any; medication prescribed now, if any.

Overall, I feel much more whole, integrated, open to my depths, compassionate without caretaking, and wise. I have been on a low dose of Citalipram since my intense anxiety a year ago, prescribed by my PCP. It may be discontinued when I see her later this month.

6) Anything else you wish you could tell people who seek therapy, given your experience?

The key to healing is trusting the healing process, however difficult, painful, or arduous the process might be. It's a journey to wholeness and to life that is worth whatever it takes, and your body and soul know the way.

Case Study 2 ~ An Interview

1) What was your life like before therapy (symptoms, problems, diagnosis, if any, and medication prescription, if any)?

I (a woman) was in a relationship living with physical and emotional abuse. First emotional then physical. My relationship was with a woman who was eight years older than me.

One day, I called the cops. I was not hospitalized, but my face, eyes, and nose were bloody. I had bruises on my arms and legs.

Despite this, I was scared of leaving the relationship. I knew it was not right for me, but I did not know how to leave it. I was taking some

201

Luc Watelet

responsibility for the abuse happening to me. But I still thought it could change.

2) Your experience with therapy before meeting Dale Goldstein.

I did therapy before. It was horrific! We talked about the problems with my significant relationship N. I was diagnosed with some depression and anxiety.

The relationship with the therapist caused more anxiety because it was very procedural and led to no better understanding. I did not know of any other therapeutic methods, but ended therapy anyway.

3) The approach of therapy with Dale Goldstein: How was it different from what you tried before? What worked for you and how did it help you find a way toward healing?

The last attack left the most visual marks on my body. I was one year into the relationship. I went to my parents for safety. Their response was quiet. They offered a calm peaceful environment.

I looked for therapists online and found one that had a book out whose title attracted me. It was called *Heartwork* by Dale Goldstein. I read a couple of pages online and checked out Dale's website. I made an appointment.

This was an incredibly different experience of therapy. First, I immediately felt safe. I noticed Dale respected pauses to be with what was being said and Dale was present to me as opposed to evaluating me. We never went into a discussion about depression and anxiety. We shared experiences, instead, without labeling or judging.

Because Dale's method accesses experiences far beyond what I knew, I've chosen to continue down that path which is about healing and awakening. I'm in my fifth year of working with him and his teachings. From this partnership, I have gained a deep understanding of so many aspects of life. Because of Dale's method and guidance and my personal commitment to healing, the quality of my life has evolved immensely. In allowing myself to completely surrender to the fear, pain, and longing buried inside, the attachment to unhealthy people, situations, and circumstances has almost completely dissolved. There is a revitalization that has started to unfold... and I can finally hear a voice I recognize as my own. Day by day, I am reclaiming myself. A journey that will likely never end (smile).

4) Your life now: symptoms or problems left, if any; medication prescribed now, if any.

I see Dale less regularly now, but do see him if I am working through something "big." Cultivating compassion and love (real love) are very much a part of my days. I have been able to forgive N, accept my role in allowing myself to stay in something that was extremely unhealthy, and let it go. Dust in the wind...

5) Is there anything else you wish you could tell people who seek therapy, given your experience?

Do it. Often times, therapy has a negative stigma attached to it. It means something is "wrong." Consequently, many people live in comfortable suffering... making the same choices that inflict pain on themselves and others. Creating the same patterns that steal their happiness. We are the only ones who can save ourselves. We are responsible for loving ourselves whole. Not our families, not our partners, not our friends. Dale has always said "Happiness is an inside job." And oh, how right he is. Therapy (specifically this kind) gives you the place, the space, and the tools to uncover your true self. It is not easy (or you would already be doing it). It is not for the faint of heart. But it is worth it.

Conclusion

I have met many people who have been doing therapy for many years without seeing any progress and others who have given up on therapy. This chapter points out that there are many modalities available to the person who wants to heal using psychotherapy. The key is to stop anything that is causing unnecessary suffering or is not helping and not to give up seeking for the right help. Help is available!

Luc Watelet

10 MENTAL HEALTH
OUTSIDE THE WESTERN CULTURE

It is no measure of health to be well adjusted to a profoundly sick society.

~ Jiddu Krishnamurti

In Chapter 4, Nature, I mentioned the book *The Spell of the Sensuous,* by David Abram, in which he describes the traditional medicine men and women who see as their primary task to preserve the balance between their people and nature. It was only when they were out of balance with nature as a community, including with the spirit world, that illnesses including mental health challenges, appeared among the people in their community. This says something about a relationship between health and nature our Western culture does not consider. Could it be that a culture may be responsible for the types of ailments that are present among its people? Could it be that depression is not just an individual struggle, but the result of a certain view of life held by the culture where it is found?

The Q'eros by Author Lissa Rankin

I refer the reader to the original blog[53] by Lissa Rankin for the full story.

---

[53] L. Rankin. *An Invitation to Peace*. Blog from September 8, 2014, still active on July 8, 2016, http://lissarankin.com/an-invitation-to-peace

The Q'eros are known as the last of the Incas, the wisdom keepers of the Andes. In essence, when Mrs. Rankin visited the Q'eros in Peru she was struck by what she found. Women gave birth alone. If they had a stillbirth, the community came together and the woman could cry and grieve surrounded by her community. Q'eros women do not experience post-partum depression. The Q'eros know no depression or anxiety. They could tell the story of one woman who had left the village. When she met with hardship with no community to support her she committed suicide.

The important question Mrs. Rankin asks is: *"Have we created a culture that feeds mental illness?"* She questions, like I do, that depression is due to a chemical imbalance, because then why wouldn't we find depression among the Q'eros with the same prevalence that we have in the USA?

Beyond that, Mrs. Rankin invites us to reclaim the peace and the joy she found among the lighthearted Q'eros.

"Alex: Crazy in the USA, Healer in Africa" by author Stephanie Marohn (Featuring Dr. Malidoma Patrice Somé)

I refer the reader to the original blog and/or book[54] by Stephanie Marohn for the full story.

When Dr. Somé first arrived in the USA, he was shocked by the way we see mental illness. In his tradition from the Dagara people, mental illness is seen as a breakthrough, not a breakdown, a transition facilitated by spirits for a human being to become a healer.

He was interested in testing his thought that the views of his people could apply to healing westerners. He came across Alex who at 18 years old had been diagnosed with schizophrenia for four years. His parents had tried everything the USA had to offer with no success. With Alex's and his parents' permission, Dr. Somé took Alex with him to Africa and

[54] S. Marohn. Blog, still active July 8, 2016, from http://www.wakingtimes.com/2014/08/22/shaman-sees-mental-hospital/. Excerpt from *The Natural Medicine Guide to Schizophrenia*, Hampton Roads Publishing (2003), pp. 183-185.

introduced him to the Dagara people.

After eight months of participation in the shamanistic rituals, Alex was quite well. He remained with the Dagara people for another four years, not because he needed more healing, but because he was not ready to face the stigma the US society attaches to mental illness. When he returned to the US, he studied psychology as a graduate student at Harvard. No one in the US ever expected Alex could even get an undergraduate degree.

Mrs. Marohn reports these words from Dr. Somé: "He [Alex] was reaching out. It was an emergency call. His job and his purpose was to be a healer. He said no one was paying attention to that."

Bruno Gröning's Approach to Healing

Bruno Gröning (1906-1959) was born in Germany. His approach to healing is closer to Eastern teachings than it is to Western teachings. So I include it in this chapter. Gröning was a man whose presence was healing to people, animals, and plants, and even to mechanical things such as radios and cars. He never claimed to be a healer. He said that God healed. He was simply a transmitter or an operator; he helped make the connection with the healing source. He never took money for the healings that happened thanks to his presence because he said that the healing power came from God not from him.

After Bruno Gröning's passing, an organization was set up in 1979 to share his teachings. Healings, which are referred to as healings on the spiritual path, continue to happen within this organization every day around the world. Today, the organization, called The Circle of Friends (www.bruno-groening.org/english), is present in about 140 countries. It is operating by donations only and everyone in the organization works by donating their time; no one is paid.

A branch of this organization, the Medical Scientific Group, composed of doctors, psychotherapists, and healing professionals, reviews the healing claims. There are thousands of reported healings published in the form of quarterly magazines and sent for free to the friends (members) of the Circle of Friends.

Bruno Gröning's teachings were simple to describe, though perhaps not always easy to put in practice. Gröning said illness is disorder. God is order. Disorder is negativity. In order to heal, we need to stop delving in negativity, because that is claiming the disease as our own and then it cannot leave us. Instead, we need to stop being concerned with any illness, or any disorder in our lives, and leave that to the medical profession, if needed. We need to open our heart to beauty and love to cleanse our body and mind, and our job is to allow this cleansing to happen. We allow this cleansing by paying attention to our sensations and allowing them without reacting to them negatively, without being scared of them. Often, the healing process involves pain or other experiences that are reminiscent of the problem. It is important to think of it as the healing process and not be scared that the disease or the struggle is back.

Dr. Hew Len, Psychologist, Uses Ho'oponopono in Hawaii

Dr. Hew Len's story can easily be found on the internet. It has been published and he tells it in his workshops. You can also hear him refer to his experience at Hawaii State Hospital in this YouTube video: https://www.youtube.com/watch?v=OL972JihAmg. I am aware that some people claim they have checked and found no records of Dr. Hew Len working at that hospital during the time he claimed to be hired there (1984-87). Some of the other criticisms state that they do not believe Ho'oponopono works without the full participation of the entire group it is applied to. I am aware of people changing without their participation within the Bruno Gröning Circle of Friends organization, and these changes are documented by medical doctors and psychologists. For example, people who had cancer or were addicts and, without their participation with the teachings of Gröning, became free of these afflictions simply by other people following the teachings of Gröning on their behalf. Therefore, I do not believe in the criticisms made about Dr. Hew Len's claim that he was able to use Ho'oponopono in the way that he did. Furthermore, Snopes.com makes no mention of this story as a hoax. I give Dr. Hew Len the benefit of the doubt until we have proof otherwise.

Dr. Hew Len was hired as a psychologist in the 1980s by the Hawaii State Hospital to head a ward for mentally ill criminals. The staff members were tired of the new directives changing with each director,

Luc Watelet

without making matters any better, and they were scared of the residents. Attacks between residents happened daily. Staff absenteeism was rampant. So when Dr. Hew Len was hired, the staff did not welcome him with anything more than skepticism.

Dr. Hew Len did not change directives and did not meet with the residents. He was simply cheerful and relaxed, went to his desk where he looked at the residents' files. For each resident he said a prayer according to the Ho'oponopono tradition. Within two or three months, the residents' behavior had calmed down enough that the staff started coming back. Within four years, they were down to only two residents and the ward had to be closed down.

In the Ho'oponopono tradition, we are responsible for the reality around us. For Dr. Hew Len, that included the state of the mental ward. Using the Ho'oponopono tradition and using its principle, he healed the part of him that held the environment in its state of affairs. In other words, he allowed the normal course of healing to take place.

A Buddhist Approach to Heal from Mental Health Challenges

In his book, *The Joy of Living: Unlocking the Secret & Science of Happiness*, Yongey Mingyur Rinpoche describes his journey healing from a debilitating case of anxiety that he started to experience in early childhood. He mentions in his book that he is considered to be a reincarnated lama supposed to have accomplished many wonderful things in previous lifetimes. Having progressed on the spiritual path does not immunize someone from mental health challenges. It also demonstrates how a Buddhist practice of recognizing the pitfalls of our mind was enough to heal him from anxiety.

In the Buddhist belief, we are already "good, whole and complete."[55] The mind gets in the way with its perception of reality (paradigm) that leads to painful habits. It is like the experience of being in darkness because the clouds are heavy and dark, but the sun is always bright and sunny above them. Our mental health challenge is to believe that the clouds are all there is and never experience reality deeply enough to

---

[55] Y. M. Rinpoche (2007), *The Joy of Living: Unlocking the Secret & Science of Happiness*, Three Rivers Press, p.11.

realize that we can let go of the clouds and the sun will be visible again.

In Yongey Mingyur Rinpoche's words:

> Buddhism is not so much concerned with getting well as with recognizing that you are, right here, right now, as whole, as good, as essentially well as you can ever hope to be.
> You don't believe that, do you?
> Well, for a long time, neither did I.[56]

Yongey Mingyur Rinpoche started a three-year retreat at Sherah Ling. His first year became the most difficult he had faced up to then. Here is how he describes his experience to liberation:

> All the symptoms of anxiety I'd ever experienced – physical tension, tightness in the throat, dizziness, and waves of panic that were especially intense during group practices – attacked in full force. In Western terms, I was having a nervous breakdown.
> In hindsight, I can say that what I was actually going through was what I like to call a "nervous breakthrough." Completely cut off from the distractions of everyday life, I found myself in the position of having to directly confront my own mind. [...]
> Finally, as the first year of retreat came to a close, I found myself having to make a choice between spending the next two years hiding in my room or accepting the full truth of the lessons I'd learned from my father and other teachers: that whatever problems I was experiencing were habits of thought and perception ingrained in my own mind.
> [...]
> For three days I stayed in my room meditating [...]. Gradually I began to recognize how feeble and transitory the thoughts and emotions that had troubled me for years actually were, and how fixating on small problems had turned them into big ones. [...] And once I began to let go of my belief in the story they seemed to tell, I began to see the "author" beyond them – the infinitely vast, infinitely open awareness that is the nature of mind itself.[57]

---

[56] Y. M. Rinpoche (2007). *The Joy of Living: Unlocking the Secret & Science of Happiness*, Three Rivers Press, p. 11.
[57] Ibid., pp. 21, 22

After these three days, he rejoined the group practices and it took him two weeks of constant attention to conquer the anxiety. After which he has never again experienced a panic attack. He had recognized by direct experience the truth in the Buddhist teachings he had received about the nature of the mind.

Yongey Mingyur Rinpoche describes the experience of the "nature of mind" as immeasurably peaceful and, with practice, he says this peace becomes unshakable.

Reflections

We have much to learn in our mainstream Western approach to treating and even understanding mental health challenges. On the one hand, we accept our mind as our highest source of knowledge, so if it is mentally ill, we understand this to mean that we have a personality disorder. In the Buddhist and Bruno Gröning approaches, the mind is not our highest source of knowledge. In these traditions, our mind is like a wild child with bad habits. We need to learn that we are in charge by learning how our mind works and how we can become master in our own being, including master of our mind.

In the West, we also operate by the opposite worldview from Ho'oponopono. We don't take responsibility for our environment and we use diagnoses as if to say to the person diagnosed: "You *are* this diagnosis and I am not, this is your problem and I will treat you for it." In other words, our belief is that this is the client's problem which we think of negatively, and by doing so, according to Bruno Gröning's teaching, we hold the client prisoner to the illness.

Our mainstream Western approach would benefit from humbly looking at the examples I listed above from the Q'eros, Dr. Hew Len and the Ho'oponopono interconnectedness worldview, Malidoma Somé and his village's wisdom in the welcoming of spirit intervention, and the Buddhist and Bruno Gröning's insights into the truth of human nature.

11 A UNIFYING MODEL FOR PSYCHOTHERAPY ORIENTATIONS

Analogy/Metaphor

In a Zen story, blind people are brought to touch an elephant. Each is guided to touch a different part of the elephant – one a tusk, one a leg, one the tail, one the trunk, and so on. Then they are asked to talk about their experience of an elephant. Of course, they disagree as to what an elephant is, as their individual experiences have all been different. This is an apt analogy and metaphor for what has been going on in psychotherapy.

David Borsos,[58] starts off a chapter, in one of the textbooks we read in counseling school, with the same story of the elephant and the blind folks and uses it as an analogy to psychotherapy today to point to the apparent divergence between psychotherapy schools of thoughts and the tensions that sometimes exist between them. Borsos describes a few steps toward an integration, but not the total integration of theories and models. In 2006, when Borsos' chapter was printed, a few parts of the elephant had been recognized to belong to the same animal, but the whole animal had not yet been identified.

---

[58] David Borsos, "Bringing Theories into Practice: Toward an Integrated Model of Psychotherapy" in *Foundations of Mental Health Counseling*, 3rd ed., Palmo, Weikel, and Borsos, 2006, Charles C.Thomas Publisher, Ltd., pp. 89-111.

By asking the blind folks to tell their individual experiences of touching an elephant, an imaginative person might realize they each touched a different part of the elephant and might suggest to them to figure out if they could see the whole picture by trying to fit together all the parts they remember touching. Try as they might, they would probably not get the whole picture unless someone already knows ahead of time all the parts of the elephant that need to be touched in order to have these folks experience everything that contributes to a whole picture. Similarly people, such as Boros, have attempted to discover the whole picture of psychotherapy from its parts. It is not the right approach because it is difficult to see how the theories and schools of psychotherapy fit together, despite their apparent conflicts, if we don't have first a whole picture of what we are looking for. What could the elephant represent in our metaphor?

Unifying Psychotherapy Orientations

At some level, different human beings think differently, so it is not surprising that so many psychotherapy theories, models and schools have been proposed. What are these theories, models and schools attempting to do? According to the National Institute of Mental Health (NIMH):

> *"In psychotherapy, psychologists apply scientifically validated procedures to help people develop healthier, more effective habits."*[59]

The American Counseling Association (ACA) defines counseling as:

> *"Professional counseling is a professional relationship that empowers diverse individuals, families, and groups to accomplish mental health, wellness, education, and career goals."*[60]

There are many psychotherapy associations and they each provide their own definition of the goal of the profession they represent. It is not necessary to list all of them here. You can check them out online if you would like.

---

[59] Active on July 8, 2016, from http://www.apa.org/helpcenter/understanding-psychotherapy.aspx.
[60] Active on July 8, 2016, from
https://www.counseling.org/aca-community/learn-about-counseling/what-is-counseling/overview.

The NIMH definition focuses on improving people's habits using "scientifically validated procedures" whereas the ACA definition appears a little more general and more explicit without limitation to a particular methodology. The apparent difference between the two definitions begs the question, "What would I ideally want from therapy?" which leads to "What is the most I can get?" Or in other words, "What can a human being ideally expect to achieve?" I think of this similarly to being offered to participate in one of two lotteries, A or B. You can only pick one, but you can ask a question first. What question would you ask? You would probably want to know which one, A or B, would give you the highest expectation to win the most, right? So let's imagine an ideal therapy!

To be fair to NIMH, our discussion in the previous chapter about the Buddhist approach to health says that what's in the way between sickness and ultimate health is bad habits, including those of the mind. But why limit therapy to known and validated procedures? Why not dream up our ideal form of therapy?

From spiritual teachings, we learn that enlightenment is an ideal to aim for. From religions, we learn about liberation. People who follow and practice Bruno Gröning's teachings seek ultimate health and associate it with a liberation of the soul.[61] In order to know what a human being can ideally be or achieve, I need to know human nature. Then psychotherapy is a discipline that uses its knowledge of human nature to bring order in human beings who feel out of order, so they can feel liberated or on their path to enlightenment.

I have devoted this book to describe human nature and how knowing about it helps in one's personal and spiritual development, as well as in the therapeutic process and the therapeutic relationship. I have described human nature as a trinity: the mind, the body, and the soul.

What if the whole elephant was a metaphor for our trinity nature? What unifies psychotherapy theories, models, and schools is that they

---

[61] Active on July 8, 2016, from
http://www.bruno-groening.org/english/default.htm after searching for the term "liberation."

each seek to help ease human suffering, and they each do so by addressing an aspect of human nature. Each theory, model, and school is only limited by the ease with which it can, or cannot, address all of human nature.

We are learning as therapists that, in order to heal as human beings, we need to be more aware of the need to engage in a relationship with our entire being: mind, body, and soul. At the same time, I suggest that the field of psychotherapy as a whole engages on a self-discovery journey of its own. As psychotherapists, we can notice the three different major schools of psychotherapy that branched out from Freud, Adler, and Jung as mind, body, and spirit related as I described in the introduction. Each of these major schools brings an important way to think of therapy and we can benefit from each one in our need to address our clients holistically.

The seed for a holistic approach to psychotherapy was already present with Freud, Adler, and Jung, except that in practice they did not think of resolving their differences. Their schools grew more or less independently to their current level of maturity. It may now be time to consider a reunification.

Lyrical Vision for Psychotherapy

Each of our journeys is a beautiful, mesmerizing, unchoreographed dance with the whole Universe. No one can be ostracized from this dance. We all have steps to bring to it. We all belong in it, no matter how we feel or how others see and treat us. Each human being has a spiritual path which I imagine as learning the steps of one's own soul dance. Humanity also has a spiritual path in which each of our dances has a place and needs to be welcomed and integrated. If one step of the dance from one of us is missing, we have a clumsy dance, which points to where we can learn to dance better together.

And this is just the beginning, as we have to learn to integrate our dance with that of all of nature.

Our dual nature of having lessons to learn and a purpose to share requires our participation in this dance with humanity and nature. There is no separation between our lessons and what we have to share. There is no shame or guilt to have for not being "perfect" or "normal" because those are cultural constructs. We are as we are and that is exactly what that dance needs.

From this perspective, psychotherapy has a more profound role to play than helping people be functional or effective in their own life, and in society. Psychotherapy can be seen as a practice to help people find their own soul dance so they can integrate with more joy into the dance of humanity, and all of life, all of nature. Each theory and school of psychotherapy can be revisited from this perspective and find its place in our unifying model and vision.

Brief Account of Major Schools of Psychotherapy and Contributions

Freud showed that we hold unconscious beliefs and drives and that we are more complex than we thought. He suggested that this complexity needs to be explored and brought to light and by doing so we can relieve ourselves from trauma. He thought that our sexual drives were of most importance on this quest. Jung discovered the beautiful world of archetypes and synchronicity. He viewed spirituality as the most important part of our quest. Adler thought our relationships with each other and our environment mattered most. These are aspects of the soul dance we each need to learn.

The psychotherapy that came from Freud and Jung, or psychoanalysis, sought to help make the unconscious conscious. The early belief was that if we made the unconscious conscious, all our problems would be solved. Freud and Jung had wonderful successes with their approaches. They made invaluable contributions without which psychotherapy would not be what it is today. We may have interpreted from this that the goal is to make all of the unconscious conscious. The problem is that our personal unconscious is intimately linked to Universal Consciousness; thus, making the unconscious conscious is impossible as the process would be infinite in nature.

It turns out that it is not necessary to make the unconscious conscious, at least not all of it. From mindfulness work, we experience that we only need to establish an ongoing conscious relationship connecting our mind-body-soul so that each part of our trinity nature works in alignment and integrity with each other. We can now be more efficient in recognizing what aspects of our unconscious wants to become conscious. We are no longer fishing the unconscious in the dark. Our inner-self is guiding the process and is letting us know when parts of our unconscious are ready for awareness. When this process is happening within one individual, it has a ripple effect, and eventually touches all of humanity and all of life.

Adler sought to bring the efforts of psychotherapy back to our daily experience in the context of the world in which we live and the people with whom we live. And he was right – psychotherapy needed to remain grounded in reality and take into account that we are not individual islands. And, in doing so, he was helping us learn to welcome and bring more grace to the dance with each other.

The existentialists brought back the ancient notion from Greek philosophy of what is essential in our lives: meaning, joy, freedom, life and death, and how we relate to them. Viktor Frankl (1905-1997) author of *Man's Search for Meaning*, gave us his incredible journey surviving the Holocaust. He held on to meaning (what gave him joy, his connection to his soul) in his life. He also helped other people survive their Holocaust journey by helping them remember their dreams. He gave us a testimonial of the power we have over our environment. We are not victims of our circumstances.

Carl Rogers (1902-1987) gave us the person-centered therapy approach informing us that we each have our answers within us. All that therapists need to do is have *unconditional positive regard* for clients and help or guide them through their inner journey.

Gestalt therapy with Fritz Perls (1893-1970) brought a more experiential rather than strictly talk therapy approach to therapy, stressing awareness and integration.

Behavior therapy, with B. F. Skinner (1904-1990) and Albert Bandura (1925-present), pointed to the correction of behavior. It does not always have to be corrected by digging back into the past. When I work with clients who have boundary issues, we don't always have to talk about them. I can hold my boundary space and respond from that perspective to my clients. They learn by experience and example. When a child is misbehaving, we can choose to talk at length about the behavior not being appropriate, or we can become curious about what led the child to behave as she did. We can let Life be the playground for experience, not put so much energy on the poor behavior which would act as a form of reward through negative attention, but instead hold the space for a healthy behavior.

Albert Ellis (1913-2007) and Aaron Beck (1921-present) brought to light the importance of one's worldview in holding the roots of our problems.

Reality therapy with William Glasser (1925-2013) gave us the importance of taking responsibility and recognizing that we always have a choice, that everything we do comes from a choice, even if unconscious.

Feminist therapy brought us back to Adler's premise that our lives cannot be taken out of the context of our environment. It brought to light that psychotherapy, so far, had been created by white men and assumed that every human being operates from the same principles as white men. It brought to light the plight of oppression suffered by minorities. Other minorities started to add their perspectives and multiculturalism found its place in psychotherapy.

Family systems therapy followed Adler with the notion that individuals are not independent islands; they belong to systems and their actions, beliefs, and problems are intertwined with the other members of that system. Instead of working with individuals, they worked with families.

The postmodern approaches showed the importance of the subjective, that truth can be very personal, and that the client, therefore, is the expert in her own life.

Viewed from the holistic trinity view of human nature, it seems clear that each theory and model I just briefly described point to different and yet compatible aspects of who we are as human beings. They all make sense and make essential contributions to our understanding of who we are.

Conclusion

Life is a multidimensional playground and each of my relationships are entire worlds that touch my mind, body, and soul. Life is the playground for learning lessons and sharing of ourselves. As a therapist, my goal is to help my clients be free to play with peace, joy, love, and harmony in this playground, while respecting their free will and without limiting them. Sometimes, a theory or model can help a client. They can be used as training wheels until both the therapist and the client are ready to let go of them and welcome the dive into the unknown to which the process of therapy leads them.

A therapist may not be able to address all of the trinity directly with a person who is deeply addicted to alcohol or drugs and is reluctant to change, showing no respect for himself or others, and taking no responsibility in getting better. An intervention may become necessary to protect others from that person. Once that person is in an inpatient institution, a therapist has several options. The most obvious one in the Western world is to use a reward/punishment system to teach responsibility and accountability to that person. That approach addresses the body-mind of that person, but not his soul. Because it is manipulative, that approach leads to relapses and rebellion until the person gets tired of the game. There are approaches from other cultures that may be more effective, as discussed in the previous chapter.

Viewing human nature as a trinity gives us a model that unifies all psychotherapeutic orientations. And it also unifies all psychotherapy specializations. Today, psychotherapists specialize in addiction therapy, mental illness therapy, career counseling, and family therapy. But since the work is the same in all cases, that is, to help people realign their mind, body, and soul, there is no need to specialize anymore. Problems and struggles and stress are the impulse to grow personally and spiritually, and, thereby, to remember our soul dance.

12 CURRICULUM IDEAS
FOR A UNIFIED MODEL
OF PSYCHOTHERAPY

Introduction

The idea for this chapter came from many directions: My experience as an online graduate student, a long talk with a student who had recently received a bachelor's degree in psychology with only notions of pharmacology and no sense that real therapy is possible, and prior therapeutic experiences. Also, the direction psychiatry has taken is a motivation to write this chapter and this entire book. A lot of what happens goes against our code of ethics that asks us to do no harm. We can do better, given what is known and possible.

Students with a bachelor's degree from any psychotherapy program should have learned basics of what is possible with therapy so they have the knowledge to seek the kind of therapy they want to study. They should also know the major authors and contributors in each school of thought, and how to discover their own natural talents for the therapy work. People should not waste so much time in therapy without seeing results, and should certainly not come out of therapy with more problems than they had when they first started. Medication can help temporarily, but to rely on medication as a lifelong treatment without searching for something better is giving up on people.

In studying my own intuitive approach to therapy, I realized that a lot of what I was doing or thinking was already published but never discussed in the program from which I got my master's degree. As I became aware that healing comes from establishing a healthy relationship between our mind, body, and soul, I saw more clearly that the world of psychotherapy was fragmented along the same lines as the split I saw within human beings: mind, body, and soul. I wanted all this information to reach everyone interested in their health and also everyone interested in helping others. And I wanted to see healing in the world of psychotherapy by unifying the cognitive-behavioral, the somatic and the spiritual.

In the world of psychotherapy, there are two areas where this unification needs to happen: among therapists and their professional associations, and in the way we teach psychotherapy.

Contribution for a New Curriculum

Experience, Experience, Experience

The most important question a human being can ask is "Who am I?" This is also the most important question we can ask in therapy (see Chapter 6, Psychotherapy 101). The most important question is not "What theory shall I live by?" Thus, it is important that a budding therapist asks herself the question "Who am I?" This is better addressed through experience than through reading books about models and theories.

Hence, I suggest that we introduce students to psychotherapy by way of experience before introducing them to knowledge. When first introduced to therapy from books, there can be a tendency to think knowledge from books is enough to be a therapist. With experience, we learn who we are and what drives us to help others, which is not found in books. Then, when we study books, we can discuss the material from experience, and not only from an intellectual perspective. As a result, we also develop both an idea of who we want to be as a therapist in the context of the world of therapy, and we develop critical thinking.

I would start the first class as a series of group work experiences before receiving any formal training and before studying the theories and practices of psychotherapy. This should be followed by a discussion of the experience – what worked, and what did not work, and why. The teacher understands that mistakes will be made and that students will learn better from them than by being protected from making any.

For instance, students receiving guidance from a student facilitator may feel that the facilitator gave too much advice without listening enough, or let the group talk too long without enough guidance. Then, they can reflect on what they wish they'd receive from a group facilitator or from a therapist. All the therapists I have consulted in my life have informed me of what I want to do and don't want to do with my own clients. This was invaluable because it helped me see I often wanted a different experience from what I received. And when left to my own resources, I found ways to my own solutions. What truly helped often surprised me and sometimes came to me differently from what I thought I wanted.

From the experience with group work, students can discuss the qualities of a group facilitator, or a therapist. It should not take many group experiences to realize that 1) listening skills and empathy should top the list, followed by 2) developing the skills to generate and support conversations that are healing or at least helpful. Then comes 3) how worldviews and cultural differences impact our ability to remain present to each other. And, 4) the importance of the facilitator/therapist's own mental health. These points are good for the teacher's awareness and to be used to compare with the list discovered by the students.

A student in psychotherapy needs to know the experience of being a client and needs to experience different psychotherapeutic approaches. This can start right away. This is also part of a therapist's self-care, so I discuss this in more detail in the section below titled: The Therapist's Mental Health.

Listening Skills and Empathy

We are taught in school (e.g., Capuzzi and Gross[62]) that listening skills include:
1. Being a non-judgmental active listener: a client needs to be and feel heard.
2. Observing clients, thereby getting silent information.

---

[62] S. E. Halverson and R. D. Miars (2005). *The helping Relationship* in An Introduction to the Counseling Profession, 4th ed., edited by David Capuzzi and Douglas Gross, Pearson Education, Inc., pp 62-66.

Luc Watelet

3. Noticing a client's verbal behavior: incongruences, abrupt switch of topics, vagueness, etc.
4. Encouraging, paraphrasing, and summarizing. All this helps clients share more and more accurately.
5. Reflection of feelings, not just content.

We are also taught about empathy. In the same chapter,[63] Halverson and Miars talk about primary empathy which is shown by natural responses from being present to the client, to what they share, and how they share it. Advanced empathy, on the other hand, brings awareness, in the conversation with clients, to underlying feelings or meanings that are not directly perceived by clients.

I discussed listening skills in depth in Chapter 6, Psychotherapy 101. I finished that chapter with advance listening skills which, to my knowledge, aren't addressed in schools. They are important to include at a later stage of a psychotherapy curriculum when students have more experience. There are three different layers of listening: direct and literal, metaphorical, and spiritual.

Listening skills should also include an introductory somatic experiential course on learning to feel one's own energy and release tension, and, also, learning to feel someone else's energy with one's body.

Conversation/Interview Process

From the book by Capuzzi and Gross, we are offered to engage in a conversation with our clients using our listening skills and a sense of direction. These are great for a student to practice.

1. Rapport building, building trust.
2. Reflection of feeling, understanding.
3. Identification of concerns, what the client wants.
4. Gathering data.

---

[63] S. E. Halverson and R. D. Miars (2005). *The helping Relationship* in An Introduction to the Counseling Profession, 4th ed., edited by David Capuzzi and Douglas Gross, Pearson Education, Inc., pp 69-73.

5. Paraphrasing/reframing, understanding the content using different words to get at a more accurate picture and engage the client in going deeper.
6. Reflection of content.
7. Goal setting.
8. Terminating the interview, bringing closure and a transition back to the client's life.

With practice, we do not need to refer back to this agenda. We know when something is missing, or if something needs to be worked on in our relationship with the client. We know to acknowledge feelings and identify concerns and gather more data and help the client get deeper.

I would also add that answers provided by the therapist are usually less life changing than asking the right questions so the client experiences his own answers. It is a skill to develop to hold off on providing answers and advice, and, instead, ask oneself: How can I help my client shift perspective? What question could I possibly ask right now to help him see what I see? One technique is to ask the client to imagine that the situation happened to someone else and ask him what he would say to that person. Another is to ask questions the client has never explored. These questions come more easily as you get to know the client better. A common question I heard from therapists whose client says he does not know the answer to a question is to ask him, "If you knew the answer what would it be?"

It makes for a wonderful course to learn to interview people using more and more listening and conversation skills. This was one of my favorite courses in the mental health counseling program I attended. Each week, we were to turn in an audio piece of interview or a video to our teacher who evaluated our work and gave us feedback. The exercise was invaluable and needs to be a part of any curriculum in psychotherapy.

Worldviews/Cultural Differences

One of the key issues that creates misunderstandings between people is worldviews and cultural differences. The therapist needs to know the role worldviews and cultural differences play in relationships. We are all here to learn about loving oneself and others. Worldviews and cultural differences are the perfect setup to engage us to learn respect and to learn to get curious about each other. This is one of the most important parts of the work in couple therapy for instance, even if both parties appear to be from the same culture. I have often found that my main role as a therapist is to help each party hear what the other party really means. When they come to therapy they have not realized yet that they use language differently so they easily misinterpret each other. In a way we each have our own worldview and our own culture. This is compounded by the hurt we still carry which leads to interpreting what we hear instead of truly hearing.

Psychotherapy was birthed from Western white men. Although Jung explored other cultures, and other healing traditions, for the most part, psychotherapy has evolved from a fairly narrow perspective that was bound to be challenged and expanded by women and people from other cultures, especially by minorities. Therefore, in today's Western academic curriculum, a large emphasis is placed on multiculturalism.

One area where the teaching of multiculturalism could improve is by including an exploration of other cultures' approaches to mental health. In the same way that women and people from other cultures put pressure on the field of psychotherapy to open up to their views and needs, I predict that the field of psychotherapy is bound to receive further pressures to acknowledge other cultural approaches to and perspectives on mental health. Why wait for those pressures, why not open up to other cultural perspectives now? That is why I encourage the psychotherapy curriculum to include the study of traditional healers and spiritual teachers.

Despite cultural differences, there are things that make us similar to each other. Human nature remains the same across cultures. If a psychotherapeutic approach is based on the knowledge of human nature, it is less dependent on cultural differences. If a psychotherapeutic approach is based on self-discovery, it is less dependent on cultural differences. To a large extent, multiculturalism only becomes an issue if cultural differences or cultural oppressions are part of the problem for which the client came to therapy in the first place or if the therapist has an issue with them.

Practicing an interview/conversation with someone from a different gender, sexual orientation, culture and/or any other worldview should be a part of the course on learning about interviews/conversations. After some experience, exploring who would be the most difficult client and why is a valuable exercise.

To me, culture is the same as everything else; if I don't know something about my client, I become curious and ask questions. Now, we each have our own unique culture, so who am I to presume to know anything about any of my clients? Assume nothing.

The Therapist's Mental Health

Capuzzi and Gross mention what they call the therapist's self-attending skills which fall in four categories:[64] self-awareness, centering or relaxing, humor, and nonjudgmental attitude toward self and others. In self-awareness they include self-knowledge, knowing one's values, beliefs, and assets. Centering is the ability to set all other concerns aside so the center of focus is the client and relaxing is essential for centering but also because, if the therapist is tense (and especially tense about feeling tense), the therapy is probably not going to be pleasant for the client, nor would it be healing. Humor is to show the lighter side of therapy; it helps the client relax. Nonjudgment is essential, and perhaps one of the most important skills a therapist can have. If I am judgmental toward myself, how can I help clients not judge themselves? And if I judge a client, how will the client trust me?

I have been asked to offer workshops about self-care for the care-giver. As I studied what services are offered on self-care, I realized that burnout is prevalent in many professions, and that the self-care discussion, accessible online, only offers general guidelines that may be missing what is key to self-care.

Here is a very brief summary of what I teach.

> For the most part, stress does not come from the outside, it comes from an inner conflict in response to the outside circumstances. If a job becomes stressful, people usually complain about the

---

[64] S. E. Halverson and R. D. Miars (2005). "The helping Relationship" in *An Introduction to the Counseling Profession*, 4th ed., edited by David Capuzzi and Douglas Gross, Pearson Education, Inc., pp. 66-67.

atmosphere at work, the attitude of one's boss or of some co-workers, the amount of work, etc. These are all external pressures. You can blame these external pressures or explore what in you is feeling the pressures. In other words, you can explore your personal resistance and conflict in response to the pressures, and learn how to pay attention to and listen to your internal reaction. You learn inner conflict management. In choosing this exploration, you notice that stress is an opportunity for self-discovery. You realize that if it wasn't for the external pressures, you would not become aware of these different parts of you that wanted your attention. You also realize that these pressures help you get clearer on who you are and who you want to be. They bring you closer to your life purpose. You then see stress as a gift.

What I also see is that unaddressed stress is the source of most challenges, physical or mental. Therefore learning to understand and grow from stress should come as one of the first topics covered in schools.

I think students who want to learn to be therapists need to understand what it feels like to be a client and to let someone else help them. They also learn best from experience. To learn to relax and be joyful and gain the self-awareness Capuzzi and Gross talk about, I make the following suggestions to include in a psychotherapy curriculum: experiencing joy and self-discovery, and experiencing therapy as a client.

1. *Joy and Self-Discovery*

As human beings, but especially as therapists, we need to experience joy and self-discovery. We cannot give what we do not have to give. In light of this, I would ask students to engage in an activity that helps with their mental health. It could be as simple as committing to a daily exercise regimen such as swimming, bicycling or jogging. Or it can be practicing martial arts, or joining a spiritual practice such as the Bruno Gröning Circle of Friends, Buddhism, Zen, Tai Chi, or Yoga. It could also be joining a creative art or writing program. It can be any hobby, something for one's own personal growth, something that helps bring balance and joy in one's life, such as nature exploration: photography, birding, camping, hiking, or trekking. Also, students should be encouraged to keep a journal. This journal is private, not to be shared in school, and is used to explore feelings, personal difficulties, and meaning in one's life.

Not all these activities necessarily help to learn how to resolve stress. Yoga and the Bruno Gröning Circle of Friends have been instrumental to me, and mainly learning to listen to my body. I experienced that any physical symptom has a message: stubbing my toe, a headache, pain, tension, including what our culture has come to call: "Oh! That's just part of the aging process!" I don't believe that aging has to bring physical problems. It is not because there is a correlation in our culture between aging and certain symptoms that these are due to aging. I have come to believe that *any physical or mental challenge can be healed* if we dedicate our self to figuring it out, for our self or others, in the highest good for all involved.

I would encourage students to keep a journal to reflect on their experience with engaging in the activity they chose, including a reflection on a daily meditation on learning to listen to one's body. They can start with a simple five minute meditation. I have found that having a meditation practice opens many wonderful doors in the therapy process.

2. Experiencing Therapy as a Client

Since I am a firm believer in experience, I would also ask students, before learning about psychotherapy theories and models, to experience three different counseling approaches, each from a different psychotherapist. If a student wants to continue a particular form of therapy I would encourage her to continue as long as she wants.

The teacher of that part of the training may need to provide the students with a list of mainstream and not mainstream therapy approaches that are available in the region where the students go to school, and ask students to find and make an appointment with a therapist. These therapists should not be associated with the school so the students can feel free to speak of their experience in school. The students would then need to evaluate their experience after the first visit and decide whether they would want to continue therapy with that therapist for two more sessions. After this first experience, students would select a second therapist with a different psychotherapy

Luc Watelet

approach and also not associated with the school. Again, the student evaluates whether he wants to continue for two more sessions with that therapist or not. After this second therapy experience, the student would select a third therapist with again a different psychotherapy approach and again not associated with the school. I recommend that each student completes three therapy sessions with at least one therapist. For this, it may be needed to make appointments with more than three therapists. After these experiences, students should reflect on and compare all therapy approaches they have experienced. The professor should review these reflections and invite the students to share them orally in class in a way that is respectful of the therapist they visited. Of course if a therapist became abusive, it should be immediately reported to the professor for further advice on how to proceed.

Human Nature

At this stage in the curriculum, students have a grasp of what it feels like to be a client, have experienced three different psychotherapeutic approaches from different therapists, have learned the basics of listening and conversation, and have become more aware of the status of their own mental health. They have also started a practice of self-reflection by journaling. Now, they are ready to learn and reflect on human nature.

I see human nature as a trinity: Mind, Body, and Soul (Consciousness). Some people may not believe in a soul while some people may not believe the body needs any attention. Since I believe it is important to respect the students' own worldview, I don't think it is helpful to teach about human nature from a theoretical point of view and impose that point of view. That would inevitably lead to endless intellectual conversations ungrounded in reality. So it is best to give students an experience of their mind and their bodies and to experience the different agendas and needs of these different parts of them. One can also give students an experience of their heart as holding other kinds of needs. The heart and the mind are often in conflict and we need to learn how to handle this if we are to help others. And then there is our consciousness, that part of us that is aware of our own experiences and our thinking without reacting to them.

Such experiences of our mind, body, and soul can come from different sources. A meditation teacher might be most adept at guiding a visualization into these different realms for students to have experiences on which they can then reflect. A massage therapist expert at releasing trauma may be extremely beneficial in helping students experience how much memory is stored in the body and how trauma can be released physically. A healer can also give a physical experience that opens a student's perspective on the relationship between mind, body, and soul.

Becoming a Therapist

Experience is not the whole story. We can only each get experience and understand it at our own level of personal growth. You cannot, in general, give heart surgery experience to a first year medical student. You cannot, in general, give an experience of driving a car in a professional race to someone who has not had any driving experience. But we can't say that this will never be possible for anyone. We each come with some expertise in some areas and some things to learn. As human beings we have a territory to negotiate, the concrete aspect of our journey. A general map can be offered from spiritual teachers who have been there before us. For a psychotherapist, it helps to study such spiritual teachings because they provide clues as to where the client may be on his journey and where we are personally.

The therapist can only help a client from the level on the path that she has reached. Rarely do we get clients who are more advanced than we are. If it happens, it may be a clue to the therapist that it is time to grow. From a client's perspective, to be in the presence of a therapist who is challenged by some of the same issues as he is, is a signal that it is time to adjust his self-perception. When Eckhart Tolle (*The Power of Now*) snapped out of his experience of depression and entered a place of happiness that was no longer disturbed by outside situations, he sought spiritual lectures to understand what had just happened to him. He realized that the speakers were describing a stage of human growth they had not experienced themselves. Since he had, he realized he was ready to be a spiritual teacher.

This book has been written from a certain perspective of therapy that believes that all solutions are within us, that anything can be healed, and that healings happen when we learn to establish a healthy relationship between our mind, body, and soul. To do this, we need very little theoretical knowledge. Instead, we need to know how to foster relationships and how to navigate the inner world, our own and that of others. It requires deep experiences of self and awareness.

This perspective may not be expected of a therapist who is beginning on the therapy journey because she may not have the experience yet to believe in these perspectives, or to know how to navigate the inner worlds. So for a period of time, some therapists need to understand theories and models as important guidelines on the path of helping others. But these theories and models should not be thought of as more than guidelines. They should not be thought of as the limit of what is possible in therapy, nor should these theories and models be thought of as defining human nature or psychotherapy. Therapists who have not yet reached a level of understanding of human nature from experience and who have not yet experienced the magic of therapy beyond applying techniques, therapists who have not yet experienced the magic of following one's intuition and seeing healing in their clients, will benefit from learning from those who have more experience by going to conferences and lectures, and by receiving therapy from a therapist who can guide them to these broader levels of understanding and experiences. On the other hand, therapists who are becoming experts in their field need the freedom to explore unchartered territories, because they pave the way to the future of psychotherapy.

Thomas relates the following story about Carl Whitaker (1912, 1995):

> *When asked how he came up with some of his outrageous yet extraordinarily creative interventions, Whitaker replied, in essence, "I have no idea what I am doing when I am doing it. A good therapist does not need to know ahead of time what he is going to do. But he must be able to provide a sound rationale for what he did afterwards."*[65]

---

[65] Thomas, V. (2003). "Experiential Approaches to Family Therapy" in L. L. Hecker, & J. L. Wetchler, (Eds.), *An Introduction to Marriage and Family Therapy* (1st ed.) (pp. 173-201). Binghamton, NY: The Haworth Clinical Practice Press, p. 187.

I repeat what I said in Chapter 6, Psychotherapy 101: An ideal for a therapist is for his behavior and words with clients to be in entire synchronicity with Life itself. Such a therapist no longer comes from personal ego or personal knowledge, but has become a humble and clear direct instrument of Life itself.

Spiritual teachings include a discussion about the various steps on the path of a student on his spiritual journey. There are similar steps on the path to becoming an expert therapist as there are from being a student of spirituality to becoming a spiritual master. It may help to explore the spiritual teachings to get a picture of where we are on the path to becoming a master at what we do.

Traditional Healers and Spiritual Teachers

We need to recognize that traditional healers and spiritual teachers came before psychotherapists. Jung and Jungian oriented psychotherapists have embraced their work. As we work toward a unification of all of psychotherapy toward a healing modality, it is important to include the work of traditional healers and spiritual teachers in our curriculum and to encourage students to learn about them, via a project, for instance.

History of Mental Health and Psychotherapy

Once students have a basic understanding of human nature and of themselves, they are ready to learn about the history of mental health before Freud and after. Now they can appreciate the evolution of practices and thoughts from personal experience and, develop their critical thinking. In this process, they will also learn about the various theories and models that have been proposed as they were often created in reaction to one another. Students will be able to evaluate how these various theories and models address the trinity of human nature and when one theory or model might work best, given a client's situation.

For the pre-Freud history of mental illness, I suggest the book by Michel Foucault, *Madness and Civilization: A History of Insanity in the Age of Reason*, originally published in 1964.

Luc Watelet

The transition of mental health practices with Freud, Adler, and Jung is particularly interesting as it propelled us into a Western vision that split into three major schools. I believe it is time for a unification of these schools today, and, with them, of all of psychotherapy.

Beers, author of a poignant autobiography, *A Mind that Found Itself (1908)*, is a big part of that transition and should be given more of a prominent place in the history of psychotherapy. He is one of the first published examples of someone healing from a mental illness. After his recovery, he went on to try to make more human the way the mentally ill were treated in America. His efforts were recognized internationally and are still worth paying attention to today. To place Beers in the historical context, his book was published when Freud, Adler, and Jung were still meeting. In Vienna, Austria, Adler had joined Freud in 1902, while Jung did in 1906. Adler distanced himself from Freud in 1911, and Jung started the process of distancing himself from Freud the following year.

The history of psychotherapy theories and models taught in mainstream programs will need to be augmented with the material covered in body-oriented schools of psychotherapy, spirituality-oriented schools of psychotherapy, and the material in this book including Chapters 9, 10, and 11.

Students could be presented that material and asked to do a research project on a Western or non-Western mental health practice from a healing paradigm.

From a Medical and Scientific Paradigm to a Healing Paradigm of Psychotherapy

I explained throughout this book the need to pay more attention to healing rather than treating, to the subjective and individual worlds rather than attempt to correct people's behaviors with outside theories and models. As human beings we have both unhealthy and healthy aspects to us. A part of our brain default network is corrupted with negative habits, and trauma still lingers in parts of our bodies that are directly related to the bad habits of our default network. On the other hand, we have dreams and a sense of purpose in our heart and soul. The experience of our unhealthy side is like a wakeup call that we need to realign our identity with our healthy side. This leads to getting to know who we are more deeply. As we connect and nurture our healthy side and stop identifying with and stop nurturing our unhealthy side, we heal and grow personally and spiritually. Ultimate health is enlightenment.

This understanding of our human nature removes the stigma of any challenges we face, removes the distinction we artificially made between normal and abnormal psychology, and leads to a shift of worldview in psychotherapy from a medical and scientific to a healing paradigm.

Statistics

My master's program in mental health counseling included a basic course in statistics. I presume that any master's degree curriculum in any psychotherapy program requires such a course.

Boredom

Statistics is not taught in a way that can be grasped intuitively. I don't know of any beginner textbook in statistics that isn't dry and technical... and boring. Students' experience is that statistics is a bunch of recipes. We can do better. I had a hard time with my first course in statistics. Luckily I was a math major. So I set the textbook aside, and I asked myself what I would do if I had to create the field of statistics from scratch. I compared what I was coming up with to what was in the textbook and something clicked in my mind, I understood.

Teaching from Practice to Concepts

Statistics should not be taught from theory first but from probability and statistical experiences. We need to start by asking students to roll a die several times and check the rates with which each number comes up. Then students can combine all of their results and see what the combined rates for each die number become. That's how you can start teaching probability and I believe some teachers do something like this. You can start statistics similarly: Starting with collecting the height of all the students in the classroom and asking students to compare the height of males to the height of females and come up with their own ways of making a decision as to who is taller, males or females. I left the question vague on purpose so students would have to think what is meant by "Who is taller?" Students are encouraged to be creative and discuss ideas with each other, conceptual, numerical or graphical. Students who already know statistics should try and come up with their own techniques.

This is how I would start a course in statistics for beginners. No theory at first. This allows the teacher to introduce basic concepts of summary statistics such as average, and other central measures, and measures of spread of the data. And it also allows a teacher to introduce visual ways to portray the data: histograms, stem and leaf plots, for instance. This approach engages the students. Each new statistical idea can be introduced by engaging students in an experiment. Then they can understand why the concept exists.

Aside

Students with a degree in statistics, no matter how old, should not be required to take this basic course. I had a PhD in biostatistics and was required to take this basic course offered as part of the mental health counseling program because my degree was more than ten years old. Statistics does not change that fast at that level that this was justified.

Teach What Is Useful

Most master's level students in psychotherapy will not go on to do research. Why not postpone the course in statistics to the PhD level? Instead of teaching the basics of statistics at the master's level, what a master's student in psychotherapy really needs is a course on how to read and understand critically the statistical part of an article. A student who takes a basic course in statistics has not necessarily acquired such skills.

Discussion of Some of the Concepts Taught in Mainstream Psychology

Because of my experience using a healing paradigm to psychotherapy, I have different ideas about certain topics covered in mainstream courses in psychotherapy. Chemical and genetic explanations for mental health challenges need to be covered here (see Prologue). Here are a few more.

The Diagnostic and Statistical Manual (DSM)

The history of the DSM shows, for instance, how homosexuality used to be considered a mental illness. Our current culture, for the most part, and the latest version of the DSM no longer consider it so. We need to learn from history. How do we know that we will not change our belief in the future about any of the other mental illnesses? In this book, I discussed the notion that mental illnesses are really only symptoms, and if the label is used that way it can be helpful, but if it is used to determine a personality trait, it can cause harm. I have clients whose psychiatric records still indicate mental illnesses, on the first page, that were deemed resolved by their psychiatrist more than ten years ago. This is at odds with our code of ethics which asks us to do no harm.

I ask for a revision of the DSM based on symptomology, which erases the notion of personality disorders, and includes a summary indicating that healing is possible. I encourage those responsible for the revisions of the DSM to do some research in this area to convince themselves.

Transference and Counter-Transference

The notions of transference and counter-transference came from Freud. Transference is defined as a projection from the client onto the therapist and counter-transference is a projection from the therapist onto the client and is often referred to as a therapist's emotional entanglement with a client. It can be used in therapy to bring out in the open the client's damaged parental-child relationship.

The danger with the transference counter-transference theory is that it assumes that the problem starts with the client. That can be unfair to the client. The client's behavior may be considered transference while completely in concordance with the therapeutic relationship (i.e., not a projection) if the therapist acted in a way to justify it. For instance, a therapist diagnoses a client and treats her by encouraging a behavior change according to some guidelines that do not come from the client herself, and continues by checking on her ability to adopt these new guidelines session after session. She can easily perceive this as a therapist acting as a parent. I don't think it would be inaccurate. Then, later in the therapeutic relationship, if the therapist does not adapt to his client's growth but the client comes to feel her own power, she may start to feel controlled by the therapist's authority. She may rebel. That is the natural development in someone's search to be themselves in the presence of authority. It happened between Adler and Freud, and again between Jung and Freud. In these two cases, although they were not patient-therapist relationships, it seems to me that Freud set it up by his own need to be seen and respected as authority.

In therapy, I think the early work with clients tends to have to do with relationships and boundary issues. This is the beginning for a client to understand who she is as she is entering the process of individuation. Imagine someone who comes with trauma from childhood such as rape or emotional abuse. Part of the work necessary at the early stage of therapy is to help the client reclaim her own voice because the child's perceptions have been distorted. Boundaries were not respected and the person victimized goes into adulthood without a clear understanding of healthy boundaries and healthy relationships, and, sometimes, may even fear them. Establishing proper boundaries in the therapeutic relationship is part of the healing process for the client. A therapist engaging in counter-transference is playing further with confusing boundaries. It is a dangerous game that needs to be made conscious.

If a client expresses some projection toward me, it is an opportunity to remain myself and not become part of a drama of relationship the client is, consciously or unconsciously, engaging in. As I remain myself, I show by example a healthy way to respond to the drama. The client cannot remain very long in her projection then, as there is no match between her projection and my behavior and attitude.

Therefore, I prefer to think of transference and counter-transference as boundary issues. Dealt as boundary issues, they become useful in the therapeutic process. When a client projects a parental figure on the therapist, the therapist may have acted in therapy as a parent without acknowledging it as role play. That is crossing a boundary and is not healthy for the client. If the therapist did not act as a parent in the therapeutic relationship then the client is somehow confused. I would immediately notice that a boundary is being crossed by the client and would address it. You address this not by blaming, but by bringing it to awareness. I would ask, for instance, if I remind her of one, or a combination, of her parents. We would explore what is happening for her, and I could offer her to role play if she is open to pursue therapy in this way.

Often clients may feel heard and understood for the very first time by their therapist and may, as a result, fall in love with him. It is natural. It is a mistake for a therapist to return the feelings. The client-therapist relationship is based on a contract, explicit or implicit, that the therapist is there to help the client, but not for the client to help the therapist. This built-in asymmetry in the client-therapist relationship could lead to abuse of power if a healthy boundary that supports this asymmetry is crossed. In order to avoid abuse of power, in my practice, I tell my client that she has the power to engage, or not, in an exercise I suggest, or to answer, or not, a question I ask. I want the client to feel her own power. Of course, I have the same power to answer or not a client's question about my personal life. This levels the playing field a little and avoids the trap of parenting the client. When clients express an interest in a relationship with me as a lover, I let them know that I am not the right person for them, but that this shows progress in their choice of a partner compared to the abusive ones from the past. So I encourage them to keep looking for someone who understands them and is kind.

Abraham Maslow (1908-1970) and the Hierarchy of Needs

The hierarchy of needs is very popular, not only in psychology, but also in management and other human disciplines. It claims that some needs need to be met before others can be met, in a specific order. One meets physiological needs first: eating, drinking, breathing, sleeping, etc. Then safety needs are addressed, then belonging, then achievement, and then self-actualization.

Pamela Rutledge, Ph.D., pointed out in 2011 that Maslow did not give enough importance to the role of social connections.[66] Rutledge's point is that needs are not hierarchical. Except for the physiological and

---

[66] P. Rutledge, Ph.D. (2011). Retrieved on December 18, 2014, and still active on July 9, 2016, from http://www.psychologytoday.com/blog/positively-media/201111/social-networks-what-maslow-misses-0.

biological needs, our other needs are "an interactive, dynamic system."

Although Rutledge's reorganizing of Maslow's hierarchy of needs is an important contribution to our ongoing refinement of psychological thoughts, I have another problem with the original model from Maslow and also with Rutledge's. First, Maslow's hierarchy of needs assumes that unmet needs automatically lead to stress and anxiety which prevents other higher needs on the hierarchy from being met. It is not necessarily the unmet needs that create stress. The stress may very well come from experiencing an unmet need in a culture that believes them to be essential. For instance, in a culture that tells me I need a shelter before I can be creative, as long as I don't have a shelter, I may choose to limit my creativity. I will experience an unmet need. But if someone's belief is that creativity comes first and does not pressure himself to have a shelter, the experience and the stress level will be very different. Hence, it can be the beliefs that cause stress, not necessarily, or not only, the needs that are unmet.

When I went through my period of divorce, foreclosure and bankruptcy (Chapter 2, Life Lessons), you could say that my hierarchy of needs was shattered at its very foundation. I went through a period of stress and anxiety trying to stay afloat. Nothing I did to generate material stability worked. In retrospect, what I tried to do was to work on my foundation according to Maslow's hierarchy of needs.

In the end, I had to give up the belief that I needed safety and financial security, and even my need of belonging (this is where I question Rutledge's revised model). My most important need was to allow myself to be joyful despite everything that was happening in my life. I had to shed all fears that things would go wrong if I did not attend first to my basic physical and social needs. This was very counterintuitive given our society's beliefs in Maslow's hierarchy of needs, which I had integrated in my worldview. I also had to let go of my need for social interactions because no one gave me advice that worked. And I had to give up my need for belonging because what I desperately needed the most was to accept myself as I was, despite what anyone else said. I discovered that the sense of belonging had to come from within, not from the outside. I had to find my joy and inner strength in being who I am and who I wanted to be. In other words, what became my top priority was self-actualization. When I started to take care of that – it was a very lonely path to understand what that meant, not a social one – my financial needs started to take care of themselves. I had to do what my teacher Yogi Bhajan said (I paraphrase): "Be you, and everything else will fall into place."

In talking with other people who have had challenges in their lives, I discovered that they had come to the same conclusion that I had come to, "Take care of the spiritual needs first, and then the material needs will take care of themselves." When I say "spiritual needs" here, I mean to reconnect with the very personal spiritual needs that come from within.

I am not certain this is true for everyone, but I am leaning in that direction. Perhaps the only possible generalization is that we each have our own path that dictates what our priorities are and, therefore, in what order our specific needs need to be met.

"Our Wounds Come from Childhood"

Our psychology culture gives us a conflicting message. On the one hand, we are told not to blame our parents for our suffering, and, on the other, we are told our wounds come from our childhood.

For instance, Virginia Satir, who otherwise gave us such wonderfully powerful teachings about life, peace, and wellbeing, wrote,

> *This book is not about blaming parents. People always do the best they can.*[67]

And, a few pages later,

> *An infant coming into the world has no past, no experience in handling itself, no scale on which to judge his or her own worth. The baby must rely on experiences with people and their messages about his or her worth as a person. For the first five or six years, the child's self-esteem is formed almost exclusively by the family.*[68]

---

[67] V. Satir (1988). *The New Peoplemaking*, Science and Behavior Books, p. 6.
[68] Ibid., p. 25.

Luc Watelet

Wayne Muller says,

> Our psychological culture sometimes falls prey that it was our
> childhood suffering that brought pain into our lives. We hurt now
> because we were hurt as children; if we were not hurt as children,
> we would not be hurting now.[69]

And,

> We tell ourselves: "The pain that happened to me could have been
> prevented; it should never have happened to me."[70]

I love Muller's method out of this dilemma. He continues,

> If pain is not our fault, then pain is not the fault of our alcoholic
> father or our inattentive mother. [...] Once we remove the question:
> "why," we may see our pain face to face, accepting it for what it is.
> Then we can truly grieve, which softens the pain. The deep hurt and
> anger and sadness can then lead us to letting go, to forgiveness, and
> to healing.[71]

My own approach is compatible with Muller's. I came to it by
questioning one of the basic premises of psychology. I do not believe we
were born empty, as could be inferred from Satir's words, although I am
not sure she believed that we were born empty. How can we explain
that different children from the same family have different self-worth
experiences? One way to understand this is that parents have different
affinities with their different children. It is often clear that a child who
behaves in a way that parents recognize and appreciate is understood
and praised more than a child who does not. This is true. So it cannot be
denied that each child lives a completely different experience in the
same family. But some children are terribly mistreated by their family
and come out with great integrity and love and do not pass on the pain
they received to their own children, or at least not to the same extent.
But others who are terribly mistreated come out imposing pain on all

---

[69] W. Muller (1992). *Legacy of the Heart: The Spiritual Advantages of a Painful
Childhood*. Fireside, p. 3.
[70] Ibid., p. 5.
[71] Ibid., pp. 8-9.

around them. How can that be explained? My view is that, already in the womb, we have our own sets of wounds and we already have our own sense of self-esteem.

I believe I came to this world with my problems. In his *Autobiography of a Yogi*, Yogananda talks about remembering his experience in the womb and from previous lives. In my own quest to heal childhood wounds, *I could not find a time when a wound was created, I could only remember when a wound came to my awareness.* I think psychology has confused the two. I started to think that my parents either triggered my memory of a wound or they did not, and they either knew how to help me with something I struggled with or they did not.

Many times I have experienced in my life that if a situation triggered anger in me, I was already angry prior to that experience, but was not aware of it. Similarly, I would say it is often the case that pain triggered by an experience was already there, perhaps unconsciously, prior to the event that led the person to feel the pain. This could be a rape, a relationship loss, a job loss, etc. Think of it this way, if we did not have a wound or pain to heal, nothing would trigger us. Things trigger us only because they awaken a pain that was already there. Thus, not only do parents do their best, it is a gift when they do something that helps us feel a wound, otherwise how else would we know what we need to heal?

This is not only about our parents. Every time we are triggered by something or someone in life, I believe the wound was already there. The circumstances or the people involved simply help us feel what we are hurting from. Blaming circumstances or people for what ails us is avoidance, it prevents us from healing, and it points to the wrong cause for our problems.

More about "Causing No Harm"

Each therapeutic approach brings a slightly different perspective to therapy and one can easily pick and choose what feels right at any time for any client. Therapists who do this are called eclectic. None of these approaches are hurtful in and of themselves. What can be hurtful is the manner in which a therapeutic approach is used.

For instance, a reality therapist thinking of depression as a choice, may approach a client who suffers from depression by asking, "So why do you choose depression?" This will probably immediately turn off some clients if it is used in a first meeting and will not establish a relationship based on trust. This approach turned off a person I met who described this as her first interaction with her therapist. The therapist would do better to ask questions to help the client understand her depression so well that it is the client who discovers that she has chosen it, or made decisions that have made her feel depressed. That is where the skill of being a therapist lies, and not on imposing a therapeutic view on clients. Sometimes, when a therapist knows a client well, the shock value of a question may very well work... but only after trust has been established and the therapist knows that the shock value will be effective with that client.

Also, ignoring a client's soul needs may lead the therapy astray. In using a behavioral approach to therapy, a therapist might be eager to guide a client on a behavior program toward the objectives they have worked on together only to create more conflicts in the client if these objectives are not aligned with his soul's deepest desires.

For instance, using a reward system to help people stop an addictive behavior can only go so far. As soon as the rewards stop, I would predict that the addictive behavior will resurge unless the person has discovered something that matters more than the addictive behavior to him. Helping someone overcome his resistance to getting a college degree may seem like a great goal unless the underlying reason for that client to want a college degree is to impress his family rather than because it is exactly what he needs for his own growth.

The best way to do no harm is to respect the client's ability to know what's next and not impose theoretical views or external objectives. We all need external objectives, but we need to keep an internal tab as to whether these objectives still serve us, or whether they were temporary objectives to get us to a new level of self-awareness, and on our way to an objective closer to our heart!

Code of Ethics

The curriculum in psychotherapy needs to include a discussion of the history of the code of ethics. The current code of ethics does not prevent harm to be done to clients. I often meet clients who were wronged either by a therapist's approach to therapy or by a system that labelled them, making them believe they were bad, or that their mental struggles had no solutions except through psychotropic medicine. Two couples experienced couple counseling from different therapists. In one case, the woman never felt heard; in the other, the man never felt heard. People do therapy for years without seeing any improvements in their lives. A woman was convinced by her therapist to continue therapy with him even though she wanted to stop.... only to find out later that the therapist was still not listening to her. She eventually left a year later feeling so much time and money had been wasted. Mental health challenges continue to be seen negatively by the psychotherapy culture and society at large. We contribute to this stigma on our clients if we continue to subscribe to the cultural view of mental illness. This leaves people, who already suffer, scarred further by society's and psychotherapists' judgments.

On the other hand, I meet more and more therapists and psychiatric nurses who don't believe in labeling anymore.

The role of health insurances complicates accountabilities to a code of ethics. Agencies and psychotherapists have given up some of their own power to health insurance companies who often dictate how and how long therapy should be done. How can treatment guidelines be dictated by health insurance companies that are not accountable to the clients about their wellbeing? Do the people who make mental health care guidelines for health insurance companies have a code of ethics like therapists do? If not, is this in the best interest of the clients? How can a therapist follow her code of ethics when she cannot decide how to best care for the client?

Not only do we need to take our power back so we can be fully accountable to our clients, we need to, and can create, a more healing psychotherapy culture today.

Pharmacology

Pharmacology has become part of the curriculum of some psychotherapy schools at the expense of real therapy. In a lot of ways, pharmacology brings an element needed to therapy, as otherwise many clients would not be able to have coherent conversations and be helped by therapy. Unfortunately, there is also a lot of abuse, and therapists have sometimes given up on real therapy thinking that pharmacology is the only viable solution for some of their clients. The experiences I related in this book regarding healing from various diagnoses of mental health challenges, including the reduction or elimination of the need for psychotropic medication, indicate that we need to review our pharmacology practice in psychotherapy.

Too often the psychiatrist who is not involved in the therapy of the patient and evaluates her over a 15 minute meeting makes a decision for the patient without respect for her free will. I had a client who wanted to reduce her medication and the psychiatrist told her that since she was going through a difficult time in her life, she would need the extra help. From my perspective, these "difficult experiences" she faced were a blessing in disguise as they were a wonderful way for the client to test how far she had come. She did not get to see how strong she was through that difficult time.

Capstone Project or Thesis, and Internship

A master's degree in psychotherapy typically includes a capstone project or a thesis, and an internship at an agency with a supervisor.

A capstone project is a proposal for a research, but the research does not have to be implemented. A thesis needs to have a research that includes data collected and analyzed.

It is important to have started an internship before starting to work on a capstone project or a thesis because a student needs to have experience before she can think of a study to research.

Getting an internship location was not easy for me because I was studying at an online school. It took serious determination to find an agency, and serious follow through to be interviewed because counselors are extremely busy. Physical schools have a relationship with local agencies and can facilitate the connection between agencies and students. This is preferable.

Licensure, School, and Student Loan Reimbursement

Before selecting a curriculum, I just trusted blindly that the licensing details would come together when the time came. Also, I did not investigate the actual differences between being a social worker and a mental health counselor as I thought the name of the discipline indicated clearly enough what the difference was. It is not so simple. Everyone who wants to be a student in psychotherapy needs to learn about licensure and about the differences between the disciplines available before applying for the program of choice.

The regulations vary from country to country and, in the USA, from state to state. Licensure is a prerogative of the state in the USA. Currently, in the state of New York, licensure for psychotherapy disciplines takes place after the degree is earned. Social workers and mental health counselors have to follow different licensing requirements in New York State. The NYS office of professions has the current information for all licensed professions.

There are variations within psychotherapy professions I was not aware of before I enrolled to become a mental health counselor. For instance it is easier for social workers to be reimbursed by insurance companies than it is for mental health counselors in New York State. Also, at the substance abuse treatment agency where I did my internship, social workers with a master's degree had an automatic pay raise from social workers with a bachelor's degree, but not so for mental health counselors. These technicalities are the responsibilities of the respective associations for social workers and mental health counselors. From what I can tell, the degree for social workers and mental health counselors is different and licensure requirements can be quite different, but career options seem very similar.

The student loan issue is also important to explore. In the USA, student loans need to start being repaid within several months of receiving one's degree. Sometimes it is difficult to get hired right away after the degree is earned. And the income received is usually smaller prior to the reception of the license. That can lead to a period of hardship for budding psychotherapists. Since schools benefit from students taking on student loans, I would like to see more involvement from schools to help deserving students find a job in the field of the degree earned.

Luc Watelet

Bullet Points Version of a New Curriculum for Psychotherapy

1. Students' experience and self-care
   a. Group work
   b. Receiving therapy
   c. Experience of their mind, body and soul
   d. A hobby or practice for one's own enjoyment
2. Exposing students to listening and interviewing skills
   a. Have students practice these skills and record them on audio and video
   b. Have work critiqued by instructor
3. Exposing students to the history of mental health
   a. Pre-Freud
      i. Practices in the West. Suggestion: *Madness and Civilization: A History of Insanity in the Age of Reason* (1988), by Michel Foucault (1926 – 1984)
      ii. Traditional healers
      iii. Spiritual teachers
   b. Freud and after
      i. Freud, Adler, Jung and their legacies
      ii. *A Mind that Found Itself* (1908), by Clifford Whittingham Beers (1876 – 1943), and Beers' legacy
      iii. Development of psychotherapy since them, including what is covered in mainstream curriculums, in body-oriented schools of psychotherapy, and in spirituality-oriented schools of psychotherapy (such as transpersonal psychology), and what I cover in this book up to and including Chapter 9
   c. Non-Western approaches to mental health (Chapter 10)
   d. Discussion of concepts of psychotherapy such as those listed in this chapter
4. Advanced listening levels (direct and literal, metaphorical, and spiritual)
   a. Practice with other students in the classroom
5. Encourage students to learn from their experiences and develop critical thinking
   a. Discussion on the ideal therapist during exposure to group work and private sessions with several therapists
   b. Private journaling

    c. Writing reports

    d. Giving presentations

    e. Reflecting on practicing therapy during the internship (and during the supervised work toward licensure provided licensure is integrated in the curriculum)

6. Exposing students to non-therapy information useful to a psychotherapist

    a. How to critically read a paper with a statistical analysis? – Statistics at the Ph.D. level

    b. Code of Ethics

    c. Pharmacology

    d. Capstone project, Thesis, internship

    e. Licensure

13 CONCLUSION

Given the situation of mental health in the USA today, the code of ethics, the licensure requirements and the overuse of pharmacology, our psychotherapy organizations may all seem like they are competing to gain the confidence of the consumer without fully addressing their concerns and well-being. We can do better!

Thinking of human beings as having a soul, not only a mind and a body, changes everything about how to help someone who has lost his or her way. The client is no longer considered to be sick or to have a personality disorder. The experience of feeling or being lost is simply an experience of feeling disconnected from the soul. The helper or therapist no longer positions herself as the expert in the therapeutic process, but more as the midwife, or the facilitator, in the process of reconnection of the client to his inner world.

Accepting this concept of human nature changes the worldview of mainstream psychotherapy from one of pathology or abnormality to one of symptomology on a spiritual journey. Human beings are no longer seen as broken and powerless, instead they are whole and creators of their own lives. Relationships between clients and therapists are a two-way street where the cognitive and emotional, the somatic, and the spiritual work together to bring healing to both parties.

It is my hope that this book has been convincing in establishing that mental health challenges are symptoms of a disconnection between the mind, the body, and the soul, and that healing is possible by working at re-establishing that connection. It is my hope that we understand the importance of love not only in psychotherapy, but also in parenting and education and in any human endeavor. It is my hope that we start to value love as a culture for the sake of humanity and for the sake of nature that has sustained us so far.

I call on psychotherapists from different schools to seek each other and learn about each other, realizing that they each participate in an aspect of the healing their clients seek. I believe that as psychotherapists heal the fragmentation of their profession, they will better be able to address the inner experience of fragmentation of their clients.

But that is only a first step. We also have a larger multicultural family to reconnect with. I am looking forward to a recognition of a kinship between psychotherapists, traditional healers and spiritual teachers. This recognition and reunion will bring multicultural healing which will contribute to a coming together of humanity.

I make the case that the DSM needs to take into account the new vision of mental health challenges as symptoms and not as illnesses or personality disorders. Mental health challenges are not abnormal, they are a natural consequence of a worldview. They show the path that needs to be embraced toward healing and even enlightenment.

And finally, I offer that we review the curriculum of psychotherapy accordingly.

Luc Watelet

To a client
frustrated
by the experience of depression,
I said,
"Let's stop thinking like a human being
for a moment,
and start being like a flower.
Would you like to try that?"
She looked at me
puzzled
"If a flower finds itself facing the shade
when the sun shines on its other side,
what does the flower do?"
I asked.
"It turns toward the sun!"
she answered.

ABOUT THE AUTHOR

Luc Watelet was 17 when he knew he wanted to be a psychotherapist. He started pre-med to study psychiatry but soon realized medical school did not interest him. He took a couple of courses in psychology to find out they bored him. So he set off in mathematics and was very happy, at first. Since he did not want to settle for a life of research, he followed his advisor's suggestion to do a Ph.D. in biostatistics. That's when life started to seem a little off to Luc. He could do the work and enjoyed some of it, like someone enjoys doing crossword puzzles. But to do it as a career?

This was the beginning of the big questions, "What am I doing here?" "Who am I?" and "Where am I going?" These questions sent Luc off on a journey back to psychotherapy in a way he did not plan. This journey is the foundation for this book.

Luc loves life and the outdoors, including camping, hiking, and photography.

Made in the USA
Monee, IL
30 June 2021